Studies in the Psychosocial

Series Editors
Stephen Frosh
Department of Psychosocial Studies
Birkbeck, University of London
London, UK

Raluca Soreanu
Psychosocial and Psychoanalytic Studies
University of Essex
Colchester, UK

Deanne Bell
Psychology
Nottingham Trent University
Nottingham, UK

Hannah Zeavin
University of California, Berkeley
Berkeley, USA

Studies in the Psychosocial seeks to investigate the ways in which psychic and social processes demand to be understood as always implicated in each other, as mutually constitutive, co-produced, or abstracted levels of a single dialectical process. As such it can be understood as an interdisciplinary field in search of transdisciplinary objects of knowledge. Studies in the Psychosocial is also distinguished by its emphasis on affect, the irrational and unconscious processes, often, but not necessarily, understood psychoanalytically. Studies in the Psychosocial aims to foster the development of this field by publishing high quality and innovative monographs and edited collections. The series welcomes submissions from a range of theoretical perspectives and disciplinary orientations, including sociology, social and critical psychology, political science, postcolonial studies, feminist studies, queer studies, management and organization studies, cultural and media studies and psychoanalysis. However, in keeping with the inter- or transdisciplinary character of psychosocial analysis, books in the series will generally pass beyond their points of origin to generate concepts, understandings and forms of investigation that are distinctively psychosocial in character.

Benjamin B. Strosberg

Anti-Semitism at the Limit

Critical Theory and Psychoanalysis

palgrave
macmillan

Benjamin B. Strosberg (iD)
Clinical Psychology
Pacifica Graduate Institute
Carpinteria, CA, USA

ISSN 2662-2629   ISSN 2662-2637   (electronic)
Studies in the Psychosocial
ISBN 978-3-031-72024-6   ISBN 978-3-031-72025-3   (eBook)
https://doi.org/10.1007/978-3-031-72025-3

This Palgrave Macmillan imprint is published by the registered company Springer Nature Switzerland AG.
The registered company address is: Gewerbestrasse 11, 6330 Cham, Switzerland

If disposing of this product, please recycle the paper.

For the displaced.

Preface

I conducted the research for this book in the year preceding the October 7th massacre in Israel and the subsequent military response in Gaza. That is, before the recent atrocities that have brought issues of anti-Semitism (and anti-anti-Semitism) into the international spotlight, with a sense of urgency and ferocity that has prompted crises—in political alliances, on university campuses, in families—and given rise to a sense that everything has changed. But, while these events have significantly impacted the study of anti-Semitism in terms of interest, pressure, and material for analysis, I regard the upsurge in anti-Semitism and political discourse surrounding it, as well as pressure for conceptual clarification, to be an escalation of an ongoing struggle rather than a paradigm shift. Concerns about anti-Semitism and anti-anti-Semitism have been pressing for me and colleagues engaged in this subject matter long before October 7th. Then as now, there was politicization of anti-Semitism to advance right-wing agendas or stifle Palestinian voices and a troubling echo of anti-Semitism within left-wing and progressive circles.

Even so, I find myself shocked, nearly paralyzed in my thinking, by the horror of the violence from Hamas and the Israeli government, the death of Palestinian children, the rise in anti-Semitic events, significant fractures within/between Jewish communities, and the intensified use of both anti-Semitic and anti-anti-Semitic rhetoric for nationalist, authoritarian, and racist agendas. Every time I sit down to think or write about the increasingly complex realities, fresh impossibilities and barriers to clear comprehension emerge, demanding constant reassessment and questioning of assumptions.

I cannot imagine a world where the abhorrent cruelty of Hamas' attacks and devastation wrought by Israel's retaliation—or any such assault on civilians—can be morally justified. Such violence and ethnocentrism stand in stark contrast to the values and moral consciousness I cherish in being Jewish. I am torn apart. These statements might be interpreted as falling into the trap of political "bothsidesism." However, as a scholar in the field of psychology, specializing in ambivalence and navigating complex realities, I advocate for embracing greater complexity rather than simplification in the moment of critical engagement. The "sides" may not be as internally consistent or homogenous as they appear. I hope that readers, whatever your current stance on Israel, Palestine, or Zionism, will resist the temptation to disengage at this point and instead, join me in embracing discomfort long enough to think together.

This heightened sense of anguish is *not* unfamiliar to me, serving as one of the driving forces behind my research. The grief and paralysis many of us feel at this moment may signal an even greater urgency for the concepts and arguments explored in this book, which take up the task of confronting the shapeshifting and multifaceted issues at hand.

Expanding on Zygmunt Bauman's concept of proteophobia, or the fear of what does not fit into clear-cut categories, the book asserts that the complexities of Jewishness, anti-Semitism, and the Jewish targets of anti-Semitism pose formidable challenges for study and thought, often evoking a sense of anxiety when confronted and sometimes prompting destructive behaviors intent on alleviating that anxiety. Readers will encounter discussions on ethno-nationalism, debates over conflating anti-Semitism with anti-Zionism, anti-Semitism across the political spectrum, and dynamics of power, privilege, and visibility, along with an exploration of complexities surrounding racism, White supremacy, and intersectionality. Through the lenses of critical theory and psychoanalysis, I explore various modes of resistance against proteophobia, anti-Semitism, and other forms of oppression. I hope that the book will contribute to the pursuit of dignity, freedom, and security for Jews and Palestinians alike—that is, together.

As I pondered how to integrate the events of October 7th into the work I had already completed, I came to the realization that doing so through revisions would either be insufficient or be excessive—it would essentially necessitate another book. Therefore, I have confined myself mostly to this preface. The book stands on its own, or rather, it only truly stands if readers can relate its provocations to the issues unraveling in their own world.

Carpinteria, CA, USA   Benjamin B. Strosberg

Acknowledgments

I want to express my profound gratitude to Derek Hook, Stephen Frosh, and Leswin Laubscher who offered contagious curiosity, inspiration, and guidance on early versions of this project. I am honored by Stephen's assistance in bringing this book to publication. Rarely have I encountered individuals as simultaneously humble and brilliant as these three.

I would like to thank the McAnulty College and Graduate School of Liberal Arts at Duquesne University, for their financial support through much of the writing process. I am also indebted to the numerous individuals who have contributed to my growth as a psychologist during my time in the Department of Psychology at Duquesne University, especially Will Adams, Joe Anderson, Suzanne Barnard, Robert Bernasconi, Pavan Brar, Roger Brooke, Michell Brown, Daniel Burston, Autumn Marie Chilcote, Jacklyn Corsitto, Elizabeth Fein, Bruce Fink, Ben Gaddes, Jessie Goicoechea, Lucas Goodwin, Emiko Hunt, Anthony Koch, Lori Koelsch, Anna Lampe, Brad Landry, Calum Matheson, Ryan Mest, Donna Orange, Louis Sass, Eva Simms, Kevin Smith, the Lacan reading group in Pittsburgh, and of course my patients and students. Special thanks to Mitchell Sjerven and Amy Sachs for generously providing a place to live and a tranquil writing space, to Sophia Strosberg and Lillian Moss for their encouragement and expertise as writers, and to Sean Leadem, a partner in intellectual crime, whose feedback has been invaluable on nearly everything I've written.

I feel compelled to thank others who, over the years, have accompanied me along the way, including in writing this first book of mine, providing inspiration, conversation, guidance, and support in various forms. Among them are Cynthia, Mark, and Seth Anderson, Greg Alexander, Amanda Clapp, Erin Currier, Omar Dahbour, Lillian Denhardt, Dick and Holly Dixon, Anna Fitzgerald, Justin George, Lisa Giordano, Nina Gonzales, Paul Guido, Lindsey Harrington, Peyton Harrison, Anthony Hassett (ז״ל), the Hook family, Madeline Kimlin, Celeste Lai, Adam and David Moss, Jack Moss, Jesse Moore, Estephania Puerta, Jessie Resnick, Daniel Schwartz, Jeffrey Strosberg, Marilyn Strosberg, Vivian Strosberg, Dara Sneddon, Caroline Sjerven, Elena Visconti Di Modrone, Becca and Jon Walley, Jon Williams, Garo Yellin, Pacifica Graduate Institute, my beloved companions in the Vermont Joy Parade, and the Library Minyan in Santa Barbara, California.

My deepest gratitude and love to Madeline and Zev, the joys of my life.

Contents

About the Author

Benjamin B. Strosberg is a professor of clinical psychology at in Carpinteria, California, and a psychotherapist in private practice.

1

Questions of Categorization in (and Against) Anti-Semitism

Mixed Messages

I arrived in Pittsburgh, Pennsylvania, in 2018 to study, and train in, clinical psychology at Duquesne University. At the time, I was participating in a practical workshop for Hearing Voices Network[1] group facilitators. On one of the workshop days, we explored the lived experience of hearing voices, which is traditionally associated with psychosis. A colleague was talking into a cardboard tube directed at my ear as I attempted to conduct everyday tasks. ["Four score and seven years ago…"] I found it difficult to concentrate with those competing voices. ["Why is he looking at you?"] It was a disorienting day, to say the least. ["Abracadabra, abracadabra!"] It was all the more disorienting when, during the exercise, I started to receive text messages from panicked friends and family asking where I was and if I was alright. Apparently, a few minutes earlier, a White supremacist had walked into a local synagogue with a large gun and

---

[1] Hearing Voices Network is an organization that helps to support people with shared experiences in voice-hearing phenomenon by offering educational workshops and facilitator training and hosting peer-led support groups (Hearing Voices Network, 2022). Though voice-hearing is generally associated with psychosis, the Hearing Voices Network promotes the idea that voice-hearing is a widely experienced phenomenon.

opened fire on a Jewish congregation in the Squirrel Hill neighborhood of Pittsburgh a few miles from the workshop and my home. I'm Jewish. I'd attended a synagogue like that as a child and still do. I remember my visceral sense of shock and fear that day, and I am reminded of it every time I walk past the guard standing sentinel at the entrance to my neighborhood synagogue.

The event has since been referred to as the deadliest attack on Jews in the United States, ever. ["Other minority groups in the United States face physical violence daily."] The intensity of the Pittsburgh massacre was certainly unprecedented in the social milieu of the United States at the time, and the chorus of voices speaking out against anti-Semitism seemed to be unanimous. ["People are paying attention because the victims are White."] Yet there is something that disturbed me about the intensity of the initial response, followed by the eventual quietness on the subject. ["We need to focus on the more deeply rooted and structural issues like anti-Black racism."] Years of analysis into structural forms of racism have taught us that bloody violence is only one form of great harm. Some anti-Semites do want Jews to die, and physical threats and attacks have increased in the United States, but that is only one form of anti-Semitism. After the Pittsburgh massacre, few people aside from other Jews seemed to be too concerned with the not-so-immediately bloody forms of anti-Semitism. ["On the whole, it's a thing of the past. Jews are White and privileged."] In fact, I feel self-conscious about writing a book on the topic. ["Jews bring everything back to anti-Semitism and the Holocaust."] I remember that after the initial shock of the massacre wore off, I was somewhat unsurprised, even prepared for the reactions that followed, given both the force of anti-Semitic rhetoric spreading on the Internet ["Jews have too much power."] and my personal experience of anti-Semitism. ["You'll never be at home."] I live in a house with a hidden room, a closet within a closet, a place to hide. ["The Black holocaust was 100 times worse than the so-called Jew Holocaust."[2]] It has only been 75 years since most of my family members were sent to death camps. ["What about the genocide of Palestinians at the hands of Jews?"]

---

[2] This phrase is taken from the beginning of Michael Rothberg's book, *Multidirectional Memory* (2009), where he is quoting Khalid Muhammad (1948–2001).

The metaphor of "hearing voices" is apt for conveying some of the disorientation and disruptions that these other contrary voices produce in me, some of which I've illustrated by the square brackets intruding into the preceding narrative. They are of course only shorthand markers—beneath "You'll never be at home" lie several lifetimes, and behind all the comparisons between Blacks, Jews, Palestinians, of who suffered and suffers "more," a dynamic that obfuscates and confuses, and which may well "belong" to neither Black nor Jew nor Palestinian. The point is that these voices—thoughts, rather than auditory hallucinations—are social, and I share them with many Jews. Were one to extend the hearing-voices metaphor, they are as much mine, individually and particularly, as they belong, culturally and generally. I carry them with me, along with the trauma of my family, and they intercede in my thinking. And as I started to research anti-Semitism, they grew louder. And I saw their echoes, interceding in the thinking of the academy. I felt like I was reading or seeing one thing while experiencing contradictory messages whose origin I couldn't quite pin down. Which was an echo, and which origin? Is such a question even answerable? These contradictions and the ambivalence they invoke became the focus of my project.

Three Questions

The Question of Categorizing Anti-Semitism

At one level, anti-Semitism[3] seems to need no explanatory introduction. History is replete with examples of anti-Semitic rhetoric and violence: executions, expulsions, and forced conversions during the Spanish Inquisition, the terror of pogroms in Russia, the implementation of Jewish racial quotas in North American universities, the millions of Jews that perished in the Nazi concentration camps. More recent examples of unmistakable anti-Semitism include[4] the 2017 event in Charlottesville,

---

[3] I explore my choice to use the spelling anti-Semitism instead of antisemitism later in the book.

[4] Here, it is important to acknowledge the North American focus and perspective that, perforce of my own location and of the numerous instances of anti-Semitism occurring in this region in recent history, significantly informs the perspective of my study.

Virginia, where marchers carried tiki torches and chanted "the Jews will not replace us"; the massacre and shooting of Jews in Pittsburgh, Pennsylvania, in 2018; Poway, California, in 2019; Jersey City, New Jersey, also in 2019; violence against Jews in the United States in the wake of renewed armed conflict between Israel and Hamas in 2021; the hostage incident at a Texas synagogue in 2022; the massacre and hostage-taking of Israeli Jews by Hamas in October 2023. "The Jews" and "Jewish power" continue to be positioned at the center of conspiracy theories adopted by some mainstream politicians around the world and mobilized by extremists to provoke violence.

The term "anti-Semitism" is used as if we all know what it means, though some examples labeled anti-Semitism are less clear and at times hotly debated. Here are a few: paintings of greedy bankers with Jewish cultural markers like big noses (e.g., Mear One's "Freedom for Humanity")[5]; the anti-circumcision movement (i.e., "intactivism")[6]; claims that Jews are in control of Hollywood; blaming Jews for Israeli policies; denying the uniqueness of the Shoah; yelling "free Palestine" and "you white piece of shit" at someone wearing an Israeli Defense Forces jacket at a public mall; protesters chanting, "settlers, settlers go home, Palestine is ours alone;" insisting that a Jewish musician declare support for Boycotts, Divestment, Sanctions (BDS)[7] before a performance; using the term "cultural Marxism" or "postmodern cultural Marxism;" the exclusion of Jews from a list of persecuted minority groups; the belief that Christianity supersedes Judaism; non-Jewish actors playing Jewish roles; non-Jewish actors wearing nose prosthetics to play Jewish roles; comparing Israel to Nazi Germany[8]; referring to Israeli policy as apartheid; using

---

[5] See Freedom for Humanity (2023).

[6] Intactivism is the name of a movement made up of anti-circumcision activists seeking an end to all male circumcision (see Intactivism, 2023).

[7] According to its website, Boycott, Divestment, Sanctions (BDS) is a Palestinian-led movement advocating for freedom, justice, and equality. It aims to secure the same rights for Palestinians as for all other individuals. The movement has been a subject of intense controversy, with debates revolving around allegations of anti-Semitism, its stance on non-violent resistance to Israeli occupation, and implications for academic free speech (BDS, 2023).

[8] See Rothberg and Lenz (2024) for a thoughtful discussion on the topic of comparisons.

terms like "Palestine will be free from the river to the sea"[9] and "the Jewish lobby." The astute reader may also already suspect that the charges of anti-Semitism (or not) in many of these examples are modified by who utters it.

Like anti-Black racism, anti-Semitism has an intuitive cachet. But the truth is, also like anti-Black racism, it has meant different things at different times and places to different people.[10] Despite its seemingly intuitive meaning, anti-Semitism is incredibly difficult to study, analyze, and fight, not least of all because people struggle to categorize this or that as anti-Semitism. The ability to categorize and define the nature of oppression and identify oppressed groups seems to go hand in hand with resisting oppression. To fight a monster, one needs to know what it looks like, where it lives, and how it wields power. It is not surprising, therefore, that contemporary debates surrounding the study of anti-Semitism revolve around the question of definition and categorization.[11] Yet the establishment of a functional definition of anti-Semitism has become part of the very problem that such definitions seek to solve—agreement on what anti-Semitism is so that it can be effectively resisted.

In 2010, the US government adopted the International Holocaust Remembrance Alliance's (IHRA) "Working Definition of Antisemitism" (USDS, 2022). The Working Definition articulates the numerous ways

---

[9] This phrase can mean different things depending on the context. Peter Beinart argues that it can mean a Palestinian nation-state without Jews or a Palestine where Palestinians and Jews live together peacefully in freedom (Demirjian & Stack, 2023).

[10] The histories of anti-Semitism and anti-Black racism are deeply intertwined (Bernasconi, 2021). Bernasconi (2021) takes this idea a step further. Whereas some scholars suggest that anti-Semitism may be worn out as a concept (i.e., being so multifaceted that it lacks specificity and critical value; see Badiou et al., 2013), Bernasconi (2021) suggests that this is no more so than the concept of racism. He makes a case for thinking about anti-Semitism in terms of racism, since racism isn't based on any real biology or hard ground to begin with. This approach leads to intersectional thinking (see Schraub, 2019).

[11] The question of definition has become central to the study of anti-Semitism (e.g., Judaken, 2018; Langmuir, 1990; Lerman, 2022; Marcus, 2015). The present project explores the logic through and by which definitions and identities are constructed, the contradictions that logic might include, and how each discourse might reproduce a facet of anti-Semitism in the very attempt to alleviate intellectual anxieties. These discourses around definition tend to produce a parallel demand to resolve the contradiction historically embedded in ideas of Jewishness—in need of categorization, and yet impossible to categorize. And ultimately, some attempts to categorize Jewishness seem to erase the historical particularity of Jewish identity, and at times, the value of particular Jewish forms of life.

anti-Semitism can manifest. On the face of it, this adoption by the US government was an effort to protect its 7.6 million Jewish citizens (nearly half of the world's Jewry), and is not particularly controversial. Here it is:

> Antisemitism is a certain perception of Jews, which may be expressed as hatred toward Jews. Rhetorical and physical manifestations of antisemitism are directed toward Jewish or non-Jewish individuals and/or their property, toward Jewish community institutions and religious facilities. (USDS, 2022)

This definition, however, is paired with a set of examples (e.g., "Drawing comparisons of contemporary Israeli policy to that of the Nazis") that lend themselves to the determination of the State of Israel as the collective Jew and thereafter the determination that a statement about Israel may also be a statement about "the Jews." The definition has proven of questionable utility in legal efforts to address hate crimes in court and has spawned controversy over political "weaponization" of the definition against critiques of the Israeli State, principally on college campuses (Lerman, 2022; Stern, 2019).

Meanwhile, debate continues (often contentious and acrimonious) in the social commons as it does the scholarly academic: on the relationship between anti-Semitism and Islamophobia, Jewishness and Whiteness, anti-Semitism, and anti-Zionism. Despite all this public and academic attention, anti-Semitic incidents in the United States could be said to have close-to-doubled in the decade preceding the events of October 7, 2023. Anti-Semitic tropes continue to proliferate. According to the Anti-Defamation League (ADL),[12] as of 2020 around 24 percent of Americans believed Jews are more loyal to Israel than the United States, and over a quarter of Americans believe the anti-Semitic trope that the "Jews killed Christ"(ADL, 2020).[13] Anti-Semitism cannot be thought of merely as

---

[12] I do not align with the ADL or its tactics. ADL and its CEO, Jonathan Greenblatt, espouse the notion that anti-Zionism equates to anti-Semitism (Chotiner, 2022).

[13] An example of this trope of Jewish responsibility for the killing of Jesus Christ and of the difficulty in thinking about anti-Semitism in general can be found in a post from the social media account belonging to actor, rapper, entrepreneur Jamie Foxx. Foxx wrote: "They killed this dude name Jesus … what do you think they'll do to you???! #fakefriends #fakelove." Over 130,000 people "liked" the post. After criticism from the Jewish community, he quickly apologized: "I want to apologize to the Jewish community and everyone who was offended by my post. I now know my

hate for Jewish people—though, it is certainly also that. Those seeking to understand and resist anti-Semitism must attend to the perpetuation of Jewish conspiracies and stereotypes that have anti-Semitic impact (like backhanded compliments about Jewish business-savvy), the willingness to join institutions and platforms that tolerate anti-Jewish rhetoric and

---

choice of words have caused offense and I'm sorry. That was never my intent. To clarify, I was betrayed by a fake friend and that's what I meant with 'they' not anything more. I only have love in my heart for everyone. I love and support the Jewish community. My deepest apologies to anyone who was offended [heart] [heart] [heart] Nothing but love always, Jamie Foxx [heart] [fox] [prayer hands]" (Vargas, 2023). Responses to the post have varied, with many individuals not interpreting his statement as anti-Semitism. The case is surprisingly complex, and careful consideration is required.

A key point of confusion arises from the use of the ambiguous pronoun "they" instead of the more common "Pontius Pilate," "Judas," "the Jews" or "we." Foxx and his followers suggest that "They killed Christ" is a common turn of phrase for many people in Black Christian culture, and that he was only using the phrase to suggest that a friend betrayed Foxx like "They betrayed Jesus." While it is very possible that Foxx posted the statement without holding conscious animosity toward Jewish people, the use of Jesus' crucifixion to convey an "us and them" mentality has anti-Semitic undertones, to say the least. This association between the historical charge of deicide against Jews and current betrayal has been used to justify persecution throughout the past two millennia.

The identity of Foxx's friend as Jewish remains uncertain. If the friend were not Jewish, it's conceivable that Foxx and his public relations team would have disclosed this information to quell the controversy. Foxx later characterized the comment as "cultural and harmless," expanding on his perspective by asserting that the "they" in his post refers to his friend and to untrustworthy people in general. He argued that the act of killing Jesus does not pertain exclusively to Jews but rather extends to humanity as a whole. This viewpoint suggests that the individuals responsible for Christ's death are not specifically identified as Jews; rather, they happen to be Jewish. Foxx maintains that he was taught to use the crucifixion as an example of betrayal by all of humanity. Nonetheless, when referring to a "they" instead of a historical figure or the pronoun "we," this framing continues to cast Jews as emblematic of untrustworthiness. A number of the responses to Foxx's post involve defenses of his statement based on the historical belief that Jews were implicated in the crucifixion of Christ, with some asserting that this absolves the post of any anti-Semitic sentiment. However, this perspective fails to align clearly with Christian teachings, as many modern churches emphasize collective human responsibility for Christ's death rather than singling out Jews specifically.

The lack of context in Foxx's post resulted in rhetorical ambiguity, giving rise to anti-Semitic reactions from some of his followers. As explored in subsequent chapters, Christianity has historically contained elements of anti-Judaism deeply ingrained within Western society, and Foxx's post may inadvertently align with these sentiments. Over centuries, Jews have been depicted as symbols of betrayal, hypocrisy, and the archetypal "they," a concept that has persisted since the crucifixion of Christ. This example underscores the enduring notion that "the Jews killed Christ." These complexities highlight the challenges surrounding discussions of what constitutes anti-Semitism, who is considered anti-Semitic, and how to address the topic without exacerbating polarization.

One additional point worth considering is the potential parallels and contrasts between this particular case and the situation involving Coleman Silk in Phillip Roth's novel, *The Human Stain* (2000).

practices, and the way that anti-Jewishness may be structurally embedded in particular worldviews.[14]

The continued proliferation of anti-Jewish practices despite (or owing to) public awareness of anti-Semitism, is nonetheless accompanied by a lagging scholarship. What could account for the discrepancy between public attention to anti-Semitism and the dearth of scholarship and scholarly consensus within the field? Perhaps, some of the problem can be attributed to what research shows as a confusion about what it is that we are measuring or even talking about when we analyze anti-Semitism. For instance, some statistics show an increase in anti-Semitic incidents, but others show a decrease (Lerman, 2022). Established methods for studying and measuring anti-Semitism are failing, perhaps owing to the changes in technology, communication, and dissemination of anti-Jewish discourse (Lerman, 2022). Anti-Semitic tropes, dog whistles, tirades, and manifestos are awash on the Internet and social media. Payton Gendron, the gunman who massacred ten Black Americans in a Buffalo, New York, grocery store wrote extensively about the "great replacement" conspiracy centering around Jewish responsibility for the replacement of White Christian Americans by non-White people. He posted his racist and anti-Semitic manifesto on the Internet—a manifesto inspired by other manifestos and theories posted on the Internet. The extent of such practices on the Internet is hard to track with older methods used by institutions like the Anti-Defamation League (see Lerman, 2022). Each repost of a meme, for instance, cannot count as one anti-Semitic incident next to the intensity of singular events of physical violence and intimidation without diluting the practice of keeping count.[15]

---

[14] In November 2022, Donald Trump had dinner with Nick Fuentes, a self-identified White supremacist and Christian nationalist. Trump was quoted as saying, "He gets me" (Haberman & Feuer, 2022). Also at that dinner was Kanye West, a celebrity who accused fellow artist and entrepreneur, Sean "P. Diddy" Combs, of being controlled by the Jews. West has since expressed affection for Adolf Hitler (Paybarah, 2022). Trump's affiliations with White supremacists and conspiracy theorists are well-known, as are his uses of anti-Semitic tropes and prejudices (Blake, 2022). En masse, Trump's voters may not be anti-Semitic in the sense of harboring hate for Jews, indeed, he may not hate Jews either.

[15] According to Merriam-Webster Dictionary (2022), a meme is: 1. "an amusing or interesting item (such as a captioned picture or video) or genre of items that is spread widely online especially through social media" and 2. "an idea, behavior, style, or usage that spreads from person to person within a culture."

It is difficult to determine how to count or even categorize rhetoric on the Internet related to Jewish tropes like "Jewish hyperpower," especially as those tropes permeate mainstream political life, mobilize attacks on Jewish people and synagogues, and function as an organizing principle for White supremacists of various intensities. Anti-Semitism remains a central tenet of a popular worldview but its multifaceted expression makes it difficult to systematically track and statistically quantify. We face ambiguity in not only defining what constitutes anti-Semitism but also effectively monitoring and measuring its occurrences.

The Question of Categorizing the Jews

To make matters more complicated, part of the confusion about how to categorize anti-Semitism might be owing to confusion as to categorizing its targeted minority group: the Jews. Who is Jewish, as well as what it means to be Jewish—in the eyes of both Jews and non-Jews—is hard to delineate and circumscribe definitively. For some, Jewishness is inherited genetically through mitochondrial DNA passed down by maternal lineage; for others, it is inherited through broader familial kinship bonds or an existential thrownness into a particular aesthetic, language, or set of values. Still for others, Jewishness is a belief system or faith one can adopt and disown. Self-identified Jews are clearly a minority group, making up only 0.2 percent of the world population and around 2 percent of the US population. Jews are the target of hate, as the examples above show. And yet, Jews are often excluded from lists of oppressed minority groups. How could this be? One explanation for this is the difficulty in categorization: Many Americans believe that Jews *are* White, and that Jews are overrepresented in the upper echelons of American society and counted among the privileged and powerful elites. They are thus categorized as a dominating and powerful minority like Whites in South Africa. One problem with this line of thinking is the number of Jews who identify as people of color. According to the Pew Research Center (2021), around 10 percent of Jews in the United States are "Hispanic, Black, Asian, Other, or Multiple Race," and the percentage may be increasing. However, some suggest the percentage of Jews of Color in the United States is more like

6 percent (Sheskin & Dashefsky, 2020). As of 2019, nearly half of all Jews in Israel are of Middle Eastern or North African descent, with only 30 percent identifying as Ashkenazi or descended from Jews who lived in European countries (Lewin-Epstein & Cohen, 2019).[16,17]

Another problem with categorizing Jews as White (with all its privileges) is the fact that the most active and violent organized hate groups in the United States attack Jews precisely because they are considered to be not White or not White enough.[18] Jews are a primary target for most White supremacists. According to one study of right-wing extremist attacks on US soil since 1980, every single perpetrator believed in a Jewish conspiracy (Allington, 2021). At the same time, many social justice groups who seek to protect minorities from oppression exclude

---

[16] Around 900,000 (no one seems to agree on a number) Jews left Arab and North African countries after the establishment of Israel and the Nakba, or the violent expulsion of Palestinian Arabs in 1948. The narrative of a Jewish "expulsion" is contested. Some scholars suggest that Israel is directly responsible for the displacement of Jews, others suggest that the Jews left voluntarily, and still others suggest that this displacement of Jews was a result of anti-Semitism and human rights violations (Basri, 2002).

[17] In discussing the question of Jewish Whiteness and privilege, it might be helpful to briefly discuss the question of race. Race, as Karen and Barbara Fields (2012) point out, is always only meaningful with reference to racism. There are no hard lines that demarcate Black bodies from non-Black bodies aside from the gaze of the racist, and there is certainly no genetic marker of Blackness. Allele frequencies used to find genetic clusters such that groups can be statistically demarcated may correspond to geographic location but not to Blackness. There may be more variation within the category Black than between Black and White. Nevertheless, race is a meaningful category, and more could/should be said about epidermalization.

Whiteness, too, is not merely a phenotypic visual marker, as if it can be determined based on Pantone color shade criteria. Whiteness, Sara Ahmed (2007) points out, is demarcated by a particular social location that affords a certain access to social and material privileges within a racialized world and granted by a racist social contract. To say that a person is White is to say that they are marked by access to power.

With the statement "Jews are White," the unique material coordinates of Jewishness are erased, and even this erasure is erased. "Insofar as Jewishness is not understood as existing as a materially distinct category from Whiteness," Schraub (2019) contends, "the failure to consider Jews as a case of a marginalized identity is not intuitively felt as an absence" (p. 384). In other words, Jews will always be seen as White as long as they are not seen as materially (marked) differently than Whiteness.

[18] Fields and Fields (2012) discuss the case of a Jew in a prison cafeteria who is unable to sit with the Black or Latino table because he is not Black or Latino, but he is also unable to sit with the White because he is not considered White. The Jewish prisoner is made to sit by himself after everyone else has eaten. I find this to be a helpful narrative account of the current situation of Jewish identity.

Jews because they are considered to be White and granted the privileges (e.g., anonymity) associated with Whiteness. David Schraub (2019) calls this precarious or conditional Whiteness. Some Jews are White in some moments and not White in others. According to Schraub (2019), "Part of the difficulty [in thinking about Jewishness in relation to Whiteness] is that Jewishness crosses over and blurs categories that theorists [...] often wish to keep separate" (p. 389). This makes Jewish identity multiform and difficult to categorize, perhaps even blurring the line between binary oppositions like Black/White, and (as I will argue in what follows) exposing some of the faulty logic behind racist thinking.

Still, there are many Jewish people who are White in the eyes of society and seem to be granted access to White privileges and in being able to feel at home in "White spaces" (see Ahmed, 2007). They are not, however, granted White privilege on the basis of their Jewishness as it might appear; they are only privileged on the basis of their assumed Whiteness or at-home-ness in White spaces. But for many people, Jewishness, especially in the Diaspora (a term derived from the Greek meaning "scattered across") is experienced as homelessness or not quite fitting in (Boyarin & Boyarin, 2002; Magid, 2006). Aside from the tension between White at-home-ness and Jewish homelessness, one of the difficulties in analyzing the intersection of Jewishness and Whiteness is the role that hidden power plays in both identity positions. Since there is an association of Jews with power, light-skinned Jews not just are registered as White but also seem to exemplify Whiteness.[19] Jewishness becomes a multiplier of

---

[19] An example may help to clarify this issue of Jews exemplifying Whiteness. There is a moment in the movie *Everything, Everywhere, All at Once* (EEAO) that comes to mind. EEAO is a movie focusing on Asian American experience, immigrant family experience, and mother-daughter relationships. Overall, I think the movie is an accomplishment on all these levels. Still, there is a moment of anti-Semitism in the movie that makes me wince every time I see it. Shortly after we are introduced to the main character Evelyn, the proprietor of a Laundromat, she repeatedly calls one of the customers by the name "Big Nose." Big Nose is played by the actor Jenny Slate. Slate has stereotypical Jewish features like curly brown hair and a prominent nose bridge. In EEAO, she is further marked as a "Jewish American Princess," with a pink jumpsuit and catty attitude. The writer/director team apologized for this representation after some Internet debate about the anti-Semitic micro-aggression (Geisinger, 2022). They said that it was a blind spot, and that it was meant to show Evelyn's character arc, and not to confirm any racial stereotypes. The nasty term "Big Nose" was used alongside other forms of racism, sexism, and fat-shaming, that the directors were critiquing and commenting on with the movie. Yet, the term "Big Nose" was used as a different kind of racial slur. It is a racial slur used in some Chinese communities to describe White people (Geisinger,

White privilege such that Jews are found to be hyper-powerful, confirming the anti-Semitic trope (Schraub, 2019).

The main category error is the contention that Jewishness is added or incorporated into, rather than intersecting/interacting, with Whiteness. Whiteness is not just a skin color; it is a social position of access to social and material possibilities that is experienced by those White people as unmarked (i.e., the slate on which cultural marks are made). To be culturally "marked" is to be more than a "mere individual." Race functions through this type of marking and "works precisely to block recourse to [...] anonymity [...] allocated through social power" (Salamon, 2021, p. 159). For an example of Jewish "markedness" and lack of anonymity, think of the TV show *The Patient* (Fields & Weisberg, 2022). The protagonist in the show is Dr. Alan Strauss, a Jewish psychotherapist played by Steve Carell. Steve Carell is not Jewish. How, then, do we, as the audience, know that Steve Carell is playing a Jewish character? Steve Carell acts "Jewish" and is marked by certain characteristics, signifiers, and "isms." He has a beard, has a proud nose, is a psychotherapist, wears glasses, has the last name Strauss. Eventually we find out more conclusively that he is Jewish because the director gives us flashbacks to Dr. Strauss' Jewish history and cultural practices.

The access to anonymity in the form of appearing unmarked seems to be both attributed to Jews and denied to Jews. "Whiteness," Sara Ahmed (2007) contends, "is only invisible for those who inhabit it, or those who get so used to its inhabitance that they learn not to see it, even when they are not it" (p. 236). The work to undo Whiteness is to make White people recognize that they not just are neutral and unmarked but also actively participate in Whiteness—that they actively practice Whiteness. Schraub (2019) argues that this undoing is different when attributed to Jews who are already marked:

2022). To my mind, it is the conflation of Jews with Whiteness that is so problematic in the scene and that the directors and many viewers see Jewishness as the epitome or caricature of Whiteness such that it erased Jenny Slate's Jewishness to such a degree that the thoughtful directors didn't recognize that it would come across as anti-Semitic. I can only imagine that the anti-Semitic moment is felt by many Jews who watch the movie, while non-Jews may miss it.

Antisemitism frequently manifests as a concern over putative Jewish hyper-power. Whereas White individuals are often seen as an unmarked category ("just" individuals), Jewishness is very much a marked identity—and the markers quite frequently center around beliefs about Jewish power, domination, or social control. The Whiteness frame by design is meant to draw attention to these attributes, revealing things that otherwise go unseen or unspoken. But when it operates on the Jewish case—where these attributes are not unmarked but instead are exceptionally visible and salient—its cultural impact can be quite different. Instead of unsettling and particularizing a hitherto "neutral" identity, it can promote, even accelerate, deeply antisemitic tropes. (p. 384).

Whiteness is the ability to hide one's markedness and to access power and material affordances. Jews (marked as Jewish) are inscribed as White by hiding their marked Jewish difference. It is not a privilege to have to hide one's minority cultural differences. Of course, the tumultuous history of Jewish assimilation shows that this hiding is never fully possible. One can say, "there are so many Jewish doctors, lawyers, media executives, and financiers" precisely because Jews are still marked as Jews. To say that Jews are hiding their Whiteness, their power and privilege, is rhetorically close to anti-Semitism.[20] This is a problem for the project of dismantling systems of power, like White supremacy, that Jews seem to be the victims of, and many, to greater or lesser degrees, participate in. This appears to be an impasse, but one that could potentially be addressed with more nuanced intersectional thinking.[21]

---

[20] A friend once told me about an incident that happened at a yoga studio in her neighborhood. In an anti-racist workshop at the yoga studio, employees were asked to sit in a circle and openly acknowledge their hidden White privilege. However, a Jewish employee found it difficult to do so without also considering her Jewish identity, which the other participants didn't understand, accusing her of White fragility. Intersectional thinking can shed light on this dynamic, recognizing that publicly acknowledging White privilege as a Jewish person might have unique consequences due to the unique intersection of Jewishness and Whiteness.

[21] It does not seem reasonable to claim that it is anti-Semitic to say, for instance, "Harvey Weinstein has too much power," or for that matter, "Israel is powerful." One way of understanding this is to explore rhetoric that one *does* something when one speaks. So, for instance, "all lives matter" is a true statement but is false as a response and rebuttal to "black lives matter." It is true grammatically while being racist rhetorically. Take this example: "The Israeli military wears green uniforms just like the uniforms worn by Nazi soldiers." That might be true but saying it within a context does something rhetorical. The way that anti-Semitism spreads on the Internet, and even in the mainstream is filled with rhetorical gestures that postpone the moment of determination. This creates an

Ongoing attempts to define and study Jewishness and anti-Semitism have been ineffective at clarifying the former or uprooting the latter. In much of the literature, anti-Semitism has been explained as bias, stereotype, prejudice, racism, psychosis, projection, and phobia; its Jewish target described as a race, religion, nationality, culture, and figure of thought. The apparent intractability of categorizing Jews may lead to an anxious confusion expressed in implicit anti-Semitic assertions; consider Whoopi Goldberg's 2022 remarks that the Holocaust was "not about race" because it was between "two White groups of people" (Gross & Vigdor, 2022). It has also led to violent anti-Semitic action: In recent attacks by White supremacists in Pittsburgh, Pennsylvania, and Poway, California, for example, Jews were characterized alternately as being *not White enough* (excluded from White Euro-American culture) and *too White* (able secretly to infect society by occupying positions of power).

I've come to believe that this difficulty in thinking about Jewishness and anti-Semitism is a defining feature of contemporary anti-Semitism. In this book, I examine this intractability: the seemingly endless efforts to categorize and define Jewishness and anti-Semitism and the implications of this endeavor for the fight against anti-Semitism and other injustices. Without diluting the complexity of the issues at hand, let me sum up what I've introduced so far. Jewish people are members of a minority group that makes up a very small percentage of the population outside of Israel. Jewish people are targeted by anti-Jewish practices. The ideas that undergird those practices are central to various worldviews (e.g., White supremacy, Christian Nationalism) and seem to play a significant role in the political life of some nations. At times anti-Semitism (as hate for Jews) is not a central political ideal but is used to signify ideals (such as White supremacy) indirectly. There are a variety of instances in contemporary society where anti-Jewish practices are enacted—shootings, bombings, Internet trolling, stereotyping, discrimination, published conspiracy theories disseminated via online social networks, etc. The target of those practices also takes many forms—the figure of Judaism in Christian

---

impasse for positive scholarship that tries to categorize something once and for all. In my thinking, this difference between grammar and rhetoric gets to the heart of much contentious disagreement around the topic of Israel/Palestine and anti-Semitism/racism. I believe that the negative approach I take here can go some way in dealing with these rhetorical issues.

doctrine, Jewish identifying people, people identified *as* Jewish, Israelis, people accused of doing something that resembles Jewish stereotypes like miserliness, Jewish institutions, values considered to be Jewish (e.g., social justice, cosmopolitanism), etc. Previous attempts to categorize and clearly define anti-Semitism through rigorous theory seem to fail, and sometimes make things less clear, as in the formulation "anti-Zionism is anti-Semitism" or the oversimplification, "anti-Semitism is the hate for Jews."

Some contemporary scholars think of the problem primarily in terms of Zionism/anti-Zionism and Israel/Palestine. It is not enough to suggest that contemporary anti-Semitism can be understood in relation to those issues. While the problem does express itself in those issues (as well as in relation to Whiteness and racism), I believe that underlying these issues in contemporary society is a problem in the kind of logical reasoning evoked in these specific historical instances of conflict. Part of this problem is related to the nature of Jewish identity which is multi-form and form-changing (e.g., Jews are thought of as White and not White). I am proposing that this difficulty in thinking about the various facets of anti-Semitism—uses, histories, practices, and targets—is itself the historically specific facet of contemporary anti-Semitism. Therefore, my wager is that to resist anti-Semitism we must first think more carefully about these difficulties in thinking that thinking about anti-Semitism evokes. This is the shore from which this book sets sail.

The Question of Uncategorizability and Proteophobia

How then are we to think about these issues that seem to be demarcated and categorized by their difficulty in thinking and resistance to clear exposition? There are thinkers over the past hundred years who have alerted us to these issues and developed concepts capable of doing justice to the historical specificity of anti-Semitism in our current era. These thinkers offer ways of studying these matters that seem to evade the trap of false confidence in settled debates—a false confidence that would lend itself to irrational justifications for action. Through that evasion they model a form of social action by way of critical and psychoanalytic thinking. I take my lead from these thinkers—sociologist Zygmunt Bauman (1925–2017) and philosopher Theodor W. Adorno (1903–1969) chief among them.

More specifically, I follow Bauman's lead in rethinking anti-Semitism in terms of what he calls "proteophobia," or the fear of what is form-changing and uncategorizable (Bauman, 1995; Cheyette, 2013; Judaken, 2018; Lerman, 2022). What is uncategorizable and form-changing challenges the fantasy of purity and order that organizes much of modern society. Anti-Semitism, especially when paired with its opposite, philosemitism (crudely, love of things/people Jewish), can be understood through the lens of proteophobia. Bauman (1998) also refers to this anti-Semitism/philosemitism pairing as "allosemitism" or the ambivalent attitude toward what is Jewish. The Jew, for example, is both loved and hated; loved for their cultural contributions and hated for those same contributions; loved as God's chosen people and hated for betraying God; loved and hated for their supposed financial prowess and survivalism. Think, here, of Jay-Z's (2017) hyperbolic backhanded compliment from the song "The Story of O.J." on the album *4:44*:

> You wanna know what's more important than throwin' away money at a strip club? Credit. You ever wonder why Jewish people own all the property in America? This how they did it.

Jay-Z (2017) is both celebrating the idea of Jewish business-savvy and participating in the perpetuation of the belief in a potentially conspiratorial, Jewish hyperpower. His philosemitism arrives with latent anti-Semitism in tow as an expression of allosemitism.

I focus on proteophobia rather than allosemitism because it (as phobia) is already in the language of the psychological, can be understood historically in relation to the totalizing modern force of social ordering, and has wide-reaching utility in the fight against various forms of oppression. This idea of proteophobia helps bring together the difficulties in thinking that I illustrated above into a network of events and discourses that can be understood as contributing to anti-Jewish practices such that it can be resisted through "dealing" with (or in) complex thinking, irreconcilable ideas, and psychic ambivalences.

The use of the concept of "phobia" exposes the complicated relationship between these anti-Jewish practices and psychology. I find that those who employ the term "phobia" in relation to anti-Semitism and racism more generally, come from outside the field of psychology. Zygmunt Bauman was a sociologist, Jonathan Judaken (who uses the term "Judeophobia") is a historian, Gavin Langmuir (who uses the term "xenophobia"[22]) is also a historian, Albert Memmi (who uses the term "heterophobia") is a philosopher, sociologist, and novelist. I am not suggesting that these scholars should not use psychological terminology, but that there needs to be more study of anti-Semitism as phobia—and specifically proteophobia—in the field of psychology. Then again, as I will show more conclusively in what follows, the notion of anti-Semitism as proteophobia is at the outer limit of the psychological, formulated as the psychological response to an otherness within the psyche—the unconscious or "the emblem of external otherness" (Frosh, 2005). Phobia and constitutive otherness are found to be central to the psychological subject capable of self-conscious interiority and sense of oneself as one's own.

An exception to this lack of attention to phobia in the psychology[23] of racism comes from Franz Fanon (1925–1961). Rooted in the psychoanalytic theory of phobia and formulated in relation to anti-Black racism and colonialism, Fanon's (1952/2008) notion of the "phobogenic object" has been a major influence in studies of racism (Laubscher et al., 2021) and anti-Semitism (Cheyette, 2013; Judaken, 2018; Rothberg, 2009) as a theoretically rigorous approach to these difficult issues. Fanon offers theoretical support from within the psy-disciplines for a characterization of oppressive practice as a counterphobic defense against psychic ambivalence. In other words, the individual attempts to resolve the unresolvable within the individual—their constitution by the other—through actions upon the phobogenic object and its representatives.

---

[22] Though Langmuir's (1990) notion of xenophobia is a clear example, his notion of chimera operates through the process of projection outward of unresolvable psychic ambivalences (in other words, a phobic response).

[23] Here, I am using psychology and psychoanalysis somewhat interchangeably for the sake of readability. I do not think they are the same thing. In fact, I see the difference as an important tension (see Frosh, 1989; Laplanche, 1991).

Stephen Frosh (2005, 2023) offers a psychoanalytic reading of anti-Semitism similar to Fanon's reading of racism, though he does not center his theory around the language of phobia. Frosh (2005) articulates a structural form of anti-Semitism characterized by the fear of complex reality and psychic ambivalence in terms of the otherness at the core of the psyche. The difference between fear of the other (Fanon) and fear of otherness (Frosh) may help to distinguish and track intersections of various identity positions leading to anti-Semitism and anti-Black racism. In what follows, I will seek to better understand the relationship between ambivalence, the other, otherness, and uncategorizability, and specifically how they may operate distinctly in racism and anti-Semitism.

Negative Methodology

Negative Psychology and Negative Dialectics

What many scholars do not account for explicitly—which I will examine and draw out from their studies—is the possible proteophobic motivation lurking in their efforts, perhaps inevitable, to better understand anti-Semitism *by categorizing* Jewishness (see Lerman, 2022). For example, much controversy surrounds the Working Definition's categorization of Israel as a "Jewish collectivity" targeted by anti-Semites (Lerman, 2022; USDS, 2022). Through the lens of proteophobia, I will examine the roles these difficulties of categorizing Jewishness and anti-Semitism play in perpetuating anti-Jewish practices. But, in doing so, I will also shed light on (re)new(ed) methods of studying identity and proteophobia that *do not settle on categorization*, but instead focus on what is left out—and therefore remains unprotected—in every social ordering of the world. The question becomes: How does one study proteophobia without reproducing proteophobia in the very study of it? Put another way, I am studying anti-Semitism because I am trying to order the world such that I can protect the vulnerable, and in the process have discovered that the anxiety that motivates such ordering—my own, included—may be inculpated in the very proteophobic process under investigation. Even if it turns out that proteophobic motivations may be inevitable in the very human striving to organize the world for the sake of self-preservation, acknowledging and resisting that proteophobia is not inevitable. I aim to uncover and develop a critical and psychoanalytic method of investigation ready for the challenge of working through the ambivalence of proteophobia without reproducing it.

To better understand this question of method, it may be helpful to compare proteophobia with its cousin xenophobia (fear of the stranger) and how previous scholars have approached this issue. Effectively protecting the vulnerable from the violence of xenophobia is achieved not by making the stranger less strange through assimilation but by welcoming the stranger as a stranger with hospitality and care (Derrida, 1998). Likewise, effectively resisting the violence of proteophobia may not be about categorizing the uncategorizable, but rather about "making a place" for what is left out of categorization. In the wake of the Shoah, German-Jewish thinker Theodor W. Adorno (1967/2004) developed "negative dialectics" as a method of research closely aligned with this welcoming hospitality.[24]

Adorno's negative dialectic is a response to Hegel's supposedly positive one. Hegel (1807/1979) offers a phenomenologically descriptive and normative analysis of reason as it develops through a dialectical process in which contradiction becomes reconciled in a supposedly higher synthesis. For example, Hegel analyzes the historical movement from Judaism to Christianity in terms of the progressive movement of a positive dialectic. The interaction between Judaism and Greek Hellenism gives way to a distinct Greek gentile Judaism as what we can now, in retrospect, think of as Christianity, but which eventually, through the synthesis of Greek

---

[24] This idea of "Adorno's hospitality" may come as a surprise for those loosely acquainted with Adorno. He is often characterized as a grumpy, stuffy, and unhappy snob. However, in Adorno's relentless and at times exaggerated model of critique, I read a hospitality for those who suffer, for otherness, nature, the stranger, and indeed, the uncategorizable. His insistence is rigorous but also playful. Adorno both recognizes the moment of satisfaction in thought grasping its object, but also calls it false. From a particular psychoanalytic perspective, the persistent denial (or negative dialectic) of origins or goals in Adorno's thinking brings us closer to understanding the dialectical nature of satisfaction itself—one's desire achieved is dissatisfying. This is epitomized in one of Adorno's (and Walter Benjamin's) favorite phrases—borrowed from Karl Kraus—"origin is the goal" (see Hullot-Kentor, 2006).

and Jew, becomes the early Catholic Church. The newly synthesized form of "Western civilization" can be thought of as "Judeo-Christian." A negative dialectical analysis might, on the other hand, uncover the way that the Jewish pole is not carried forward in the synthesis toward "Judeo-Christianity" but is erased in that very assumption of a positive synthesis. In this example, the part of Jewishness that is not a religion, but a particular form of life[25] is erased in the notion of a universalizable (i.e., religious or Christian) "Judaism." As I will explore more thoroughly below, historically, there was no "Judaism" as a religion before Christianity formulated an anti-Judaism (Boyarin, 2019; Nirenberg, 2013). Christianity as a synthesis was always already an anti-Judaism. Subsequently then, negative dialectics reveals what is left out (or unconscious) in any investigation (in the above example, aspects of Jewishness are erased in the positive dialectical movement/synthesis toward Christianity). What is left out, moreover, is left out because it troubles efforts at clear-cut categorization (e.g., what is Jewish beyond the Judeo-Christian) and may lead to proteophobia.[26] Hence, negative dialectic becomes a critical concept for my research and for psychology more generally.

I understand the psychological subject—the object of psychology—to be produced through a similarly positive dialectical synthesis, the ordering of distinct moments into a higher synthesis of self-consciousness, and the ordering of the world through the unification of experiences into a sense of "me" and "mine."[27] Anti-Semitism through the lens of proteophobia at once demands psychological analysis and paradoxically exposes

---

[25] I borrow the term "form of life" from Boyarin (2019, p. 24) who borrows it from Wittgenstein (1953/2009, p. 11) and Hacker (2015). Since culture is a relatively modern concept and may not have existed in the historical periods discussed in this project, the term "form of life" can serve a similar purpose without importing the modern concept. "Form of life" refers to a life organized through a particular and historical symbolic system and language. For Boyarin (2019), for example, since the Jewish form of life lacked a word like "religion" in its symbolic system, it also lacked what we think of as religion (p. 25).

[26] Accordingly, it may seem that Jews should be at home in Judeo-Christian society but end up being left out by a Christianity that supposedly supersedes Judaism.

[27] It could be noted that Hegel's formulation of self-consciousness is a "negativity," yet it is also always the identity of identity and non-identity—the very process of unification. Hegel always makes the positive synthetic move toward progress of reason. There is in Hegel, though, a troubling of the "me" and "mine." Desire is always the desire of the other. Self-consciousness always undermines itself. Still, I'm not convinced by recent readings of Hegel that ignore the positive Hegel of the absolute.

the inadequacies of thinking about anti-Semitism in terms of psychology. This seems to indicate the need for something like a "social psychology" or a "psychological sociology," but in practice those approaches tend to move too quickly to positively reconcile the dialectical tensions between the psyche and the social. The fields of psychosocial studies and human science psychology are two notable exceptions to this trend toward reconciliation. I refer to the application of negative dialectics in psychology as "negative psychology" (Strosberg, 2021). In this light, the analysis of otherness and what is uncategorizable requires a negative psychological approach.

Negative psychology, as I employ it here, is a method of tracing the contradictions within identity and conceptual boundaries (e.g., between self/other, psyche/society) through the employment of psychological terms to show the failure of those terms to do justice to the matter-at-hand.[28] My aim in this study is *not* to make anti-Semitism—or Jewishness—fit neatly into a categorical box, since such an effort mirrors the very proteophobia I wish to eschew. Instead, I aim to examine the reproduction of anti-Semitism and to employ a negative psychology to model resistance to proteophobia in the very study of anti-Semitism itself.

I believe that the field that offers the most compelling analysis of these tensions is psychoanalysis. Yet, psychoanalysis is a broad and very diverse field, and many contemporary psychoanalytic theorists—as far as I can tell—do not maintain this tension. Hence, I also use the term "negative psychology" to characterize those psychoanalytic theories[29] that offer analyses of these very inadequacies of psychology[30] to maintain a tension with the social domain and a constitutive otherness.

My attention to Adorno's negative dialectics and negative psychology has the secondary benefit of being explicitly formulated in relation to anti-Semitism. In the *Dialectic of Enlightenment* (1947/2004), Adorno and his colleague Max Horkheimer (1895–1973) illustrate the need for a

---

[28] This is something akin to what Lacan (1966/2006) calls *Mèconnaissance*.

[29] The psychoanalytic theories I have in mind that explicitly do this, are many of Freud's, as well as the work of Lacan, later Lacanian theorists, and post-Lacanian psychoanalysts, but many other psychoanalytic theories would fit the bill.

[30] It should be noted that the term "psychology" refers to a field, a discipline, a concept, an object, and a subject. Here, the term refers to psychology as the concept of individual conscious interiority.

negative dialectical approach (though not yet named as such) specifically in relation to the problem of ambivalence and psychology in anti-Semitism. Adorno's work on anti-Semitism in *The Authoritarian Personality* (1950/2019) is rooted in the tension between the psyche and the social in psychoanalysis, and I have come to understand Adorno's thinking in that period to be expressly a negative psychology (see also Adorno, 1951/1982). The connection between negative dialectics and anti-Semitism is reciprocal—negative dialectics helps us understand anti-Semitism, and anti-Semitism helps us understand negative dialectics.

Although Adorno's contributions to the study of anti-Semitism (Adorno et al., 1950/2019; Horkheimer & Adorno, 1947/2004) are significant and agenda-setting (e.g., Bauman, 1995; Langmuir, 1990; Nirenberg, 2013), the scholarly treatment of his work on the subject is lacking. This book fills a gap in the literature by focusing specifically on what Adorno's theory and negative psychology can contribute to the contemporary study of anti-Semitism. If, indeed, Adorno's theory can be used to study and combat anti-Semitism through the lens of proteophobia, it may also be able to contribute to protecting Jews and other oppressed groups by clarifying the unique situation of anti-Jewish practices.

Recent critical studies of anti-Semitism (Judaken, 2018; Lerman, 2022; Schraub, 2019) introduce the subject in a similar fashion to the way I introduce it here, explaining how the study and resistance to anti-Semitism are permeated with confusion and contradiction. Moreover, this study fits in with a loosely affiliated, interdisciplinary, and international field of critical anti-Semitism studies. The "critical" qualifier here means a rigorous scholarship and difficult theoretical thinking that questions epistemological and ontological assumptions, and that situates both the scholar and matter-at-hand within history, and not beyond it.

Scholars of prejudice and anti-Semitism often rely on psychology and psychoanalysis (Allport, 1979; Burston, 2021; Cheyette, 2013; Fanon, 1952/2008; Frosh, 2005, 2023; George & Hook, 2021; Judaken, 2018; Langmuir, 1990; Mbembe, 2015). As phobia, proteophobia is undeniably connected to the psychological, yet anti-Semitism is also undeniably social—a rather obvious dynamic which nonetheless is seldom analyzed by psychology and psychoanalysis in recent years. Further, it is not often that scholars working on the critical studies of anti-Semitism are housed in psychology departments. Therefore, I am hoping that this critical psychology of anti-Semitism can add unique perspective and interdisciplinary weight to contemporary debates. In particular, I believe that Adorno's critical, indeed, negative psychology of anti-Semitism is primed to be mobilized in critical anti-Semitism studies. In the next sections, I offer some methodological touch points for a negative psychology of anti-Semitism.[31]

Negative Phenomenology and Negative Dialectics

Since its inception, science unlocked new avenues for precision and exactitude in human understanding, measurement, and prediction of the natural world. However, the benefit of these new processes comes at a price. To remain true (to its own pretensions), this process must be totalizing and has continued to objectify and categorically systematize everything, including the human individual who carries out and interprets these scientific operations. Since the beginning of the twentieth-century phenomenology has offered an important corrective to both the natural scientific and earlier folk-mythical approaches to psychological research by emphasizing the uniquely human lived experience of self-evidence. Phenomenology is a philosophical method for understanding that experience through the "reduction" to the invariant structures of experience and not—as was the trend—to reduce the particularity of that experience to a universal category given deductively from without.

Jean-Paul Sartre (1946/1965), Jean Améry (1966), and Albert Memmi (1962) produced phenomenological studies of anti-Semitism in the wake of the Shoah. Sartre (1946/1965), for instance, formulated anti-Semitism phenomenologically as the "fear of the human condition" (p. 38) and the uncertainty of that condition. "How," Sartre (1946/1965) asks in response to the overwhelming anti-Semitism in France, "can one choose to reason falsely? It is because of a longing for impenetrability" (p. 12). He continues:

---

[31] My critique of psychology and psychoanalysis presented here closely aligns with the perspectives found in psychosocial studies.

The rational man groans as he gropes for the truth; he knows that his reasoning is no more than tentative, that other considerations may supervene
to cast doubt on it. He never sees very clearly where he is going; he is
"open"; he may even appear to be hesitant. But there are people who are
attracted by the durability of a stone. They wish to be massive and impen-
etrable; they wish not to change. Where, indeed, would change take them?
We have here a basic fear of oneself and of truth. What frightens them is
not the content of truth, of which they have no conception, but the form
itself of truth, that thing of indefinite approximation. It is as if their own
existence were in continual suspension. (Sartre, 1946/1965, p. 12)

Michael Walzer (1995) perceptively notes, in his preface to the work,
that Sartre's formulation is remarkably similar to Adorno's idea of the
"intolerance of ambiguity" (Walzer, 1995, p. x). With psychoanalytic
resources, Fanon (1952/2008) developed Sartre's phenomenological ideas
in relation to anti-Black racism and colonialism and continued (if only
secondarily so) the phenomenology of anti-Semitism in relation to that
anti-Black racism (Cheyette, 2013).[32]

Phenomenology is, at its best, a method of revealing hidden assumptions and categories, and an attention to the radical particularity of
human experience. In this way, it can be a tool to uproot proteophobia.
However, phenomenology is often used pragmatically to thematize and
categorize human experience. Since the very outset of the phenomenological corrective, there have been trenchant critiques leveled at the
assumptions that even phenomenology seems to take for granted (e.g.,
the metaphysics of presence, the postulate of a defined self of self-
evidence, the myth of origins and authenticity, social conditions). In
many ways, these critiques of phenomenology do not come from outside
of phenomenology but are found at the heart of phenomenology. The
Jewish French phenomenologist Emmanuel Levinas (1974/2006), for
instance, suggests that responsibility in the face of the otherness of the
other is precisely the resistance within the very process of conducting

---

[32] Phenomenology continued to develop as a human science research protocol, and some more
recent studies take a traditionally empirical approach to the phenomenological study of anti-
Semitism. Using an experimental design, Dion and Earn (1975) studied the phenomenological
experience of being the target of anti-Semitism. Flasch (2020) studied the phenomenological experience of being Jewish and experiencing anti-Semitism on American college campuses.

phenomenology to the kinds of thematization performed *by* phenomenology. In *Totality and Infinity* (1961/1969), Levinas writes, "The void that breaks the totality can be maintained against an inevitably totalizing and synoptic thought only if thought finds itself faced with an other refractory to categories" (p. 40). In other words, to resist oppressive objectification in thinking is to resist the totalizing force of categorization in thinking about that which escapes our categorizing impulses.

Some of these critiques have remained under the auspices of phenomenology as a philosophic subdiscipline (e.g., Sartre, 1946/1965; Fanon, 1952/2008; Levinas, 1961/1969, 1974/2006; perhaps Derrida fits in with this group) and some come from adjacent fields like psychoanalysis (e.g., Lacan, 1966/2006, Laplanche, 1996) and Critical Theory (e.g., Adorno, 1967/2004, 1960–1961/2019b). Many of these thinkers seem to suggest that if we take the logic of phenomenology to its logical conclusion, that logic undermines itself. Most of these critiques emphasize the moment of self-undermining and offer a challenge to the project of knowledge production and categorization (i.e., philosophy and science) from the precarious standpoint of critical reason. They often come as a challenge to the unified and self-enclosed subject of that knowledge production (*cogito*, ego, self, consciousness, the Same, perhaps even *Dasein*). They emphasize not what comes after phenomenology in refuting phenomenology—as if lived experiences of individual human subjects are unimportant—but the negative moment of thought at the limits of phenomenology. If I understand her correctly, this could be what Drucilla Cornell (1992) refers to as "philosophy of the limit."

It is in this negative moment of self-undermining that the critique of phenomenology becomes a helpful lens through which to approach the study of anti-Semitism, which Horkheimer and Adorno (1947/2004) aptly referred to as the hate for the negative principle in thought, or what I believe can be and has been reformulated as proteophobia. More specifically, Adorno's (1960–1961/2019b) formulation of "negative dialectics" *as the failure of phenomenology when measured against its own claims* can help scholars rethink anti-Semitism today. Elad Lapidot (2021) refers to Adorno's approach as "negative phenomenology" (p. 56). Adorno (1960–1961/2019b) insists that phenomenology and dialectics are not distinct philosophical standpoints from which one can choose. When taking phenomenology at its word, phenomenological analysis fails to make good on its own claims and commitments, and according to Adorno (1960–1961/2019b), this failure *is* dialectics. Phenomenology and dialectics are aspects of a non-identical matter-at-hand. In other words, they are not merely different methods of accessing a universally self-same world since they are not merely methods but also part of the world; but they are also not merely different aspects of the same self-identical fabric of reality because reality itself is not self-identical. The matter-at-hand is, especially in the case of anti-Semitism, non-identical and contradictory. Phenomenology fails but is only untrue when it ignores this dialectical movement which exposes what is left out (*as* left out and not merely latent) in any analysis, categorical or otherwise. This is Adorno's hospitality—also a psychoanalytic hospitality—to the new, the left-out, the uncategorizable, the unsayable. It is in this hospitality, that I find an opening for responding justly to the other's suffering and a way of studying anti-Semitism that does not repeat the dialectical process of supersession that reduplicates the formal structures historically expressed as anti-Semitism.

Contradictions and Constellations

Contradictions

Horkheimer and Adorno's *Dialectic of Enlightenment* (1947/2004), a text that contains their first sustained investigation of anti-Semitism, opens with the lines:

> Enlightenment, understood in the widest sense as the advance of thought, has always aimed at liberating human beings from fear and installing them as masters. Yet the wholly enlightened earth is radiant with triumphant calamity. (p. 1)

Our world is still one of contradiction: where mastery (scientific, technological, and personal) simultaneously turns out to be calamitous lack of control; where psychological subjects undermine their own psychological subjectivity; where individualism and conformism collide; where resistance to oppression can also be the infringement on the right of free speech; where humans survive at the expense of innocent animals; where technological advancement is militarized; where slave labor is used to make cheap clothing for the poverty stricken; where reparations made to slave owners are ignored in public discourse; where transnational institutions force countries to produce crops they don't need and can't afford; where European countries send billions of dollars to invading armies out of duty to the stability of capitalism; where democracy rests on the threat of state force; where the invisible hand is given a human face; where faced with utter annihilation caused by global warming, we postpone an inevitable catastrophe with green capitalism; where to build better batteries for a more sustainable world, cobalt is mined like blood diamonds; where faced with the Covid-19 pandemic many reasonable people demanded that shutdowns be lifted because in the long run the failure of our economic system could lower the quality of life for many, thereby justifying the sacrifice of the vulnerable; where the value of life is assessed like an insurance adjuster; where there is war for the sake of peace; where cancer is the main side effect of medicine for multiple sclerosis; where anti-depressants are implicated in suicide. Anti-Semitism, when examined in the context of the unique and ever-changing historical position of Jews, Jewishness, and Judaism, and in relation to the central concepts mobilized in modernity to make sense of the world (e.g., nation, gender, race, and religion), can be understood as one attempt to resolve the anxious fear in response to the ineradicable contradictions inherent in this complex social landscape (as highlighted in the above-mentioned sets). This conception of anti-Semitism offers relevant challenges to contemporary scholars, researchers, and clinicians overreliant on a logic of non-contradiction.

Horkheimer and Adorno (1947/2004) ask how knowledge production—which is at once enlightening and leading to calamity—can still work to end oppression and suffering if it is always already an act of domination (benevolent as it might seem). If philosophy is still necessary (and I think it is), it is only as critique: the resistance to heteronomy and the resistance to an inevitable freezing into untruth. This critical theory not unlike the work being done concomitantly by Levinas (1961/1969), who suggests that "to know or to be conscious is to have time to avoid and forestall the instant of inhumanity. It is this perpetual postponing of the hour of treason [...]" (p. 35). So, the methodological conundrum arises: What steps does one take to postpone this hour of treason in the determinations required in the process of research? An answer can be found in Adorno's (1967/2004) statement that "lending voice to suffering is the condition of all truth" (p. 17). In other words, already in thinking directed at truth there is something dialectically being left out and yet sought: *the voice of suffering.*[33] Instead of focusing on the synthetic moment of categorization where that voice is left out—the synthetic moment must necessarily leave something out by the very nature of being historical—the methodological imperative is to focus on the moment of disintegration and deconstruction, the trace as it perpetually evades seizure, precisely in its evasion. This is the condition of truth I set for myself, here.

Horkheimer and Adorno (1947/2004) insist that the projective operations of reasoning subjects must be exposed. And since all perception, they suggest, is projection, any effort to analyze projection by way of perception in any purity—as in natural scientific empiricism or phenomenology—is at odds with itself. As such, human perception is stuffed full of concepts, and concepts already with percepts. Horkheimer and Adorno offer, instead of reconciliation, a negative dialectic of enlightenment as critical reasoning which is not unreason or merely reason. Since to reason is to identify categorically, critical reasoning is the recognition of the non-identity that eludes its own operations.

An extension of this methodology applied to the study of anti-Semitism can be found in *Anti-Judaism: A Western Tradition* (2013), where historian David Nirenberg explicitly looks to Horkheimer and Adorno (1947/2004) for methodological inspiration. Nirenberg's (2013) project

---

[33] In *Eclipse of Reason* (1947/2004) Horkheimer writes:

The real individuals of our time are the martyrs who have gone through infernos of suffering and degradation in their resistance to conquest and oppression, not the inflated personalities of popular culture, the conventional dignitaries. These unsung heroes consciously exposed their existence as individuals to the terroristic annihilation that others undergo unconsciously through the social process. The anonymous martyrs of the concentration camps are the symbols of the humanity that is striving to be born. The task of philosophy is to translate what they have done into language that will be heard, even though their finite voices have been silenced by tyranny. (p. 109)

is a historical investigation of how the concepts associated with Jewishness and Judaism have become a latent aspect of our perception in the West—the genome of Western civilization. The figure of the Jew amounts to the antithesis of historical unfolding. And taken as such, each attempt at synthesis produces "Judaism out of its entrails," a phrase borrowed from Karl Marx and used throughout Nirenberg's (2013) book. In other words, in the constellation of ideas that make up the so-called Western canon, what is left out and unconscious is a Jewishness that haunts the Western traditions of religion, philosophy, and science. This is not to say that the West is merely a response to Judaism. The genome of the Western tradition is overdetermined (e.g., by gender, sexuality, class, Blackness, Orientalism, colonialism).

Though Western civilization and Christianity have historically understood themselves through various forms of anti-Judaism, they are not inherently pathological or anti-Semitic if this self-understanding is explicit and reflective. With this, Nirenberg (2013) is echoing Horkheimer and Adorno (1947/2004), who argue that projection is not pathological in itself, since all subjectivity involves projection. However, they identify non-reflective projection as pathological, terming it "false projection"(Horkheimer & Adorno, 1947/2004, p. 155). Nirenberg (2013), working within the history of ideas, writes that "what is perhaps the most spectacular modern failure of critical thought was constituted in large part by a failure to think critically about the history of its own ideas about 'Judaism'" (p. 456). As hyperbolic as this statement may be, its significance cannot be understated.

Constellations

I have been building a case that the form of a study should resemble the object of study, since the method of investigation contributes to the nature of the subject being studied. The study of anti-Semitism in terms of proteophobia, therefore, should be one that resists systematization. One of the best places to look for such a methodology (which is just as rigorous or even more so than systematic thinking) is Adorno's "Essay as Form" (1958/2019a).

Written between 1954 and 1958, "The Essay as Form" is one of Adorno's most influential essays on methodology (Rose, 1979). The essay as a form of research is impure and disorganized compared to systematic science, but representationally and narratively organized enough to also fall outside (or just on the hither side of the border) of art. The academic tradition, as well as science more generally, is blind to what does not partake in the scientific universal, on the one hand, or the irrationalism of artistic particularity, on the other. Academia insists on a dichotomy of science and art as the whole of the world. Adorno makes the case that this duality of art and science leaves out critique. The essay deals with something historically specific—"culturally pre-formed objects" (Adorno, 1958/2019a)—as opposed to the universal, and treats that specific thing as a fragment of something never once whole nor universal, or an image frozen in time.[34]

The essay form relies on over-interpretation, as something like an exaggerated, though careful, deliberation. Apropos the study of anti-Semitism, Adorno (1958/2019a) points out that historically this over-interpretation is linked to Jewish forms of thinking and "marked with the yellow star" (p. 4). This summons to mind the Western tradition of accusing both Jews and non-Jews of "Judaizing" through this kind of over-interpretation. "Judaizing" is a pejorative term which has meant, among other things, hiding the truth that is given in its "self-evidence" through the use of obscurantist Talmudic-style over-interpretation or over-intellectualism. This "Jewish" over-interpretation is seen as looking or speculating too far

---

[34] As an image frozen in time, Adorno's culturally pre-formed object is akin to Walter Benjamin's (1927–1940/1999) dialectical image or "dialectics at a standstill" (p. 462) which functions like the dream image that disintegrates in the moment of awakening. For Benjamin, on the other hand, the text is not the image but the image in decay upon awakening. The truth is not the wholeness but this very decay. This idea that the image is not meaningful in itself but only meaningful when we awaken, or only when the dialectic begins to move again upon awakening. The image, for Benjamin, is not meaningful as an image but is a snapshot only understood *in* language and *through* linguistic processes which make the image other than it is. The dialectical image takes the form of free-association, or what Benjamin calls "constellation," where ideas are to objects as constellations are to stars, a decentered network. The constellation is fixed in the presence of its totality, like a Jungian archetype. Yet, for Benjamin, this fixedness of the constellation as image (as with free-association and meaning) is a sign of its commodity fetishism, its falseness and deception. It is a snapshot, which when taken is already false. Falseness does not mean we can or should escape the image; its limit is also its critical potential. There is no original, it is always already a substitution, hence we only encounter it in language which is governed by the laws of substitution.

and interpreting beyond what the person or text "intends" to say or what a phenomenon seems capable of offering for thought. With great esteem, Harold Bloom wrote (somewhere) that alongside Kafka, Freud (1900/2001) is one of the great Jewish over-interpreters.[35] And in this

---

[35] Simultaneous accusations of Jewish over-interpretation and Jewish literalism seem to contradict each other. It would be reasonable to think that a literal reading—a form of reading also considered "Jewish" by early Christians—would lead to an absence of interpretation, as such. For example, Jews read the commandment to circumcise male children literally as a commandment to circumcise male children. So-called literal interpretation by the Rabbis, however, led to the Talmud, a prolific work of over-interpretation. The command for circumcision, for instance, is overdetermined and begs many questions: What day does one circumcise? Who does the circumcising, and with what kind of knife, blessing, etc.? It is as if both Jewish literalism and over-interpretation are linked by a refusal of obvious, singular, or anagogical interpretation. But does reading literally mean reading what is obvious and on the surface, as opposed to interpretation that reaches beneath the surface?

Rainer Nägele (1982), constellating the work of Adorno with Lacan, discusses an alternative literal way of reading *a la letter* (to the letter):

Truth is not on the surface, but neither is it behind or beneath. [...W]hatever appears in speech acts and utterances is product of a displacement, of a cover up, a secondary process; however, the truth is not simply behind this deceptive surface and process, it will not be found by a simple act of uncovering and particularly not by negating the surface. The truth is nowhere else but in the deceptive secondary process itself. The process of hiding is the structure of truth. (p. 75)

In other words, the letter itself contains the process of displacement that leads to the need for interpretation. Language is already a displacement. I understand this to be a very Jewish way of reading and a very psychoanalytic one.

The psychoanalytic attention to the letter of the patient's speech resonates with Talmudic (and Jewish) forms of reading and thinking. A helpful example is found in Mendelsohn's *The Lost* (2006), where he discusses a passage from the renowned French rabbinic commentator, Rashi, regarding the story of Cain and Abel. Rashi offers a literal reading of a specific sentence from the biblical narrative, resembling psychoanalytic methods of listening.

Rather than opting for a more intuitive or natural interpretation, Rashi offers a literal reading of the biblical statement, "Therefore, whoever slays Cain will suffer vengeance sevenfold." An intuitive, perhaps also literal, interpretation might suggest that anyone who kills Cain will suffer retribution sevenfold or "*shiv'ahthayim.*" An alternative reading might view this statement as a metaphor for justice, punishment, or vengeance. Rashi's approach represents a distinctly Jewish form of literal reading, reminiscent of psychoanalytic methods (e.g., Freudian and Lacanian). As Mendelsohn (2006) notes, Rashi divides the sentence into two parts:

The first, he insists, is the half-sentence "Therefore, whoever slays Cain...!" Adducing syntactical parallels from elsewhere in the Hebrew Scriptures, Rashi insists that this half-sentence be read as an implied but unspecific threat against anyone who might be tempted to harm history's first murderer: "This is one of the verses which cut short their words," he argues, "and made an allusion, but did not explain. 'Therefore, whoever slays Cain' expresses a threat—'So shall be done to him!' 'Such and such is his punishment!' But did not specify his punishment."

This manipulation of the text leaves Rashi with a two-word fragment, *shiv'ahthayim yuqqâm,* "will suffer vengeance sevenfold." Rashi insists, however, that the implied subject of this statement is not, as we may be tempted to think, whoever might be tempted to slay Cain, but rather Cain

spirit, Adorno (1951/2005) asserts that "in psycho-analysis nothing is true except the exaggerations" (p. 29).

For Adorno (1958/2019a), interpretation is too often reduced to intentions or psychological impulses, and such a reduction or circumscription hides the contribution of the interpreter:

> Nothing can be interpreted out of something that is not interpreted into it at the same time. The criteria for such interpretation are its compatibility with the text and with itself, and its power to give voice to the elements of the object in conjunction with one another (p. 4)

The essay must in some way mimetically resemble its subject matter and *give voice to the elements of the object*. This is particularly important for my project on the strange proteophobic logic found in the constellated image of anti-Semitism. To develop a *systematic* study of anti-Semitism would too clearly resemble the categorizing force of anti-Semitism that reconciles contradictory categories. The task, then, is to give voice to the object of study as it is dominated and subsumed by the concept we have of it; to constellate the objects and concepts without a central axiom. Examples of this approach can be found in Nirenberg's (2013) constellation of discourses of anti-Judaism, and Walter Benjamin's constellation of images from nineteenth-century Europe in the *Arcades Project* (1927–1940/1999). "The essay," Adorno (1958/2019a) explains, "draws the fullest conclusions from the critique of system" and "[...] allows for the consciousness of nonidentity, without expressing it directly; it is radical in its non-radicalism, in refraining from any reduction to a principle, in its accentuation of the partial against the total, in its fragmentary character" (p. 9). While this may render the essay challenging to apply or implement, as a form of critique, it already serves a practical purpose by preventing concepts or underlying presuppositions from being exploited to justify injustices.

One possible objection to this interpretation of the essay form—that it is fragmentary, incomplete, and abstract—gives the impression that it is

---

himself. What G-d is saying here, according to Rashi, is, "I do not wish to take vengeance from Cain now. At the end of seven generations I take My vengeance from him, for Lamech will arise from among his children's children and slay him"—as indeed happens in Genesis 4:23.

unsystematic *in contrast to something which is not*. This something else is assumed to be systematic, whole, concrete, and universally ordered. What a fantasy! Both the essay form and the systematic form are aspirational and grounded in certain underlying ethical assumptions. Systematic thinking is the hallmark and a requirement for anything we call a "scientific method," and an essay (as a constellation of fragments) may be the only way to challenge this need for a system without collapsing into irrationalism and undermining the emancipatory project of philosophy and science—a project we need now more than ever.

According to Rose (1979) Adorno rejects Descartes' principle of preceding from the simplest self-evidence to the more complex, since thinking always starts with complexity. It is foolish, Adorno (1958/2019a) suggests, to think that concepts only function (or function more adequately) when defined beforehand. Science (in its quantitative form), which relies on strict definitions, can never really offer definitions of the concepts it uses while staying within its boundaries. It can offer operational definitions but not meaningful ones. Concepts are always defined and concretized in relation to the "language in which they stand" (Adorno, 1958/2019a, p. 12); in other words, where a signifier is in relation to other signifiers, each having their place within the particularity of a given symbolic network at a given instant. A symbolic network is necessarily both diachronic and synchronic. Synchronically, a symbolic network is a system, yes, but only when frozen in time.[36] Since language is only meaningful when used, the frozen language-as-system is always already false, an outdated snapshot or at best a dictionary definition (or

---

[36] Discourse is the clearest example of diachrony. When speaking, a statement is in time and doesn't take on a final meaning until punctuation marks it (as in the full stop at the end of a sentence). Even then, its meaning can change when the next sentence starts. For example: "I really love books...fed to the fire;" or "'I hate my mother'... I would never say something like that." In German, the main verb doesn't come until the very end of the sentence, as in "*Ich werde meinen Vater töten*" (I will kill my father). We don't know what is going to happen until the end. It can be noted that Boyarin (2023) considers this structure to be the signature of Jewish language, as in "Throw mamma from the train—a kiss." Written language is associated with synchrony. A book is like a snapshot where the beginning and end exist simultaneously. On the other hand, for the reader, the book is not so systematic. One starts at the beginning and continues through the book. As the book progresses, what was read at the beginning is retained but also changes in the diachronic act of reading. A concept as it is established at the beginning—anti-Semitism, say—is different at the end. Or so is the purpose of the book. I hope that you have a different idea of anti-Semitism by the end of this book than you do right now.

what Walter Benjamin [1999] refers to as "dialectics at a standstill" [p. 462]). As language is used diachronically, on the other hand, its basic components change, and the system morphs like stars in a constellation. This is one of the main challenges of relying solely on a dictionary to learn a language or translate works of literature. The essay form, then, expands language by using concepts in new ways, and in so doing, the essay does something to (and with) what, like anti-Semitism, may at first seem determinate.

Adorno (1958/2019a) expands the example of learning to speak a new language to explain the development of concepts in an essay. Anyone who has traveled to a place where the inhabitants speak a foreign language knows that a dictionary can be helpful for ordering off a menu and asking for the bathroom, but does not help very much in conversing, thinking, or entering into the form of life assembled by that foreign language system. In listening carefully to how the signifiers of that language are used again and again in a constellation of different cases and contexts, the speaker can eventually enter into the language, instead of merely applying it from the outside. Likewise, an essay uses concepts over and over in various ways in a process through which the reader enters into the material presented. The reader cannot assume the knowledge contained without going through the process; no scholarly abstract or introduction is sufficient. In the context of this book, I hope to offer a constellation of material related to the history and study of anti-Semitism (as a culturally pre-formed and per-formed object) that is difficult to think about such that the reader is welcomed into the matter-at-hand. In this sense, reading and writing can become an opening outward into the world, a social practice, a doing, a performance that aims toward conveying truth.

Adorno (1958/2019a) writes: "The demand of continuity in one's train of thought tends to prejudge the inner coherence of the object, its own harmony" (p. 16). This harmony is an "epistemological impulse" that Adorno (1958/2019a) wants to dispel as an intolerance of the anxiety that comes with uncertainty and uncategorizability (p. 16), or to put it in terms I am developing here, the experience of proteophobia. In many ways, this book is a long essay on contemporary anti-Semitism which, to borrow a fragment from Adorno, "thinks in fragments, just as reality is fragmentary, and finds its unity in and through the breaks and not by glossing them over" (Adorno, 1958/2019a, p. 16).

Matter-at-Hand or This Book in Other Words

Although one can say that anti-Semitism is on the rise (and it does seem to be), it is perhaps more accurate to say that reported anti-Semitic incidents are on the rise, or even that anti-Jewish practices of all kinds have come out of the shadows. But even that does not feel quite right. Anti-Semitism seems to have always been with us, and not just in the shadowy corners of the world or obscure conspiracy theories. Yet, Hannah Arendt (1951) points out that this seemingly "eternal anti-Semitism" is a myth rooted in the logic of unchanging history and stagnant Jewishness; a myth that undergirds some of that very same anti-Semitism. This presents a challenge when critically and historically examining anti-Semitism.

While intuitively, anti-Semitism seems ancient and consistent across time, the concept itself emerged relatively recently in the nineteenth century, tied to the modern nation-state (Arendt, 1951).[37] Still, if nothing else holds anti-Semitism together as a concept, anti-Jewish practices are marked across epochs by their multi-form and contradictory expressions: The early Church fathers formed their thought both as and against the figure of the Jew. Not so long ago, science was described by contrast to an ever too spiritual and irrational Jewish thinking. Jews were, soon after, accused of over-rationalism and dangerously abstract mathematics. Capitalism was blamed on the Jews. Communism, the Jews. The excesses of modernism, post-modernism, and anti-modernism have all, at one point or another, been blamed on the Jews. Economic and social disorder, Jews. Wealth disparity, Jews. Problems in the Middle East, Jews. Slave trade, Jews. Technology, Jews. Even the Holocaust, Jews. Etcetera, etcetera.

---

[37] For this reason, many theorists argue that Judeophobia (Judaken, 2018), anti-Judaism (Nirenberg, 2013), or antisemitism (Lerman, 2022) fit better as a broad conceptual umbrella.

Despite the persistence of discourses related to Jews, Jewish history, and Jewish ideas and literature, and confusion surrounding anti-Jewish practices, it is still considered taboo to study Jews and anti-Semitism in certain corners of the academy. Bryan Cheyette (2019), a scholar focusing on Jewish and postcolonial literature, posted on social media about a job interview with the head of the English Literature Department at a red brick university in England where the first question posed was: "Don't you think writing on Jews is rather narrow?" This, in relation to not even writing on anti-Semitism but also writing on Jews!

It is not uncommon to think of anti-Semitism as a fringe phenomenon, for instance, a rhetorical device to smear the UK Labour Party or to deter criticism of Israel. It may be both of those latter things, but it is never just that. Jews are often thought to be privileged *as Jews*, White *as Jews*, wealthy *as Jews*, and no longer marginalized *as Jews*, etc. The idea of universal inclusion into privilege and Whiteness also contribute to contemporary forms of anti-Semitism which exclude Jewish particularity, culture, diversity, and embodiment from discussion.

Nevertheless, questions of Judaism and anti-Judaism seem ineradicable from "Western" traditions of Christianity, democracy, capitalism, science, and even mathematics. These questions play an important role in the thought of central figures of the so-called Western Canon as diverse as Jesus Christ, Paul the Apostle (died ~64), Augustine of Hippo (354–430), Muhammad (died 632), Baruch Spinoza (1632–1677), Gottfried Wilhelm Leibniz (1646–1716), Renè Descartes (1596–1650), John Locke (1632–1704), Thomas Hobbes (1588–1679), Immanuel Kant (1724–1804), Georg Wilhelm Friedrich Hegel (1770–1831), Heinrich Heine (1797–1856), Karl Marx (1818–1883), Friedrich Nietzsche (1844–1900), Sigmund Freud (1856–1939), Carl Jung (1875–1961), Martin Heidegger (1889–1976), and on and on. These questions also appear to haunt the scholars critiquing that "Western Canon" in terms of Blackness, colonialism, and racism such as W.E.B. Du Bois (1868–1963), Aimè Cèsaire (1913–2008), James Baldwin (1924–1987), Franz Fanon (1925–1961), Charles Mills (1951–2021), Frank B. Wilderson (1956-), and Achille Mbembe (1957-), to name a few such scholars. I'm not suggesting that all these thinkers focus singularly on the figure of the Jew, though some do. And I'm not suggesting that anti-Semitism is unchanging or monolithic across thinkers. Instead, I am suggesting, following David Nirenberg (2013), that Jewishness and anti-Judaism have been insufficiently examined though figural constellations in the history of the West, changing as those constellations do. Judaism has represented—disproportionately to the presence or influence of actual "real" Jews in any time and place—the test of various constitutive ideas in the Western world. Over the past two plus millennia, Judaism has been seen as the limit case for humanity (e.g., salvation, emancipation, progress, art, racism). Leo Strauss wrote that "the Jewish problem is the most manifest symbol of the human problem insofar as it is a social or political problem" (quoted in Nirenberg, 2013, p. 343). I believe that in many ways the Jews continue to play this role, though less obviously so, and that the confluence of the Jewish problem and the human problem meet at the logic of proteophobia.

Jewishness is a form of constituting otherness, along with Blackness, orientalism, gender, sexuality, and class. The study of anti-Semitism can contribute to the broader struggle against oppression in all its forms. The philosopher and social theorist Slavoj Žižek (1992/2009) suggests that the "purest, that is to say distilled, form of racism" is anti-Semitism (p. 128). With this, another difficulty in categorization arises: Anti-Semitism is meaningfully related to anti-Black racism, but collapsing them into each other reduces the particularity of anti-Semitism and anti-Black racism in a way that links it to a logic of making everything the same; a logic we might associate with anti-Semitism (see Horkheimer & Adorno, 1947/2004). A deeper investigation of the intersecting histories of anti-Semitism and anti-Black racism is needed. The theory of anti-Semitism I am proposing here is not a challenge to the idea that anti-Black racism is a structural and constitutive force in Western society (e.g., Fanon, 1952/2008; Mbembe, 2015; Mills, 1997/2019; Moten, 2018; Wilderson, 2020). I see structural theories of anti-Black racism and anti-Semitism as intersecting and interacting. Blackness is understood to constitute non-Black subjectivity through a logic of the other that cannot be incorporated into the system and the outside that constitutes the inside (an inside that may or may not exist). The other is kept in inhuman conditions, abject poverty, forced into dehumanizing slavery, deported, and given a slow death. The Jew is the invisible parasite that ruins social order from the inside out, hence the rhetoric of being replaced in slogans like "the Jews will not replace us" and the emphasis on extermination rather than separation or incarceration. The Jew is the other that makes society question the inside*ness* of the inside. Further still, intersectionality (see Schraub, 2019) and multidirectional thinking (Rothberg, 2009) are needed to do justice for those left out in such a schema (e.g., Black Jews) and to better understand the intersection of Blackness and Jewishness, anti-Black racism and anti-Semitism, as well as Whiteness and Jewishness.[38]

I didn't merely encounter proteophobia one day and begin seeing it everywhere. I observe contradictions and complexity all around me. I witness significant anxiety in response to this complexity, and irrationality in the act of reasoning about it. Still, I have not given up on the capacity of critical reasoning faculties to lead us toward justice. In fact, worse than not thinking at all, is giving up on thinking in mid-thought, since the conclusions born from such a half-thought still looks reasonable even when it may not be.[39] This giving up in mid-thought takes the shape of anti-intellectualism and premature activism. The desperation for action can too easily redouble suffering by reproducing violence (for more on this see Adorno, 2001 and Butler, 2020). To act in the world without critical thinking is to act wrongly—even if it is to break off thinking for the sake of social utility—just as to think without the impact of human suffering is to think empty thoughts. There is good reason to defend against anti-intellectualism. What is simple seems correct, what is satisfying seems right, what is oldest seems truest. Critical and psychoanalytic investigation helps to uncover the danger and rigidity of these assumptions.

Let me return, now, to the specificity of the phenomena: Where does this unreason in reason manifest? Discursive tropes, representational images, dialectical syntheses, what the academy has appropriated and rejected, epistemological assumptions, cultural appropriations, ontological grounds, academic and cultural tropes, epistemological congealed assumptions. I will inevitably draw from that experience, as well.

---

[38] See Frosh (2023), for a sustained analysis of the relationship between antisemitism and racism.

[39] Horkheimer and Adorno (1947/2004) developed a similar idea into a theory of *Halbbildung* or "half-education" associated with anti-Semitism. I return to this theory in Chap. 6.

I cringe to admit that as I birthed the concept for this endeavor, a nagging thought crept into my mind: "Is the topic of anti-Semitism truly relevant today?"[40] Ironically, that skepticism itself became the confirmation I sought. In that moment of uncertainty, echoes flooded my mind: people shouting at me in a Berlin train station, "fuck you *Juden*" and "go back to Israel," bullies chanting "Jew bag" amidst schoolyard scuffles, the moniker "dirty Jew" casually thrown by classmates. A friend's unsettling assertion to "shut up already about the Holocaust." The demand to ignore Jung's anti-Semitism.[41] Fanon's trivializing portrayal of anti-Semitism as a domestic squabble.

Then, I recalled the countless occasions when colleagues casually tossed crude Jewish jokes in my presence. "Now, isn't this peaceful?" my professor queried, ushering us beneath a colossal 15-foot cross, its shadow a

---

[40] Part of this concern comes from the idea that talking about anti-Semitism can distract from the pressing issue of justice for Palestinians. Journalist and professor Peter Beinart (5 June 2023), for instance, started one vlog by saying "I feel a little guilty that I'm talking again about antisemitism this week because it's so clear to me that antisemitism is used by American politicians and establishment American Jewish organizations to prevent a conversation about the realities for Palestinians on the ground by always focusing on the alleged antisemitic kind of motivations of critics of Israel" (np). In the public sphere, discourse surrounding anti-Semitism acts to silence Palestinians struggles. Of course, Beinart (5 June 2023) is talking about antisemitism to insist that we not use antisemitism to distract from Palestinian struggles and critics of Israel. It is a thorny rhetorical issue tied to competitive memory, competitive oppressions, and competition for resources (see Rothberg, 2009).

[41] In a seminar I attended in 2021, a psychologist sought to describe the difference between Freud and Jung by invoking the Question of Nicodemus, the bible parable that Jung himself used to articulate his difference from Freud. In the lecturer's version of the story, Nicodemus was a Roman soldier, but in the original bible parable, Nicodemus is a Rabbi (a curious substitution):

"How can a man be born when he is old?" Nicodemus asked. "Surely he cannot enter a second time into his mother's womb to be born!" Jesus answered, "I tell you the truth, no one can enter the kingdom of God unless he is born of water and the Spirit. Flesh gives birth to flesh, but the Spirit gives birth to spirit.

Reasoning by analogy, Freud doesn't understand this question and "gets stuck there," the psychologist continued. This appears to affirm Freud's (typically Jewish) inability or unwillingness to recognize the spirit and the truth of his own works, of being tied to the flesh; an ancient Christian calumny that suggests an innate deficiency shared by all Jewish people. Jews in such calumny open the door but refuse to walk through it (as Hegel puts it). Jung, accordingly, is read as superseding Freud as Christianity supersedes Judaism. It is true that Freud's psychoanalysis is undeniably connected to the Jewish. However, Jung famously calls Freud's psychology—both his psychoanalytic method and the psychological matter discovered by that method, "Jewish psychology," suggesting not only that was psychoanalysis Jewish but also that it was for the uniquely Jewish psyche, distinguished by its perverse sexuality and stunted development. Supersession was, for Jung, connected to the natural development of the psyche—of which Jews suffered stagnation.

stark contradiction, at least in my experience, to the phenomenological mood it purportedly exuded for my professor. The text message during a lecture on Lacan reading, "Jew-issance," with an eye roll emoji, while a Jewish student was asking a question. The random woman in the Berlin U-Bahn (subway) who told me, "You look just like in the Spielberg movie." I remembered my grandfather—a survivor—keeping a car in the garage until the end of his life, just in case, a small bit of cash, just in case, always, just in case, so many things, just in case.

A non-Jewish friend, complaining about rent, didn't just say "my landlord" but instead "my Jewish landlord." A Jewish friend this time tells me about the overrepresentation of Jewish doctors leading to the mass mutilation of children in the form of circumcision. Kanye West tweets about going "def con 3 on Jewish people." Protesters chanted "the Jews will not replace us" and "blood and soil." In Buffalo, New York, a young White man from my hometown drove three hours and killed ten Black shoppers at a grocery store. In his manifesto, he wrote: "Jews are the real problem."

At an academic conference someone pronounced "Ashkenazi" with an emphasis on the "nazi." Was I just hearing things? Would other Jews have heard this too? Amidst the sea of vitriol in a social media onslaught against a colleague, Derek Hook, anti-Semitic epithets like "Derek Hooknose" and "Rabbi Hook" and "Loxist" mingled freely with accusations of Nazism.[42] Putin's explanation for the unprovoked invasion of Ukraine: ousting the Jewish president in order to rid the country of Nazis.

Christians are a majority in two-thirds of all countries and territories in the world, with 2.2 billion believers (Pew Research Center, 2011).

---

[42] In online anti-Semitic circles, a Loxist is a Jew who discriminates against White people. Here is an excerpt from one such email (see Hook, 2024):

I'm just gonna go out on a limb here and guess your jewish.....I am certain I am right on this and though you lo[x] ism is not being exposed there is a truth in your speech. That jews.......and there jealously to be that of the real chosen race......the White race have yet again shown that everything a jew does or says is so massively inflated to make them look better that it only takes a mere sec. Or 2 for the truth of there real goal in destroying White people of jealously comes to life. But I'm here to tell you know money changer...you are yet a mut who has tried to claim your pure breedness yet the world let's you talk cause they have learned that you never stop promoting yourselves and hurting others. Good day Mr. Jewish Professor cause I know you probably trying to take some Palestinians house for your own and saying God gave it you is way more important then talking to a smart and definitely more knowledgeable White guy then you claim to be. Did you get your degree at Aushwitchs University? Double majors and 6 million lies?

There are close to 1.9 billion Muslims and 50 Muslim majority countries. There are only 15 million Jews in the world and around six and a half million of them live in Israel. Most Jews live in the diaspora. Is the price of keeping Israel a Jewish state, the Jewishness of Jews? Palestinians fight for their self-determination, and Israelis fight for self-preservation. What are the boundaries of this self? On Yom Kippur, the Jewish day of atonement, at the start of the Jewish year 5782, I went to a member-led synagogue, Dor Hadash, where members of my congregation said a blessing for their loved ones who were brutally murdered in 2018 by a White supremacist who stormed their synagogue. The congregation asked the attorney general to forgo the death penalty.

These examples form a constellation. Anti-Semitism is undeniably real and remains a pressing issue in the United States and many other parts of the world. Despite its significance, it remains challenging to think about, write about, read about. However it comes to be defined, anti-Semitism certainly requires more study and better understanding.

References

Adorno, T. W. (1982). Freudian theory and the pattern of fascist propaganda. In A. Arato & E. Gephardt (Eds.), *The essential Frankfurt School reader* (pp. 118–137). Continuum. (Original work published 1951)

Adorno, T. W. (2001). *Problem of moral philosophy* (T. Schröder, Ed. & T. Livingstone, Trans.). Stanford.

Adorno, T.W. (2004). *Negative dialectic* (E. B. Ashton, Trans.). Routledge. (Original work published 1967)

Adorno, T. W. (2005). *Minima moralia: Reflections from damaged life.* Verso. (Original work published in 1951)

Adorno, T. W. (2019a). *Notes on literature* (R. Tiedemann, Ed. & S. E. Nicolson, Trans.). Columbia University Press. (Original work published 1958)

Adorno, T. W. (2019b). *Ontology and dialectics: 1960–61* (N. Walter, Trans.). Polity.

Adorno, T. W., Frenkel-Brunswik, E., Levinson, D. J., & Sanford, R. N. (2019). *The authoritarian personality.* Verso. (Original work published 1950)

Ahmed, S. (2007). A phenomenology of whiteness. *Feminist Theory, 8*(2), 149–168. https://doi.org/10.1177/1464700107078139

Allington, D. (2021). Conspiracy theories, radicalisation and digital media. In *The Global Network on Extremism and Technology (GNET)*. King's College London.

Allport, G. W. (1979). *The nature of prejudice*. Addison-Wesley. (Original work published 1954)

Amery, J. (1966). *At the mind's limit*. Indiana University Press.

Anti-Defamation League (ADL). (2020). Antisemitic attitudes in the U.S.: A guide to ADL's latest poll. Retrieved March 10, 2021, from https://www.adl.org/news/press-releases/anti-semitic-stereotypes-persist-in-america-survey-shows

Arendt, H. (1951). *Origins of totalitarianism*. Schocken.

Badiou, A., Hazan, E., & Segrè, I. (2013). *Reflections on anti-Semitism*. Verso.

Basri, C. (2002). The Jewish refugees from Arab countries: An examination of legal rights - A case study of the human rights violations of Iraqi Jews. *Fordham International Law Journal, 26*(3), 656–720. https://ir.lawnet.fordham.edu/ilj/vol26/iss3/6

Bauman, Z. (1995). *Life in fragments. Essays in postmodern morality*. Basil Blackwell.

Bauman, Z. (1998). Allosemitism: Premodern, modern, postmodern. In B. Cheyette & L. Marcus (Eds.), *Modernity, culture, and "the Jew"*. Polity Press.

BDS. (2023). *Boycott, divestment, and sanctions*. https://bdsmovement.net.

Benjamin, W. (1999). *The arcades project*. Harvard University Press. (Original work drafted 1927-1940)

Bernasconi, R. (2021). Racism. In S. Goldberg, S. Ury, & K. Weiser (Eds.), *Key concepts in the Study of Antisemitism. Palgrave critical studies of antisemitism and racism*. Palgrave Macmillan. https://doi.org/10.1007/978-3-030-51658-1_19

Blake, A. (2022) Trump's long history of trafficking in antisemitic tropes. *The Washington Post*. Retrieved January 2023, from https://www.washingtonpost.com/politics/2022/10/17/trump-history-antisemitic-tropes/

Boyarin, D. (2019). *Judaism: The genealogy of a modern notion*. Rutgers University Press.

Boyarin, D. (2023). *The no-state solution: A Jewish manifesto*. Yale University Press.

Boyarin, J., & Boyarin, D. (2002). *Powers of diaspora: Two essays on the relevance of Jewish culture*. University of Minnesota Press.

Burston, D. (2021). *Anti-Semitism and analytical psychology*. Routledge.

Butler, J. (2020). *The force of nonviolence*. Verso.

Cheyette, B. (2013). *Diasporas of the mind: Jewish and postcolonial writing and the nightmare of history*. Yale University Press.

Chotiner, I. (2022). Is anti-Zionism anti-Semitism? *The New Yorker*. Retrieved April 30, 2024, from https://www.newyorker.com/news/q-and-a/is-anti-zionism-anti-semitism

Cornell, D. (1992). *Philosophies of the limit*. Routledge.

Demirjian, K., & Stack, L. (2023). In congress and on campuses, 'from the river to the sea' inflames debate. *The New York Times*. Retrieved April 30, 2024, from https://www.nytimes.com/2023/11/09/us/politics/river-to-the-sea-israel-gaza-palestinians.html

Derrida, J. (1998). *Of hospitality*. Stanford University Press.

Dion, K. L., & Earn, B. M. (1975). The phenomenology of being a target of prejudice. *Journal of Personality and Social Psychology, 32*(5), 944–950. https://doi.org/10.1037/0022-3514.32.5.944

Fanon, F. (2008). *Black skin white masks* (C. L. Markmann, Trans.). Pluto Press. (Original work published 1952)

Fields, B. J., & Fields, K. E. (2012). *Racecraft: The soul of inequality in American life*. Verso.

Fields, J., & Weisberg, J. (2022). *The patient* (TV series). HBO Max.

Flasch, P. (2020). Antisemitism on college campuses: A phenomenological study of Jewish students' lived experiences. *Journal of Contemporary Antisemitism, 3*(1).

Freud, S. (2001). The interpretation of dreams. In J. Strachey (Ed. & Trans.), *The standard edition of the complete psychological works of Sigmund Freud, volumes IV-V*. Vintage Books. (Original work published 1900)

Frosh, S. (1989). *Psychoanalysis and psychology: Minding the gap*. Macmillan.

Frosh, S. (2005). *Hate and the 'Jewish Science': Anti-Semitism, Nazism and psychoanalysis*. Palgrave Macmillan.

Frosh, S. (2023). *Antisemitism and racism: Ethical challenges for psychoanalysis*. Bloomsbury.

Geisinger, G. (May 2022). Everything everywhere all at once directors are glad to talk about 'Big Nose' controversy. *Digital Spy*. Retrieved December 27, 2022, from https://www.digitalspy.com/movies/a39902848/everything-everywhere-all-at-once-big-nose-jewish-antisemitism/

George, S., & Hook, D. (2021). *Lacan and race: Racism, identity, and psychoanalytic theory*. Routledge.

Gross, J., & Vigdor, N. (2022, February). *ABC suspends Whoopi Goldberg over Holocaust comments*. Retrieved January 2023, from https://www.nytimes.com/2022/02/01/us/whoopi-goldberg-holocaust.html

Haberman, M., & Feuer, A. (2022, November). Trump's latest dinner guest: Nick Fuentes, white supremacist. *New York Times*. Retrieved December 28, 2022, from https://www.nytimes.com/2022/11/25/us/politics/trump-nick-fuentes-dinner.html

Hacker, P. M. S. (2015). "Forms of Life," in "Wittgenstein and Forms of Life," special issue. *Nordic Wittgenstein Review, 17*, 1–20.

Hegel, G. W. F. (1979). *Phenomenology of spirit* (A. V. Miller, Trans.). Oxford University Press. (Original work published 1807)

Hook, D. (2024). Whiteness at the abyss: Reflections on a scene of attack. Special issue. *Psychoanalytic, Culture, and Society*.

Horkheimer, M. (2004). *Eclipse of reason*. Continuum. (Original work published 1947)

Horkheimer, M., & Adorno, T. W. (2004). *Dialectic of enlightenment: Philosophical fragments* (G. S. Noerr, Ed. & E. Jephcott, Trans.). Stanford. (Original work published 1947)

Hullot-Kentor, R. (2006). *Things beyond resemblance: Collected essays on Theodor W. Adorno*. Columbia University Press.

Freedom For Humanity. (2023, July 22). In Wikipedia. https://en.wikipedia.org/wiki/Freedom_for_Humanity.

Intactivism. (2023). https://www.circumstitions.com/

Jay-Z. (2017). "The story of O.J." In 4:44. ROC Nation.

Judaken, J. (2018). Introduction. *The American Historical Review, 123*(4), 1122–1138. https://doi.org/10.1093/ahr/rhy024

Lacan, J. (2006). *Écrits: The first complete edition in English* (J. A. Miller, Ed. & B. Fink, Trans.). W.W. Norton & Co. (Original work published 1966)

Langmuir, G. (1990). *Towards a definition of antisemitism*. University of California Press.

Lapidot, E. (2021). *Jews out of the question: A critique of anti-anti-Semitism*. SUNY Press.

Laplanche, J. (1991). *New foundations for psychoanalysis*. Basil Blackwell.

Laplanche, J. (1996). Psychoanalysis as anti-hermeneutics (L. Thurston, Trans.). *Radical Philosophy, 79*(12), 7–12. https://www.radicalphilosophy.com/article/psychoanalysis-as-anti-hermeneutics

Laubscher, L., Hook, D., & Desai, M. (Eds.). (2021). *Fanon, phenomenology and psychology*. Routledge.

Lerman, A. (2022). *Whatever happened to antisemitism?: Redefinition and the myth of the 'collective Jew'*. Pluto Press.

Levinas, E. (1969). *Totality and infinity: An essay on exteriority*. Duquesne University Press. (Original work published 1961)

Levinas, E. (2006). *Otherwise than being, or beyond essence*. Duquesne University Press. (Original work published 1974)

Lewin-Epstein, N., & Cohen, Y. (2019). Ethnic origin and identity in the Jewish population of Israel. *Journal of Ethnic and Migration Studies, 45*(11), 2118–2137. https://doi.org/10.1080/1369183X.2018.1492370

Magid, S. (2006). In search of a critical voice in the Jewish diaspora: Homelessness and home in Edward Said and Shalom Noah Barzofsky's Netivot Shalom. *Jewish Social Studies: History, Culture, Society, 12*(3), 193–227.

Marcus, K. (2015). *The definition of antisemitism*. Oxford University Press.

Mbembe, A. (2015). *Necropolitics*. Duke University Press.

Memmi, A. (1962). *Portrait of a Jew*. Penguin.

Mendelsohn, D. (2006). *The lost: A search for six of six million*. Harper Perennial.

Merriam-Webster Dictionary. (2022). Meme. *Merriam-Webster dictionary online*. https://www.merriam-webster.com/dictionary/meme

Mills, C. (2019). *The racial contract*. Cornell University Press. (Original work published 1997)

Moten, F. (2018). *Stolen life*. Duke University Press. https://doi.org/10.2307/j.ctv111jj9x

Nägele, R. (1982). The scene of the other: Theodor W. Adorno's negative dialectic in the context of poststructuralism. *Boundary 2, 11*(1/2), 75. https://doi.org/10.2307/303018

Hearing Voices Network. (2022). Voices and visions. Retrieved December 28, 2022, from https://www.hearing-voices.org/voices-visions/

Nirenberg, D. (2013). *Anti-Judaism: A Western tradition*. Norton.

Paybarah, A. (2022, December). *Kanye West draws fresh denunciation for Hitler praise in Alex Jones interview*. Washington Post. Retrieved December 28, 2022, from https://www.washingtonpost.com/politics/2022/12/01/kanye-west-alex-jones-hilter-interview/

Pew Research Center. (2011). Global Christianity—A report on the size and distribution of the world's Christian population. Retrieved December 28, 2022, from https://www.pewresearch.org/religion/2011/12/19/global-christianity-exec/

Pew Research Center. (2021). 9. Race, ethnicity, heritage and immigration among U.S. Jews. *Jewish Americans in 2020*. Retrieved December 28, 2022, from https://www.pewresearch.org/religion/2021/05/11/race-ethnicity-heritage-and-immigration-among-u-s-jews/

Rose, G. (1979). *The melancholy science*. Verso.

Roth, P. (2000). *The human stain*. Houghton Mifflin.

Rothberg, M. (2009). *Multidirectional memory: Remembering the holocaust in the age of decolonization*. Stanford University Press.

Rothberg, M., & Lenz, R. (2024). We need an ethics of comparison. *Medico International*. Retrieved March 14, 2024, from https://www.medico.de/en/we-need-an-ethics-of-comparison-19392

Salamon, G. (2021). The place where life hides away: Merleau-Ponty, Fanon, and the location of bodily being. In D. Hook, L. Laubscher, & M. Desai (Eds.), *Fanon, phenomenology, and psychology*. Routledge.

Sartre, J. P. (1965). *Anti-Semite and Jew: An exploration of the etiology of hate*. Schocken. (Original work published 1946)

Schraub, D. (2019). White Jews: An intersectional approach. *AJS Review, 43*(2), 379–407. https://doi.org/10.1017/S0364009419000461

Sheskin, I. M., & Dashefsky, A. (2020). How many Jews of color are there? *eJewishPhilanthropy*. Retrieved April 30, 2024, from https://ejewishphilanthropy.com/how-many-jews-of-color-are-there/

Stern, K. (2019). I drafted the definition of antisemitism. Rightwing Jews are weaponizing it. *The Guardian*. Retrieved December 28, 2022, from https://www.theguardian.com/commentisfree/2019/dec/13/antisemitism-executive-order-trump-chilling-effect

Strosberg, B. B. (2021). Adorno's negative psychology. *Social and Personality Psychology Compass, 15*(2). https://doi.org/10.1111/spc3.12578

USDS. (2022). Working definition of Antisemitism. Office of the special envoy to monitor and combat antisemitism. https://www.state.gov/defining-antisemitism/

Vargas, R. A. (2023, August). *Jamie Foxx apologizes after Instagram post draws accusations of antisemitism*. The Guardian. Retrieved August 6, 2023, from, https://www.theguardian.com/film/2023/aug/06/jamie-foxx-apologizes-instagram-post-antisemitism

Walzer, M. (1995). Preface. In J. P. Sartre (Ed.), *Anti-semite and Jew: An exploration of the etiology of hate*. Schocken.

Wilderson, F. B. (2020). *Afro-pessimism*. Liveright.

Wittgenstein, L. (2009). *Philosophical investigations* (G. E. M. Anscombe, P. M. S. Hacker, & J. Schulte, Trans.). Wiley-Blackwell. (Original work published 1953)

Žižek, S. (2009). *Sublime object of Ideology*. Verso. (Original work published 1992)

2

Excursus on a History of Anti-Semitism

Epochs of Anti-Semitism

Throughout history, instances of anti-Jewish practices have occurred and evolved in response to both the changing reality of Jewish life as well as the changing socio-economic and political contexts. The history of anti-Semitism can be organized around a series of important moments, routinely described in historical accounts of "anti-Semitism."[1] These are moments when anti-Semitism seems to manifest more intensely or distinctly than other moments in history and can be read as marking epochs in the history of anti-Semitism. One such historical schema looks like this: ancient, Christian, medieval, modern, post-Holocaust. One benefit of such a periodization is to position these moments of manifest anti-Semitism in the socio-historical context in which they are embedded in order to illustrate the changing forms of anti-Jewish practices in relation to changing social, political, and economic history. With this, we can challenge ahistorical readings of anti-Semitism as a single, consistent, and

---

[1] I use quotation marks here because, I am asking readers to put aside the potential difference between antisemitism, anti-Semitism, anti-Jewish practices, anti-Judaism, and Judeophobia and to tolerate the term *anti-Semitism* as a "culturally pre-formed object" (Adorno, 1958/2019).

eternal problem guilty of naturalizing (and therefore concealing) historical processes.[2]

The anti-Jewish practices in each epoch are historically specific yet in
some way constellated by difficulties in thinking and categorizing
Jewishness in relation to what is not Jewish (e.g., "Jewish" minorities in
antiquity, Jewish life in Christendom, Jewish particularity in relation to
enlightenment universality, Zionism, and anti-Zionism). Problematizing
the categorical delineation of historically specific forms of anti-Semitism
reveals that these categories break down under scrutiny, giving way to
blurring, blending, and mixing of categories and historical boundaries.
What seems to be produced takes the form of an inconsistent and contingent though historically renewed problem—the difficulty in categorization and reactions to that difficulty.

Historical Complexity of Jewishness and Anti-Semitism[3]

Historically, Jewishness has defied easy categorization, sparking various
forms of anti-Jewish practices that have changed over time, presenting
their own challenges for classification. In the following pages, I provide

---

[2] In this study, there are a series of mythological concepts that need to be bracketed, in the phenomenological sense of making unfamiliar so as to question generally accepted assumptions and natu-
ralizations: religion, nation, antisemitism, race. These are all concepts invented and changing in
history. Part of my effort to better understand these mythological concepts is to analyze them as a
cultural production which "transforms into nature" (Barthes, 1957/1991, p. 127). Barthes
(1957/1991) makes a helpful distinction between demythology and semiology. The dymythologist
deconstructs mythology by positing an original meaning or truth, a semiologist suspends assumptions of an original so as to recognize how those myths distort or construct but do not disappear
the truth. According to Barthes (1957/1991), "Myth hides nothing: its function is to distort, not
to make disappear" (p. 117). The distortion is a matter of form, and "Semiology is a science of
forms, since it studies signification apart from their content" (Barthes, 1957/1991, p. 110). I am
taking the stance of the semiologist, the (critical) phenomenologists, also perhaps the psychoanalyst, the deconstructionist, the lay Talmudist, the negative dialectician.

[3] I hang the beads of anti-Semitic events on a string of historical storytelling such that they are not
isolated events but interrelated ones. I am not, on the other hand, trying to write a history of anti-
Semitism in any sense of a rigorous or comprehensive historical accounting (for such an account
see Langmuir, 1990; Nirenberg, 2013; Poliakov, 2003). It is a historical account of various Jewish
and anti-Jewish events, but also, following Langmuir (1990) and Nirenberg (2013), I would like
to emphasize the history of the figure of the Jew and the way the concept "Judaism" has been (re)

examples from different historical contexts where contradictions and difficulties related to Jewishness and anti-Semitism become focal points. From the earliest Diasporas to the complexities of medieval Europe, and from the advent of Christianity and Islam to the expulsions from Spain in 1492 and the French Revolution, Jews occupied a unique position that challenged conventional social organization and posed questions central to each epoch.

Between the eighth and sixth centuries BCE, the Judean kingdoms of Israel and Judah fell to the Assyrians and Babylonians, leading to the Diaspora of the Judeans to foreign lands. The Roman conquest of Jerusalem in the first centuries CE precipitated a second Diaspora. During this early Diasporic existence, Jews occupied a position that challenged previous categories, as demonstrated in places like Greek Alexandria, where they were, as David Nirenberg (2013) puts it, "neither disenfranchised nor citizen, neither conquered nor conquering, neither powerless nor free" (p. 46). Before this time conquered peoples were absorbed by the conqueror's cosmology. The Jews, on the contrary, packed up their cosmology and carried it into the Diaspora to thrive among other peoples. The Diasporic and minority status of the Jews marked a qualitative shift of social spacing in the ancient world.

Christianity emerged from the interaction between Jews and their non-Jewish neighbors. Early Christian universalism, conceived as a matter of faith rather than a specific way of life, positioned itself both in opposition to and as a successor to what Christians termed "Judaism." According to Boyarin (2019), prior to Christianity, Jewishness was tied to language, laws, and rituals that circumscribed a form of life and lacked what we now recognize as religion.[4] Christianity regarded itself as an anti-Judaism but also the new or more authentic expression of Judaism. The

---

formulated by those who use the concepts to better understand and control their worlds. Both accounts—history of events and history of concepts—provide material for a proteophobic analysis. Moreover, the irreconcilable interval between living and breathing Jewish people and the concept of "the Jew" or "Judaism" is often a site where thinking becomes murky and justice seems to be blocked (see Cheyette, 2013, for a discussion of the gap between the "real" and "imagined" Jew). To my mind this irreconcilability indicates not that we are on the wrong track, but that we are on the right one, save that more thinking is needed.

[4] Kant, in *Religion Within the Limits of Reason Alone* (1793/2008), makes a similar argument from the perspective of anti-Judaism.

emphasis shifted from adhering strictly to the letter of the law to embodying its spirit—or so it was articulated. While Jews adhered to the physical
rite of circumcision, Christians emphasized a metaphorical circumcision
of the heart.[5] Yet the Judaism used by Christians as an antithesis, was not

---

[5] As Jordan Osserman (2022) notes, Christianity didn't invent the idea of reading circumcision
"spiritually." The notion of the circumcision of the heart is itself rooted in Jewish teaching:
"Circumcise yourselves to the Lord, and take away the foreskins of your heart […]" (Jeremiah 4:4).
According to Osserman (2022) St. Paul's "truly novel gesture"—that is, which establishes the distinction that is Christianity—"consists in his subtracting the 'spiritual meaning' of Jewish law from
the ritual practice altogether, seemingly eviscerating the bond between the Jewish spirit and the
Jewish flesh" (p. 67). The idea of circumcision and contemporary reactions to circumcision rituals
evoke questions related to both anti-Judaism and anti-Semitism. Osserman (2022) offers an interpretation of Daniel Boyarin's logic of circumcision which grounds Jewish identity in the Diaspora's
lack of self-enclosure and an openness to otherness:

> In Boyarin's version, the ritual is less about "branding" the Jew in opposition to the Gentile than
> it is a matter of performatively embodying one's constitutive relation to otherness or "not having."
> Circumcision becomes […] the opening of a void within the organic body. An intimate part of the
> self is marked by a lack, subjected to an originary wound imposed by the Other. Whereas the typi-
> cal masculine strategy is to disavow or try to fill in this void, in Boyarin's reading of circumcision it
> becomes the ineradicable origin-point of the (Jewish) self, linking man to a divinity beyond him.
> That the rabbinical approach to the rite invokes symbolic signifiers of femininity— menstrual
> blood, sexual receptiveness, and so on—suggests, in Boyarinian/Lacanian logic, an attunement to
> this feminine relation to castration, releasing the logic of feminine subjectivity from an exclusively
> anatomical referent. (pp. 89–90)

Osserman (2022) then distinguishes this perspective from Alain Badiou's anti-Judaic reading of
circumcision. Summing up his argument, Osserman concludes that

> […] circumcision functioned, for Alain Badiou, as a "form of branding," a way of constituting
> an identitarian (phallic) order: St. Paul needed to express his "indifference" to Jewish circumcision
> in order to "cut" through communitarian Jew/Pagan differences and offer a universal form of
> belonging situated in the void of being. For Daniel Boyarin, circumcision represented the very
> inverse of this, a mark of one's subjection to symbolic castration that resisted sublation into phallic
> Christian transcendence and that held out the promise for a more genuinely open and embodied
> relation to otherness. Although they offered divergent interpretations of Paul, and Paul on circum-
> cision, both authors, I argued, took a stance in opposition to phallic mastery, which I identified as
> closely related to the "feminine" side of Lacan's formulas of sexuation. The fact that they offered
> such opposing readings on circumcision could be explained, I concluded, by the inherent ambiva-
> lence of the practice itself. (p. 214)

This reading situates circumcision squarely in the Jewish relation to the formulation ambivalence, otherness, and negativity that I develop throughout this book. It is an ambivalent practice
that situates the Jewish person in relation to ambivalence. This is what I will later refer to as the
non-identity of Jews that doesn't erase identity. This reiterative performance is a non-identity historically belonging to Jews and is opposed to phallic identity and the achievement of a retroactive
wholeness. Osserman (2022) suggests that in thinking critically about one's circumcision, that
circumcision offers an opening to the encounter with one's own desiring subjectivity: "To be sub-
jected to circumcision is to be confronted with one's inconsistent inscription in the symbolic order;
to *subjectify* one's circumcision is to claim this inconsistency as one's own" (p. 218).

necessarily connected to any actual Jewish people. In fact, "Judaism," as a term, wasn't used by Jews, a fact that supports David Nirenberg's (2013) formulation that "Judaism" emerged out of the entrails of Christianity. These moments in history display a complicated picture brimming with new concepts and new forms of life, such as 'religion of faith' and minority peoples, as well as nuanced distinctions between Jews, Judeans, Jewishness, Judaism, Christians, and the figure of the Jew.[6]

During the Middle Ages, Christian doctrinal anti-Judaism was codified into law, extending its influence to broader European legal and institutional realms. This period witnessed the emergence of popular anti-Judaism in Northern Europe, culminating in violent episodes such as the Rhineland Massacres of Jews in 1096, carried out by Christian crusaders. Despite being coerced into moneylending, Jews faced condemnation for usury and were accused of profiteering from the holy crusades they were compelled to finance, leading to the confiscation of their assets. Notably, a significant portion of England's total revenue at certain historical junctures was derived from appropriated Jewish assets, placing Jews in a precarious position vis-à-vis the dominant institutions of the time. These historical dynamics further compounded the already complex and vulnerable situation of the Jewish people.

The precarious situation of Jews persisted, leading to further dispersion and the instability of Jewish communities. For instance, Jews had inhabited France for a millennium until 1180, when King Philip Augustus imprisoned them across his realm, subsequently releasing them for a ransom, confiscating all Jewish assets, and expelling them from his kingdom (only to readmit them less than 20 years later, albeit subject to heavy taxes). The Jews of France experienced a cycle of expulsion and readmission until 1394, when they were once again expelled, only to return in the seventeenth century. Similarly, Jews were expelled from England in 1290 and, like their counterparts in France, did not return until the

---

[6] While supersession was reassessed in some Christian doctrine after the Shoah, the logic of supersession continues to dominate Western civilization in a displaced and secularized form (Cheyette, 2013). Take for instance, the notion of "Judeo-Christian" culture. Judeo-Christian culture is attributed to a secular culture rooted in what is thought of as a secularization of the "Judeo-Christian." By this, they mean societies that developed out of Christianity and Judaism. But this term "Judeo-Christian" hides a secularized supersessionism. The Jewishness that is not captured or subsumed by Christian forms of universalism is erased from the equation.

seventeenth century. The changing power dynamics between monarchs and church authorities continued to complicate the status of Jews, making it challenging to fit them into existing categories. As Cohen (2008) observes, "Competing legal systems complicated [the status of Jews], and [...] the 'law of utility' inevitably led to arbitrariness and ultimately to the isolation of Jews into a special legal category, subject to the authority of various ruling powers" (p. 195). The control over Jews underscored the delicate relationship between religious and secular authorities, both of which exploited Jewish communities for divergent purposes.

As the historical landscape evolved, so did the manifestations of anti-Jewish sentiment. During the Bubonic Plague (1347–1351), for example, Jews were scapegoated for the spread of a disease that decimated half of Europe's population. While Jews may have been somewhat protected from the worst effects of the plague, potentially due to their legal isolation and adherence to sanitary laws, they became targets of blame in the societal upheaval. The convergence of material changes in social dynamics and continued cosmological anti-Judaism gave rise to a new strain of conspiratorial anti-Jewish assertions and triggered mass persecutions.

Moving to a different part of the world, Islamic cosmology, emerging in the eighth century CE, superseded both Christianity and Judaism while inheriting elements of the former's anti-Judaism. Islamic scripture struggled to classify Jews. Muslims, while honoring Jewish prophets, utilized Judaism and anti-Judaism to construct their worldview, engaging in what Nirenberg (2013) describes as a "double gesture of inclusion and exclusion," allowing Islam to incorporate Judaism while simultaneously excluding it (p. 169). While Islamic tradition and rituals, such as the Muslim temple mount and prayer direction, explicitly reference the supersession of Judaism, anti-Judaic practices within Islam did not lead to the same frequency or intensity of massacres and expulsions as witnessed in Christendom.

Muslim societies largely served as a haven from Christian persecution and generally afforded Jews minority rights and protections as custodians of scripture. However, historical tensions, misunderstandings between Jews and Muslims, and various political and economic factors periodically led to instances of persecution and discrimination against Jews. *Dhimmi* codes, ostensibly implemented for protection, relegated Jews to lower-class status, curtailed their rights and access to sacred sites, and mandated distinctive clothing. The scholarly discourse on the treatment of Jews by Muslims has become politicized, particularly in the context of the Israel-Palestine conflict. Some highlight the oppression endured by Jews under Muslim rule, while others emphasize the cultural achievements of Jews during the so-called Golden Age of Jewish-Muslim interfaith relations.

In 1492, Christian King Ferdinand II and Queen Isabella I expelled both Jews and Muslims from Spain, followed by similar expulsions from Portugal as part of the Spanish Inquisition (1478–1840). The edict of expulsion was not officially lifted until 1968, even though Jews lived in relative safety in Spain since the mid-nineteenth century. During the Inquisition, Jews and Muslims were forced to either convert to Christianity, leave the country, or face execution. Both Jewish and Muslim converts were distinguished from their "pure" Christian neighbors and labeled with the pejorative category, *Conversos*. *Conversos* were never fully accepted by their Christian-born neighbors. In fact, *Conversos* were sometimes seen as an even greater threat to Christian purity, now incorporated into Christian society as the outsider within. Jews and Muslims were said to have impure blood that could taint the *Limpieza de sangue* or purity of Christians. This suspicion seems contrary to Pauline doctrine which asserts universality: "There is neither Jew nor Greek, there is neither slave nor free, there is no male and female, for you are all one in Christ Jesus" (Galatians 3:28, English Standard Version Bible, 2001). Accordingly, Jews should be able to convert to Christianity and have their souls "saved," regardless of history, "blood," or genealogy.

The failure of these conversions during the Inquisition, but also later with the failure of Jewish assimilation into the secularized Christian universalism marked by the French Revolution, exposes some complications in formulating Jewishness as merely a matter of faith or religion. It was presumed that something essential—perhaps the Jew's historical particularity or spirit of their "race"—remained after Christian faith (and later national identity) was "proven." These ideas later evolved into the pseudo-scientific notion of race, and the belief that one's racial inheritance and inner essence were inseparable.

The term "Semitic" was originally coined within philological discourse to categorize a group of Afro-Asiatic languages (Hebrew, Arabic, Aramaic) according to their common ancient roots and manifesting as racial identification. Mielants et al. (2009) point out that for Christian Europeans, Jews were outsiders from Africa and West Asia, whereas for many Muslims, Jews "were accepted as of similar if not the same origin" (p. 2) expressing a "unity in the face of Christendom" (p. 3). Mielants et al. (2009) mark the expulsion in 1492 as the original discriminatory practice against a Semitic culture, as such, arguing that anti-Semitism was fused with Islamophobia since its inception *as* anti-Semitism (though not yet called that). Edward Said (1979/2003) makes a similar argument for the common roots of anti-Semitism and Islamophobia in the orientalist concept of arrested cultural and racial development.[7] More recently, Achille Mbembe (2015) has characterized Islamophobia as the "mimetic counterpart" of a "renewed Judeophobia" (p. 6). This connection offers hope and substance to coalition and solidarity between Jews and Muslims who too often find themselves in conflict.

The expulsions of 1492 coincided with the start of the colonial enterprise, which involved the dehumanization, subjugation, and enslavement of Black and Indigenous populations globally. According to Aimè Cèsaire's (1950/2001) colonial boomerang theory, the paradigm-shifting racial consequences of colonialism reverberated back to Europe, and soon Jews and Muslims were racially excluded from the White European social contract. Complicating the picture of anti-Semitism once again, this boomerang effect instilled "old forms of discrimination with new meaning" (Mielants et al., 2009, p. 5). Colonial racism and anti-Semitism are intertwined and mutually reinforcing systems of oppression that have far-reaching and lasting impacts on both the colonized peoples and Jews. Categories of race, religion, and nation form an inseparable constellation

---

[7] Developing on Said's work, Gil Anidjar (2007) argues that though there may be no really existing "Semitic peoples," Semites had a real enough place within discourse. "The Semitic hypothesis in this context," Anidjar (2007) writes, "refers to the invention of the Semites, which is to say, the historically unique, discursive moment whereby whatever was said about Jews could equally be said about Arabs, and vice versa" (Anidjar, 2007, p. 18). The Semitic hypothesis, if nothing else, brings together Jews and Arabs in the history of a particular discourse.

of intersecting discourses (Anidjar, 2007).[8] And, like the link between Islamophobia and anti-Semitism, the connection (or inseparability) between racism and anti-Semitism can be coalition-building (see Frosh, 2023).

Understanding the inherent connection and similarity between struggles can be harnessed for liberatory ends, but it can also leave out the historical specificity of each. Yes, Jews and Muslims were both expelled from Spain in 1492, and there is good evidence that Jews sided with Islam in conflicts between empires because they were persecuted less violently in Islamic societies. But at the time of expulsion, Islamic empires had immense political power, enough for the Muslim-controlled Emirate of Granada to wage war with Christian Spain for a decade leading to the expulsion. And at the time, there were other Muslim powers engaging in diplomacy with the Christian world, such as the Ottomans and Berbers. This is not to suggest that the Muslim population of the Iberian Peninsula was not persecuted in 1492, or that Jews and Muslims had no common interests, but that the historical and material positions of Jews and Muslims were not necessarily "united" by their supposedly common (racialized) Semitic origins in opposition to Christendom. Islam was a major religion and form of life of the Iberian Peninsula for over a millennium, and Christian Spain felt perpetually threatened by Islamic empires through the seventeenth century. The Jews, living in the Diaspora, were expelled from over a dozen European countries around that time and had virtually no direct political or military power. These complications challenge clear-cut categorization as historical context and power shifts.

The expulsion from the Iberian Peninsula was not the first or last time Jews were expelled for being Jewish. Virulent, irrational, and characterological forms of anti-Semitism took root well before the fifteenth century. Langmuir (1990) classifies antisemitism (as opposed to anti-Judaism) by its general irrational and chimerical quality developed during the thirteenth century, while Mielants et al. (2009) mark it with a specific racial inflection of fifteenth-century colonialism. This is a good example of the way historical analysis constructs an object of study. In what year did

---

[8] To be religious is not necessarily to think in terms of race, but to be anti-religious seems to quickly slide into racism.

anti-Semitism begin, in the fifteenth century or the thirteenth? Before the Slave Trade, were Jews merely Europeans, such that the Shoah was merely a turning of colonial tactics back on Europe, as categorized by Aimè Cèsaire (2001) and Charles W. Mills (1997/2019)? Is it appropriate to use the term "Semitic" prior to its invention as a term? The difference in historical marking is related to defining concepts like chimera, race, and Semite.

The Protestant Reformation of the sixteenth century left a profound impact on Christians and neighboring Jewish communities. The Reformation emphasized individual spiritual responsibility, detached from institutional or communal ties. Much like the birth of Pauline Christianity, "Judaism was central to the self-definition and identity of the Protestant Reformation" (Po-Chia Hsia, 2018, p. 50). Reformers viewed themselves as the new chosen people superseding the old, leading to the study of Hebrew and Jewish scriptures as integral to Protestant salvation (Po-Chia Hsia, 2018). However, the continued existence of Jewish communities posed an existential paradox for Protestant reformers who pronounced the death of Judaism (see Newman, 1993). During the Protestant Reformation, various categorization issues arose, including the blurring of lines between philosemitism and anti-Semitism, ongoing accusations of Judaizing between Protestantism and Catholicism, and a shift from institutionalized religion to individual salvation through faith. This complicates the straightforward periodization of anti-Semitism, as the revival of anti-Judaic doctrine coexisted with emerging pseudo-racial theories of anti-Semitism, alongside persisting blood libel accusations and violence in the sixteenth century.

Protestantism also significantly influenced Jewish life and the potential for Jewish assimilation, leading to the conceptualization of Judaism as a distinct religious practice separated from other spheres of life. As Boyarin (2023) asserts, religion

[…] is notoriously difficult to define, but in its modern usage it almost always devolves to the essentially Protestant—even essentially Lutheran—notion of a belief system, disembedded from other forms of belonging, identity, and practice within a given nation. Such a view is embodied in

English usage when we refer to "the Jewish faith," as if belief in certain propositions were what made one a Jew. (p. ix)

Boyarin (2023) humorously terms this phenomenon "Jewtheranism" (p. 38), likening a form of Judaism to Lutheran faith and religiosity.

During the Enlightenment, beginning in the late seventeenth century, anti-Semitism evolved into a more secular form. However, this transformation did not signify a complete departure from previous iterations but rather a continuation of existing patterns. The structure of Jewish life, rooted in Diaspora, posed distinct yet interconnected challenges for Christianity and the emerging modern socio-political order. This prompted fundamental questions about religious faith, national identity, and universality, and persisted among Enlightenment thinkers (e.g., Marks, 2010) and subsequent philosophers who continued to employ the language of Judaism and anti-Judaism in their discourse to understand problems of their time (Nirenberg, 2013).

The Jewish Naturalization Act of 1753 in England marked another turning point in the status of Jews in Europe and sparked a public debate about their rights and place in society (Yuval-Naeh, 2018). Meanwhile, the French Revolution marked a fundamental shift in the political landscape of France and had far-reaching consequences for the rest of Europe, including the rights of minorities. The granting of citizenship to Jews during the French Revolution (1789–1799) led to much debate and was conditional on Jews assimilating into the ostensibly neutral European civilization based on universalist ideals. Jews were required to renounce minority privileges and loyalties, embracing civic allegiance to the nation-state while practicing Judaism privately. Consequently, Jews had to relinquish many aspects of their cultural identity that were not strictly "religious" in the Christian sense of the term. It is noteworthy that during this period, Jews began to adopt the concepts of "Judaism" and "religion" to refer to themselves (Boyarin, 2019, p. xi).

The idea of the "Jewish Question" can be traced back to the late eighteenth and early nineteenth centuries, during times of significant social, economic, and political change in Europe. Debates surrounding assimilation came to a head during the Dreyfus Affair (1894–1906), bringing the Jewish Question to public discourse with the question of dual loyalty. It centered around the wrongful conviction of Captain Alfred Dreyfus, a French Army officer of Jewish descent, for espionage on behalf of Germany. Among other things, the Dreyfus Affair represented the growing anti-Semitism in response to Jewish assimilation in France. Jews were initially encouraged to assimilate into French society, yet they soon faced accusations of being a hidden threat, cast as the dangerous other within, echoing similar accusations made during the Spanish Inquisition.

By the late nineteenth century, both Jews and non-Jews were seeking solutions to the Jewish Question. For Jews, enlightenment, assimilation, and persecution brought to the fore new questions about what it meant to be Jewish. This period was also marked by a series of violent pogroms in western Russia, which were often sanctioned by political and religious authorities. The pogroms, along with increasing anti-Semitism and discrimination in general, led to widespread fear and insecurity among Jews. In response to these challenges and as potential solutions to the Jewish Question, various movements emerged, including Bundism (a culturally Jewish labor movement) and Zionism in both cultural and political variations. These movements offered different visions for the future and identity of Jewish people, ranging from socialist revolution to cultural autonomy to the establishment of a Jewish State. By the 1930s and 1940s, the Jewish Question was part of political discourse in the United States (see Nock, 1941). The Shoah was formulated as the Nazis' "Final Solution" to the Jewish Question. Today, White supremacists and other racist groups who subscribe to anti-Semitic conspiracy theories around the world use the term "JQ" to refer to the "Jewish Question" (Kestenbaum, 2016).[9]

As I have brought to focus in the preceding pages, a constellation of anti-Judaism and anti-Semitism is observed through an uncanny repetition of contradictions and uncategorizability: A Jewish identity forged in

---

[9] Jewish assimilation following the enlightenment led to the fear of a secret other inside of society that was eating away at society from the inside out. One way to understand this is as a product or side effect of the newly minted social order of nationalism and internationalism. Jews were seen as either too different or not different enough from the "imagined community" of the majority in a given nation (Anderson, 2016). On one level, the Jewish Question is about real Jewish people and their specific and historical position in relation to social power. On another level, the Jewish Question is about the inconsistency of liberal and modern ideas in and of themselves (see Marx, 1844/2012).

diaspora; the Christian and Muslim as both Jewish and not Jewish; Judaism as both preceding and produced by Christianity; the Jew as both capable and incapable of conversion to Christianity during the Inquisition; the Jew as challenging the universality of "the rights of man," and the Jewish particularity that must be protected by the universality of "the rights of man"; the Jew as too isolated and too assimilated in an age of nationalism. The issues with categorization extend beyond the scope outlined above and permeate many facets of history, persisting well into the twentieth century and continuing to shape contemporary narratives.[10]

Navigating Conceptual Quandaries in Historical Writing

One problem with writing about anything whose contours and definitions are themselves a problem, or contested, is that any declarative statement about the object of study assumes what it has set out to define or examine. This calls for a methodological response and not a cynical one. It seems that before writing about anti-Semitic events throughout history, the concept of anti-Semitism must be defined. And yet, as I indicated in the previous chapter, concepts are defined through intellectual work itself. Instead of giving up in the face of this potential paradox— giving up in the sense of giving in to the impulse to rely on rigidly preformulated definitions or giving up in the sense of not writing at all—I resign myself to begin in the middle, as it were, with what Adorno (1958/2019) refers to as a "culturally pre-formed object" (p. 3): anti-Semitism.[11] I hope that in acknowledging this starting point, we can mitigate some of the risk of making ahistorical claims.

---

[10] Many Germans experienced ambivalence after the Holocaust, balancing efforts to fight discrimination with feelings of resentment for their collective guilt. The saying "Germans will never be able to forgive the Jews for the Holocaust" speaks to this. A recent poll by the Allensbach Institute for Public Opinion Research found that one in ten people in Germany have witnessed physical attacks on Jewish individuals (AJC, 2022). Anti-Semitism remains a major problem in German society and across Europe (Kovacs & Fischer, 2021).

[11] Adorno, since his inaugural lecture at Frankfurt in 1931, argued to replace reliance on verbal definitions with constellations or models (Adorno, 2001, p. 151, footnote). One intervention that this project makes into the debates surrounding anti-Semitism is to suggest that definitions of anti-

What is it to write history? Common sense suggests that history is the story of the past or the chronicle of events "exactly as it happened" (Ranke, 2011). History—what it is and how it should be recorded and studied—is not so clear or straightforward. History, unlike the past, necessitates choices of inclusion and exclusion that form a narrative emphasizing certain moments and not others, depending on conscious and unconscious normative commitments and intentions. These narrative decisions form boundaries of epochs, categories, and concepts, and are often presented as natural or primordial archetypes or myths. Not only is a story defined by its content; just as essential are the decisive cuts and breaks that constitute the story's beginning and end, but also the punctuation throughout. To tell the story of the past, the simple past, the past "as it *really* happened" would be akin to the cartographer from Borges' (1998) famous story who, attempting to draw up a map that so perfectly represents the territory such that it covers over everything, creates a useless relic.[12] Who could use such a map? It is a truism that acts of writing history leave out what they do not select for inclusion or focus; in this sense, history is as much about what is left out as what is included.[13] The past may be viewed from an infinite number of angles, can be cut in an infinite number of ways, and contains historical depths which cannot be re-presented. The question becomes: If history is not the past as it happens, and we made decisions in telling the story of history, what is determinative of those categorical decisions? Are they arbitrary or natural? Are they found in the past or the present?

Semitism fail because the idea of definition is not adequate to the matter of anti-Semitism. Only constellations will do.

[12] This theme has been developed by a number of authors such as Umberto Eco (1995), Jean Baudrillard (1994), Lewis Carroll (1893), and Slavoj Žižek (2002). Ted Chiang (2019) is another author wrestling with this idea of history as a chronicle of events. In his sci-fi short story, "The Truth of Fact, the Truth of Feeling," Chiang (2019) describes a future where humans create video logs of their lives that allow them to access supposedly "objective" eidetic memory. Even such a chronicle of the past "as it really happened," his story shows, needs to be interpreted and is lived differently than it is recorded.

[13] According to scholars like Auerbach (1946/2003) and Mendelsohn (2020), the gaps and cracks in Jewish literature and modes of thinking reveal an ambivalent and multilayered reality that for some people may seem to better represent human experience which doesn't seem like a chronicle of events "as they really happen."

This issue of selective historicizing—that histories necessitate decisions of inclusion and exclusion—is especially important when examining questions about the nature of anti-Semitism in different historical moments. In writing history and defining terms like "anti-Semitism" or "racism" the same problems with categorization arise. Philosopher Charles W. Mills (1997/2019) has argued that there are "ontological joints" at which one can divide the world into clear-cut categories (p. 79). Like carving a chicken carcass, these joints seem like natural division points. History is, likewise, divided by these joints. The joints in history are conceptual—a matter, in each case, of categorization and ontologizing. According to Mills (1997/2019), there is a parsimonious "elegance and simplicity" to these joints, as in the conceptual racial binary of "white/ non-white" which "map the essential features of racial polity accurately" (p. 78). Yet, Mills also acknowledges the fuzziness in harmonious racial polarities related to the figure of the Jew who is perennially excluded from Whiteness *and* nonwhiteness. Mills (1997/2019) writes: "Nevertheless, these problem cases [and Jewishness, above all] are useful in illustrating—against essentialists—the social rather than biological basis of the Racial Contract" (p. 80). Mills (1997/2019) offers "off-white" as a way of closing the gap in order to continue to mobilize the "elegant" binary of White/nonwhite, where the figure of the Jew might otherwise make such a binary inoperable. To continue where Mills leaves off, I do not want to close the gap or give a final solution to the question, even while I agree that the White/nonwhite binary *does* operate in our society. This binary, however, seems to erase the Jewish experience, whereas Mills' "off-white" solution explains away the Jewish experience of being explained away. The category of Jewishness challenges the simplicity of such clear-cut categories through which racial concepts and historical epochs are delineated. The figure of the Jew requires us to question intuitive assumptions and what seems natural or original.

The Racial Contract (1997/2019) tells the story of a founding myth of racialized society. Carole Pateman argued, in *The Sexual Contract* (1988), that there are other contracts, other narratives through which modern society is organized, specifically referring to systematic sexism. I would argue that Edward Said's *Orientalism* (1979/2003) conveys a similar contractual binary between so-called Western (Occidental) and non-Western (Oriental) forms of life. Nirenberg (2013), in turn, makes a case for the way that anti-Judaism constitutes the "West." Each of these narratives is distinct and intersecting but not equal. Numerous other scholars have also contributed such narratives, including Luce Irigaray (1985) and Frank B. Wilderson (2020). Each of these elegant narratives does a kind of violence, like ripping a chicken apart at its joints, in order to organize a historical telling. As this book is exploring, the prospect of a proteophobic "contract" is different in that it is rooted in the categorical exclusion of those deemed to be contract breakers, or rather, those who don't fit into the terms of each ontological contract.[14]

The story of anti-Semitism—and the ontological joints that story relies on—may seem clear-cut at first glance. Suggesting that anti-Semitism is "the oldest hate" and has been experienced since antiquity presupposes that some facet of anti-Semitism is ahistorical or archetypal. Yet, anti-Semitism, as a concept, was only developed in the nineteenth century. Such an ahistorical anti-Semitism (also called eternalism, an idea analyzed in the next chapter), then, presupposes an essentially ahistorical Jewishness consistently oppressed in antiquity as it is today—a persistent anti-Semitic trope of its own. The difficulty in giving a historical account of anti-Semitism may be related to the difficulty in writing history in general or finding the right ontological joints that constitute the subject of that historical writing, but something specific about anti-Semitism seems resistant to definitive cuts, as it defies straightforward common-sense representation such as, *"People have hated Jews for thousands of years and anti-Semitism is the name for this hate."* One could give a history of anti-Semitism starting in ancient Egypt, running continuously through

---

[14] It could be argued that Queerness also doesn't fit into this category, especially as formulated by Josè Esteban Muñoz (2019) and Lee Edelman (2004). Though Muñoz is critical of Edelman's project, I read them as very close on this point. Edelman's *No Future* (2004) presents something of a systematic anti-Queerness, in that Queer is always a disturbance of identity categories. Edelman formulates his projects as formulating a critique of reproductive futurism in favor of an "opposition to the logic of opposition" (p. 4). His project resonates with my critique of proteophobia. He formulates all identity as operationally defined, and Queerness as a resistance to this identity formation. Edelman lobbies for the "primacy of a constant no in response to the law of the symbolic" (p. 5), and as it is for Shoshana Felman (2003), it is a "no" of nonopposition and not an oppositional (Queer) negative as it is sometimes read.

modernity. In some ways, it would be a reasonable endeavor given the fact that Jews have been the target of anti-Jewish practices for more than two thousand years. But within that statement there are a number of ambiguities that ruin such a linear narrative of the consistency of anti-Semitism. For example, does hate for someone who happens to identify as Jewish count as anti-Semitism, or only if it is the hate for Jews *because* they are Jewish? What about the use of anti-Semitic rhetoric leveled at non-Jews, and the notion of "Judaizing" (attributing to non-Jews certain, usually negative, "Jewish characteristics")? Is a Jewish stereotype anti-Semitic (considering, as well, that stereotypes—theoretically—can be "positive"), or is it only so if "negative" and/or accompanied by discrimination? What about prejudice without overt discrimination? What about hate for the State of Israel?

Principally, does the referent of what we call anti-Semitism preexist the word we have to describe and categorize it? Jews, Judaism, Jewish forms of life, and the figure of the Jew—each a target of anti-Jewish practices—are, without a doubt, different now than they were two thousand years ago. Is there an essence in/to Jewishness, then, that the anti-Semite has always hated, and that I can point to as the eternal essence of anti-Semitism? A way of reading, a set of practices, an emphasis on the body, a history, a dual loyalty? Or to borrow language from the anti-Semite (for dramatic and sarcastic effect): a putrid smell, a specific gait, a corrupt intent, a greedy or perverted character? No. The examples I explored above show that Jews are hated for various changing and often contradictory reasons, some relating to Jews and some relating solely to those who commit the anti-Jewish practices.

What I will develop, though, is not the persistence of a specific content or feature that makes up the essence of the category of anti-Semitism across historical epochs. What persists in the history of anti-Semitism is a constellation, contingent dynamic (perhaps the dynamic of the contingent), shapeshifting image, and the difficulty in thinking (historically or categorically), as such. Anti-Semitism manifests in historically specific ways that differ across times and places—the rootlessness of the Diaspora in relation to the world historical context of antiquity, the advent of Christianity out of a Judaism it produced, the continued Diaspora of

Jews in the modern age of nationalism and ethno-science, the continued Diaspora of the Jews in relation to the attempted annihilation of Jews, the rise of a Jewish ethno-state, the continued Diaspora of the Jews in relation to that Jewish ethno-state. What constellates these—and perhaps also what cuts into and across them—may well be the reaction to this dynamic of uncategorizability related to Jews, Jewishness, and Judaism reflecting a broad complex reality.

I have challenged the idea that we can essentialize anti-Semitism or what it is to be the objectified figure of the Jew for the anti-Semite. There is no essence there, or so it seems. I have offered the concept of "uncategorizability" for the constellation that does appear to persist across many of these settings. Still, appearances are deceiving. I don't offer "uncategorizability" as a satisfying alternative to essence. Indeed, as I will show, I want to do justice to the experience of Jewish identity as something that is not *merely* uncategorizable but also lived as a constellation of ethical relations and practices by those who identify as Jewish. Now, Jews don't agree on what it means to be Jewish, but there are certainly Jews. The Jews who made animal sacrifices, the Jews of Berlin in 1924, the Jews of Berlin 2024, and my own family have all asked, for example and across the centuries, "how is this night different from all other nights" during the Passover seder.[15]

The concept of proteophobia is not without its theoretical challenges, posing difficult questions relating to historical particularity, universality, and eternality. It is not my intention to reduce anti-Semitism to a mere instance of proteophobia. Instead, I organize this exploration around proteophobia, making a critical examination of anti-Semitism via proteophobia, and vice versa, in order to better lay bare both a clearer picture of the object of my study—anti-Semitism and the challenges it has posed in attempts to explain and categorize it—and a productive critique of those

---

[15] My association to this line of thinking is the Ship of Theseus. Is there something essential about anti-Semitism that would stay the same throughout history as the planks that make it up are replaced with new planks? If someone gathered all the decayed and replaced parts of the ship and used those to build a second one, which would be the "original"? It points to the question rather pointedly, of something essential about the Jew or not, and if not, then by which marker is there a historical Jew (as, by extension, anti-Semitism). Perhaps the only constant is the story of a story; perhaps the only constant is of waiting—for Elijah and the Messiah, a story of Rosencrantz and Guildenstern, which is to say a story of all of us.

efforts that in one way or another have suffered from an overreliance on or an uncritical embrace of *categorization*—of Jews, of Judaism, of prejudice, etc. I advance the claim that proteophobia does not *necessarily* lead to anti-Semitism, but remains a *proto-anti-Semitic potential*.[16] And with these concepts, one might find tools to counter anti-Semitism in its many guises. Still, the charge that I make of anti-Semitism an instance or exemplary case of proteophobia is not so much one to contest, dismiss, or devalorize, as one that helpfully illuminates some of the problems and (I hope) promises of my conceptual orientation and methodology: primarily, critical theory and psychoanalysis.[17]

As I will describe in greater detail in the following chapter, David Nirenberg (2013) has developed a theory of anti-Judaism as something that is consistent and recognizable across epochs, and in doing so he has been accused of positing a universal, ahistorical underlying principle giving that anti-Judaism its conceptual consistency. I will do some work to challenge that reading. Instead of an underlying principle of anti-Judaism, I will argue, Nirenberg (2013) offers historical evidence that various non-Jewish peoples have used varied and sometimes contradictory concepts of Judaism and anti-Judaism, and employed these same signifiers across epochs in very different ways. When analyzed historically, this shapeshifting though historically concrete anti-Judaism troubles clear-cut categories, even if the signifier "anti-Judaism" is the best fit as an analytic tool.

---

[16] I am borrowing this idea of the "proto... potentials" from Herbert Marcuse who coined the phrase "protofascist potentials" (Marcuse cited in Macdonald & Young, 2021, p. 3) and Walter Benjamin who used the term "fascist armature" to characterize Jung's early work (Benjamin in Scholem & Adorno, 2012, p. 542). The definition of fascism is contentiously debated, as is its usefulness as a broad analytic tool. Nevertheless, it has come to represent an important signifier for what must be avoided—both politically and conceptually—in the struggle against oppression and untruth. Fascism is first and foremost a historically specific phenomenon, as in Italian Fascism and German Nazism. Yet, the term has been used in critical theory to reach beyond these historical manifestations to a "minimal" fascism at the level of epistemology and ideology—e.g., striving toward wholeness, purity, origins, completion, an authority that reduces anxiety. Protofascism is a potential, sometimes explicit but at other times just below the surface of a fragile democracy (as in the examples of the United States and Israel). These potentials, deeply embedded within epistemological foundations can readily manifest as tangible consequences and realities. Therefore, it remains imperative to critically examine the implicit epistemological foundations of this protofascism, as I am suggesting is the case with proto-anti-Semitic potentials.

[17] The concept of "critical" helps to constellate various methodological ideas developed in the previous chapter and employed throughout the book. In the critical process, thought folds back on itself toward an awareness of its processes, axioms, and ideological assumptions.

This is not positing anti-Judaism as a universal but as what Nirenberg (2013) refers to as a "mask" under which various historical particularities can slide, and "a pedagogical fear that gives enduring form to some of the key concepts and questions in the history of thought" (p. 10). I am offering proteophobia as a name for that fear. This offers an alternative to the opposition between the universalist approach and the argument for specificity—perhaps something close to what Judith Butler (2013) refers to as "universalization in the name of the inassimilable" (p. 23).[18]

References

Adorno, T. W. (2001) *Metaphysics: Concepts and problems* (R. Tiedemann, Ed. & E. Jephcott, Trans.). Stanford University Press.

Adorno, T. W. (2019). *Notes on literature* (R. Tiedemann, Ed. & S. E. Nicolson, Trans.). Columbia University Press. (Original work published 1958)

American Jewish Committee (AJC). (2022). American Jewish committee surveys German general and Muslim populations on antisemitism. Retrieved February 10, 2023, from https://www.ajc.org/news/american-jewish-committee-surveys-german-general-and-muslim-populations-on-antisemitism

Anderson, B. (2016). *Imagined communities: Reflections on the origin and spread of nationalism.* Verso.

Anidjar, G. (2007). *Semites.* Stanford University Press.

Auerbach, E. (2003). *Mimesis: The representation of reality in Western literature.* Princeton University Press. (Original work published 1946)

Barthes, R. (1991). *Mythologies* (A. Lavers, Trans.). Noonday Press. (Original work published 1957)

---

[18] Here is a larger passage that articulates Judith Butler's thesis in *Parting Ways* (2013), where they articulate an ethical imperative related to Israel and Zionism rooted in Jewish literature at a specific intersection of the universal and particular. The resonances with the current project should be obvious:

The modes of universalization that contest those regimes of power most effectively are the ones that simultaneously expose the "inassimilable" as the precondition of a current mode of universalization and demand a dissolution and reformulation of the process of universalization in the name of the inassimilable. The point is not to convert the inassimilable into the assimilable, but to challenge those regimes that require assimilation to their own norms. Only when those norms break apart does universalization have a chance to renew itself within a radically democratic project. (Butler, 2013, p. 23)

Baudrillard, J. (1994). *Simulacra and simulation*. University of Michigan Press.

English Standard Version Bible. (2001). *ESV* Online. https://esv.literalword.com/

Borges, J. L. (1998). *Collected fictions* (A. Hurley, Trans.). Viking.

Boyarin, D. (2019). *Judaism: The genealogy of a modern notion*. Rutgers University Press.

Boyarin, D. (2023). *The no-state solution: A Jewish manifesto*. Yale University Press.

Butler, J. (2013). *Parting ways: Jewishness and the critique of Zionism*. Columbia University Press.

Carroll, L. (1893). *Sylvie and Bruno concluded*. Macmillan and Co.

Cèsaire, A. (2001). *Discourse on colonialism*. Monthly Review Press. (Original work published 1950)

Cheyette, B. (2013). *Diasporas of the mind: Jewish and postcolonial writing and the nightmare of history*. Yale University Press.

Chiang, T. (2019). The truth of fact the truth of fiction. In *Exhalations: Stories*. Alfred A Knopf.

Cohen, M. R. (2008). *Under the crescent and cross: Jews in the Middle Ages*. Princeton University Press.

Eco, U. (1995). On the impossibility of drawing a map of the empire on a scale of 1 to 1. In *How to travel with a salmon & other essays* (pp. 95–106). Houghton Mifflin Harcourt.

Edelman, L. (2004). *No future: Queer theory and the death drive*. Duke University Press.

Felman, S. (2003). *The scandal of the speaking body: Don Juan with J.L. Austin, or seduction in two languages*. Stanford University Press.

Frosh, S. (2023). *Antisemitism and racism: Ethical challenges for psychoanalysis*. Bloomsbury.

Irigaray, L. (1985). *This sex which is not one*. Cornell University Press.

Kant, I. (2008). *Religion within the limits of reason alone* (T. M. Greene & H. H. Hudson, Trans.). HarperOne. (Original work published 1793)

Kestenbaum, S. (2016, December 21). "White nationalists create new shorthand for the 'Jewish Question'". *The forward*.

Kovacs, A., & Fischer, G. (2021). *Antisemitic prejudices in Europe: Survey in 16 European countries*. Action and Protection League.

Langmuir, G. (1990). *Towards a definition of antisemitism*. University of California Press.

Macdonald, B., & Young, K. E. (2021). Critical theory, fascism, and antifascism: Reflections from a damaged polity. *Emancipations: A Journal of Critical Social Analysis, 1*(1), 1–33. https://doi.org/10.54718/WOOW5695

Marks, J. D. (2010). Rousseau's use of the Jewish example. *The Review of Politics, 72*(3), 463–481. https://www.jstor.org/stable/20780332

Marx, K. (2012). On 'the Jewish Question'. In J. J. O'Malley (Ed.), *Marx: Early political writing.* Cambridge University Press. (Original work published 1844)

Mbembe, A. (2015). *Necropolitics.* Duke University Press.

Mendelsohn, D. (2020). *Three rings: A tale of exile, narrative, and fate.* University of Virginia Press.

Mielants, E., Gordon, L., & Grosfoguel, R. (2009). Global anti-Semitism in world-historical perspective: An introduction. In L. Gordon, R. Grosfoguel, & E. Mielants (special guest co-editors), *Anti-Semitism in the world system: Past, present and future*, special issue of *Human architecture: Journal of the sociology of self-knowledge, 7*(2), 1–14.

Mills, C. (2019). *The racial contract.* Cornell University Press. (Original work published 1997)

Muñoz, J. E. (2019). *Cruising utopia, 10th anniversary edition. The then and there of queer futurity.* New York University Press.

Newman, A. (1993). The death of Judaism in German protestant thought from Luther to Hegel. *Journal of the American Academy of Religion, 61*(3), 455–484. https://www.jstor.org/stable/1465125

Nirenberg, D. (2013). *Anti-Judaism: A Western tradition.* Norton.

Nock, A. J. (1941). *The Jewish problem in America.* The Atlantic. Retrieved February 10, 2023, from https://www.theatlantic.com/magazine/archive/1941/06/the-jewish-problem-in-america/306268/

Osserman, J. (2022). *Circumcision on the couch: The cultural, psychological, and gendered dimensions of the world's oldest surgery.* Bloomsbury.

Pateman, C. (1988). *The sexual contract.* Polity Press.

Po-Chia Hsia, R. (2018). Judaism and Protestantism. In J. Karp & A. Sutcliffe (Eds.), *The Cambridge history of Judaism, volume 7: The early modern world 1500–1815.* Cambridge University Press.

Poliakov, L. (2003) *The history of Anti-Semitism: Vol 1–4* (G. Klin, Trans.). University of Pennsylvania Press.

Ranke, L. (2011). *The theory and practice of history* (G. G. Iggers, Ed. & W. A. Iggers, Trans.). Routledge.

Said, E. (2003). *Orientalism.* Vintage. (originally published in 1979)

Scholem, G., & Adorno, T. W. (Eds.). (2012). *The correspondence of Walter Benjamin: 1910–1940.* (M. R. Jacobson & E. M. Jacobson, Trans.). University of Chicago Press.

Wilderson, F. B. (2020). *Afro-pessimism.* Liveright.

Yuval-Naeh, A. (2018). The 1753 Jewish naturalization bill and the polemic over credit. *Journal of British Studies, 57*(3), 467–492. https://doi.org/10.1017/jbr.2018.82

Žižek, S. (2002). *Welcome to the desert of the real.* Verso.

3

A History of the Study of Anti-Semitism

Defining Anti-Semitism

In *The Definition of Anti-Semitism* (2015), Kenneth Marcus[1] invokes Marx's iconic epigram from *Thesis on Feuerbach* (1888/1994): "The philosophers have only interpreted the world, in various ways. The point, however, is to change it." Marcus (2015) implores his readers that where previous scholars have worked to understand anti-Semitism, we must work to stop it. And as an attorney, he argues that a clear definition of anti-Semitism is required to harness the force of social policy and institutional power. According to Marcus (2015), for the definition of anti-Semitism to be logically coherent and practicable, it must take into account essential aspects of the phenomenon, including the rhetoric of anti-Zionism as previous definitions have failed to do so. Defining anti-Semitism is complicated by issues such as criticism of the self-proclaimed Jewish State and boycotts of Israeli institutions run primarily by Jewish people. Marcus gives a surface acknowledgment that not all criticism of Israel is anti-Semitic, but his criteria for identifying anti-Semitic criticism

---

[1] Kenneth Marcus was Donald Trump's pick to head the US Office of Civil Rights during his presidency.

© The Author(s), under exclusive license to Springer Nature Switzerland AG 2024
B. B. Strosberg, *Anti-Semitism at the Limit*, Studies in the Psychosocial,
https://doi.org/10.1007/978-3-031-72025-3_3

of Israel are broad. These include criticism that is intentionally hostile to Jews, unconsciously hostile to Jews, perpetuates irrational ethnic stereotypes, transmits "negatively coded cultural myths, images or stereotypes," (Marcus, 2015, p. 32) or contributes to a "climate of opinion that is hostile to Jews" (Marcus, 2015, p. 193). Based on these criteria, Marcus (2015) advances the adoption of the IHRA's "Working Definition of Antisemitism." Are Marcus' criteria for identifying anti-Semitic criticism of Israel really practical? How, to illustrate, can the validity of claims related to unconscious hostility be determined? If unconscious hostility is found to be a motivating factor for criticism, can it be considered the same as conscious anti-Semitic hostility? Don't these issues highlight the difficulty in identifying and defining anti-Semitism in a clear and objective manner?

As an attorney, Marcus has devoted considerable effort to combating anti-Semitic and anti-Zionist trends among college students and professors. It is undeniable that anti-Semitism has also been present in progressive circles on campus and off. It can be challenging, however, to distinguish between anti-governmental activism and anti-Semitism, particularly as the former inherently transmits negative images of some Jewish people or groups and when the latter is unconscious or implicit. This requires a careful and nuanced approach, which the Working Definition does not seem to provide. The language of the Working Definition is easily weaponized and not only against anti-Semitism but also against those who, like me, oppose ethno-statism and Israeli governmental policies. Marcus' (2015) definition appears to create as much ambiguity as it does resolution.

Marcus' (2015) strategy is to emphasize the importance of a comprehensive definition of "anti-Semitism" that covers all possible contingencies as a means of supporting effective legal interventions against it. He prioritizes listing the essential phenomena categorized under the term, and focuses on anti-Israel and anti-Zionist activism. However, it remains uncertain whether such an approach is feasible, particularly in the case of anti-Semitism. What if every definition *must* leave something out? What if anti-Semitism stems from the fear of what is always left out? The call for a clear definition of anti-Semitism that includes the essential phenomena, and the reliance on that definition for just interventions are challenged by the idea that something essential about anti-Semitism *resists* definition. This is not a reason to give up on thinking about anti-Semitism, or justice for Jews. Here, the insistence on an answer to the question of definition may enact a closure to justice, whereas new forms of justice may be found in thinking about the question while suspending the need to answer it with finality. The latter is more like answering the call of the question rather than answering the question, as such. It may be that the search for an answer to the question of definition enacts a resistance to thinking from *within* the question. And, as we will see, this is the Jewish Question at hand.

Antony Lerman (2022) has been working in the field of anti-Semitism studies and public policy for decades and concedes that the question of definition has indeed become the central question for the contemporary study of anti-Semitism. He argues the IHRA's Working Definition of Antisemitism makes the problem of definition worse. Lerman (2022) traces the path by which the question of definition became the central issue, attributing the trajectory to the discourse surrounding the so-called new anti-Semitism or the near conflation of anti-Zionism with anti-Semitism. The term "new anti-Semitism" became popular around 2001 at the outset of the Second Intifada, a period of intense violence and conflict between Israelis and Palestinians. For Lerman (2022), this striving for a new definition resulted in the new term (re)producing the problem of definition in the very attempt to resolve it. For scholars like Lerman (2022), it is absurd to suggest, as it sometimes is, that Jews and those in the field of anti-Semitism studies did not know what anti-Semitism was before 2001, or that they did not consider anti-Semitism related to Israel. There were ways of describing the phenomenon in question without requiring a new and supposedly more "definitive" definition that included Israel; ideas that were not definitive were nonetheless workable in practice. What, then, we need to ask, does the Working Definition and the discourse of the "new anti-Semitism" do?

I disagree with a not insignificant aspect of Lerman's (2022) approach to the problem, despite finding much of the literature critiquing the new definition of anti-Semitism and the "new anti-Semitism" well-argued and convincing. It is not enough to suggest that scholars know what they are talking about even if they can't define it. We could say, following Justice

Potter Stewart, "we don't know how to define anti-Semitism, but we know it when we see it," but that is hardly a case for critical thinking nor reasonable grounds for the kind of democratic debate required by the standards of contemporary science and philosophy. This notion that we (vaguely) know what we are talking about seems to foreclose critical reflection. Certainly, the act of legal justice requires determinate decisions, and the act—the gavel blow—is the end of deliberation. As Derrida (1992) puts it, justice "is that which must not wait" (p. 26).[2] But Derrida (1992) also reminds us that the end of deliberation is always premature, even if it is necessary. The very practical work of justice in scholarship that relies on theoretical rationality, however, is not a gavel blow; it is the continuation of this deliberation process. Justice requires reflection especially when we think we know what we're talking about. Put another way: To act justly, we must reflect on our concepts, especially where we think we already know how to define them. It is important not to ignore the call to action *and* for further deliberation toward defining anti-Semitism. Yet, redefinition can lead to less clarity, especially in the case of the "new anti-Semitism." This problem highlights the need for reflection, perhaps even redefinition, but it also reveals a more complex problem related to the project of definition itself and anti-Semitic phenomena more specifically.

The Talmud, which is the central text in the Rabbinical Jewish tradition and scholarship, is regarded by many Jews as something essential to Jewish identity, especially for Jews in the Diaspora (Boyarin, 2023). The Talmud provides an excellent example—perhaps even a model of sorts—of how to continue the work of justice in the face of ambivalence and the lack of definitive answers. Jewish laws and practices are determined not in spite of, but according to, endless deliberation between Rabbis in the Talmud. As Mishnaic sage, Rabbi Tarfon said, "הוּא הָיָה אוֹמֵר, לֹא עָלֶיךָ הַמְּלָאכָה לִגְמֹר, וְלֹא אַתָּה בֶן חוֹרִין לִבָּטֵל מִמֶּנָּה" or "It is not your responsibility

---

[2] Here is a passage from Derrida's (1992) work on deliberation and justice that offers more clarity:

The undecidable is not merely the oscillation or the tension between two decisions; it is the experience of that which, though heterogeneous, foreign to the order of the calculable and the rule, is still obliged—it is of obligation that we must speak—to give itself up to the impossible decision, while taking account of law and rules. (p. 24)

to finish the work, but neither are you free to desist from it" (Pirkei Avot, 2:16).

In focusing on the question of definition, Marcus (2015) is in good company with historian Gavin Langmuir (1996). Distinctively if not misleadingly, however, Marcus (2015) uses a conclusive "*The Definition of Anti-Semitism*," where Langmuir (1996) puts forward a more tentative "*Towards a Definition of Antisemitism*," in the title of his book. I say misleading because he does not conclude the book so definitively. Judaken (2018) points out that Marcus' (2015) in-depth analysis leads only to a provisional definition, and that Marcus' (2015) criteria for categorization "depend upon what researchers seek to include in the classification they adopt" (Judaken, 2018, p. 1131). In other words, a definition is always tied to the aim one has prior to investigation. Instead of recognizing a failure in his task—to give *the* definition—and thus potentially seeing in that failure something productive, Marcus (2015) seems to endorse a form of foundationalism. If the foundation of an argument is untouchable—that is, if the foundation itself cannot be examined or critiqued—how do we ensure that this foundation is not itself participating in injustices the argument seeks to address or resolve? We cannot. For all that, reading Marcus' (2015) arguments as part of a Talmud-like constellation of voices on the topic of anti-Semitism can transform failure and foundationalism into fodder and what Adorno (1958/2019a) refers to as "culturally pre-formed objects" (p. 3). This is how I will proceed.

In the rest of this chapter, I offer a selection of significant scholarship surrounding anti-Semitism over the past century; a selection subject to similar narrative cuts and exclusions found in all historical accounts.[3] These works offer the possibility to analyze the epistemological and ontological arguments that undergird contemporary debates and provide insights into how, as scholars, we ground such debates. I highlight the preoccupation with finding a definition of anti-Semitism and how the preoccupation gives way to thinking about the nature of definitions as a

---

[3] I have left out in-depth analysis of many important works in the study of anti-Semitism. I'm thinking here of Sartre (1965), Memmi (1962), Lyotard (1990), Badiou et al. (2013), and Judith Butler (2013), among others. I also did not address some scholarship that I consider misguided but important in the history of the study of anti-Semitism, like the work of David Hirsh (2018) and Bari Weiss (2019).

mechanism for control of ambivalence and otherness. As it turns out most scholars conclude that anti-Semitism has something to do with ambivalence. It is here that I intervene with the concept of proteophobia and a hospitality for ambivalence and otherness afforded by aspects of critical and psychoanalytic theory.

As a clinical psychologist, I emphasize the way that psychological and psychoanalytic resources have been employed to understand—but also to explain and resist—anti-Semitism. Scholars in the field of psychoanalysis have, since its inauguration, employed psychological resources without reducing anti-Semitism to a psychological phenomenon. Nevertheless, the relationship between a social and psychological understanding of anti-Semitism remains an irreconcilable tension within the scholarship. This chapter emphasizes these irreconcilable tensions and inner contradictions in the literature surrounding anti-Semitism in order to explore the way this irreconcilability may constitute the phenomena in question. This lays the groundwork for a deeper exploration in the later chapters of Theodor Adorno's negative psychology developed in his theory of anti-Semitism. It is my contention that this negative psychology can help psychologists (and others) think rigorously about the tension between the social and the psychological without reducing one to the other, and offers a model of thinking about anti-Semitism that resists proteophobia.

Many of the scholars I will discuss are, to point out another tension, actors in the history of anti-Semitism which is unfolding here and now. Just as the Christian fathers accused each other of Judaism, so too, scholars of anti-Semitism can be found to accuse each other of anti-Semitism and even Christianity. This difficulty in thinking about anti-Semitism, this participation of the scholar in the thing studied, this confusion of categories may be a defining feature of anti-Semitism in this contemporary historical moment. We are still in a historical moment defined in large part by what Horkheimer and Adorno (1947/2004) called, more than 75 years ago, a totalized society.[4] In such a totalized society, what

---

[4] Totality is a key concept for Western Marxism. It is sometimes thought of as thinking of the whole society. Totality, however, as a holistic thinking has also been part of many intellectual traditions from structuralism to systems theory and gestalt. Adorno's intervention, as it is relevant for thinking about anti-Semitism, is the idea of a negative totality (i.e., where the whole is the false), such that the Jew represents that which exposes the illusory totality of the orderable world.

disrupts social order becomes subsumed, erased, repressed, or destroyed. The work of social justice, then, may take the form of exposing the falsity of the totalized system so as to give voice to those who are suffering erasure under this oppressive order. The particularities of Jews and Jewishness produce questions of otherness and ambivalence which makes it a prime target of the proteophobic violence of totalization in the form of anti-Semitism *and* a potential mode of resistance to it.

Groundwork for the Study of Anti-Semitism

Boyarin and Nirenberg on Judaism and Anti-Judaism

As we have seen and will continue to see, it is difficult to determine the boundaries between what is anti-Semitism and what is not *not* anti-Semitism. Anti-Zionism may not be the same as anti-Semitism, but what about anti-Judaism? Take, for example, Friedrich Nietzsche, whose philosophy has been cited as offering a critical ground for contemporary counter-hegemonic theory, but whose work has also been regaled by anti-Semitic regimes for its hostile categorization of the figure of the Jew. The question of Nietzsche's anti-Semitism provides an exemplary case of the difficulty in demarcating anti-Semitism. *Is* Nietzsche anti-Semitic? Nietzsche (1895/2005) is explicit in his renunciation of anti-Semites. Nietzsche (1895/2005) reviles anti-Semitism as exemplary of a kind of decadence, of weakness, of slavish morality par excellence—though, Nietzsche might also add—of *Jewishness*. What would it mean for anti-Semitism to be essentially *Jewish*? Nietzsche (1895/2005) formulates a theory of the "Jewish type" that seems unrelated to Jewish people and characterized by what he calls *ressentiment*, or something like a bitter and vengeful resentment. For Nietzsche (1895/2005), "the Jew" is the ascetic priest cleaving to the authority of "the Church," gaining power through intellect rather than brawn, and eschewing nature and what is "noble" in the Christ narrative (essentially, freedom from *ressentiment*). The anti-Semite is, then, paradoxically defined by this so-called Jewish *ressentiment*.

Nietzsche's (1895/2005) primary target is the institution of Christianity, here represented by the priestly and ascetic Jew. Without examining this for its accuracy—we know that most rabbis in the time of "the priests" referred to by Nietzsche (1895/2005) were opposed to asceticism and spiritualism, values that were in fact deeply Christian—we can see that the figure of the Jew for Nietzsche exemplified an anti-Judaism that may not fit squarely into anti-Semitism as hate for Jewish people. Nevertheless, Nietzsche's idiosyncratic and sometimes convoluted views inform the history of both intellectual anti-Judaism and virulent anti-Semitism, lambasting anti-Semites while being wielded as a weapon by anti-Semites.[5] Although he seems a special case, I offer Nietzsche's approach as exemplary of the difficulty in thinking about anti-Semitism. It doesn't seem to matter whether or not Nietzsche hates Jewish people. The boundaries of anti-Semitism do not align with the usual boundaries assigned to prejudices since anti-Semitism seems to persist irrespective of intergroup conflicts or even psychological prejudices against Jewish people.

In the rest of this section, I outline Nirenberg's (2013) argument that anti-Judaism (like the one espoused by Nietzsche) is central to Western civilization, owing to the fact that the abstract figure of the Jew was produced "out of the entrails" of a now hegemonic Christianity. This structural anti-Judaism has at times had grave anti-Semitic effects, most obviously in the Nazi era, but in other times as well. I then discuss Boyarin's (2019) provocative "addendum" that Judaism as a religion was and is itself a product of Christianity, and Jewishness a relation to otherness and to what is not Jewish. These are important developments for the study of anti-Semitism.

Boyarin (2019) follows Foucault and Wittgenstein in the idea that a language system used by a collective constitutes the form of life of that collective and what is possible and imaginable within that collective. According to Boyarin (2019), the word "Judaism" didn't exist in the premodern world (p. xi). As I suggested in the previous chapter, Judaism as a "religion" did not really exist for Jews in the way we think of religion

---

[5] A similar dynamic between anti-Semitism and anti-Judaism can be found in contemporary thinkers like Alain Badiou who seem to want to abolish the idea of a uniquely Jewish identity—or group identities, in general—in favor of an enlightenment universalism or humanism (see Samuels, 2016, p. 176).

today. There was, however, a people of the Kingdom of Judea displaced from their land and spread around the world. Boyarin (2019) shows, in fact, that Jews themselves did not use the word "Judaism" in terms of religion until the nineteenth century (p. xi). On the other hand, the word "Judaism" was used in Christian writing from the second century forward. Paul is a prime example of someone who was a Jew and distanced himself from Judaism, producing a split between Jews as a people and Judaism. Judaism as a concept was a product of Christianity (perhaps the world's first "religion" in the modern sense of the term).

As I outlined in Chap. 1, constellations offer a way of understanding that does not rely on the definition of a term prior to its use. This is particularly helpful when thinking about something like religion which seems to have no consistent definition (Boyarin, 2019). Still, religion is a meaningful category. Constellating modern usage of the term "religion," Boyarin (2019) argues that religion has become synonymous for anything that resembles modern Christianity, and that Christianity paradigmatically brought "religion" as a concept to other forms of life.

For the ancient people of Judea (and for many Jews still today), what we now refer to as separate categories of sacred ritual (something like religion), political identity (something like nation), and ethnic identity (something like race) are inseparable in Jewish "peoplehood." But in the ancient world, this was true of most collectives. Unique to the Jews, however, was a peoplehood carried into Diaspora. The Jews lived among other peoples and remained—or perhaps, more accurately, became—Jews through this cohabitation. According to Boyarin (2019) the ancient Greek word for the Jewish people, *Ioudaismos*, does not mean Judaism as a religion but an allegiance to a political body (Judean) and set of laws that govern a form of life (p. 38; see also Cohen, 1999). With the advent of Christianity among Second Temple Jews, this unique historical situation of the Jewish people exploded into a set of questions that have come to define a major portion of the world today.

Like Boyarin (2019), Nirenberg (2013) looks to Adorno (this time in his collaboration with Horkheimer) for methodological inspiration. He employs critical theory to reveal the concepts that seem the most taken for granted and to explore the effect of those concepts as they structure human perception (as, for example, mythologies, ideologies, and hidden assumptions). Anti-Judaism has become one of these structural yet taken-for-granted concepts. Nirenberg (2013) traces the figure of the Jew and the concept of anti-Judaism through Christianity, Islam, enlightenment philosophy, German idealism, twentieth-century developments in science and mathematics, and Nazism. The Jews, Judaism, and anti-Judaism took different forms and were employed for different social and material reasons across historical epochs.

Boyarin (2019) concurs with Nirenberg's (2013) methods and findings but contends that his interpretation of those findings does not go far enough:

> David Nirenberg has shown over and over [...] the myriad ways that "Judaism"—or in his terms, "anti-Judaism"— has functioned both to enable analysis and also to provide the terms of polemic throughout western thought [...] The point that Nirenberg does not, perhaps, emphasize the importance of which sufficiently (although he manifestly understands it and points to it) is that this "Judaism" thing is not something real that is being treated stereotypically and distortedly in all these western discourses but is, indeed, being produced by those very discourses themselves. (Boyarin, 2019, pp. 128–129)

According to Boyarin (2019), Judaism (as a religion) is produced in relation to Christianity, even for Jews. "Something about the difference between Judaism and Christianity," Boyarin (2019) goes on to say, "is captured precisely by insisting on the ways that Judaism is not now, and never was, a religion—for Jews" (p. 153). But Boyarin may be overstating for rhetorical reasons, here, and for the most part he takes an ambivalent stance where the Jews is "neither quite here nor quite there" as a religion or political entity (Boyarin, 2019, p. 154).[6] For modern Jews, Judaism is a religion to be protected by religious freedoms and converted to by non-Jews; and yet it is also a form of life that is not divorced from notions of nation, ritual, ethnicity, culture, languages.

---

[6] It is important to consider, here, Gil Anidjar's (2007) study, *Semites*, which shows that the categories of religion, secular, Semitism, Race, etc., are not even as clear as Boyarin here makes it seem, or perhaps as I am making it seem in my reading and retelling of Boyarin's arguments.

This shapeshifting constellation of Judaism and anti-Judaism charted by Nirenberg (2013) and Boyarin (2019) gives evidence in favor of my hypothesis connecting Judaism, Jewishness, anti-Semitism, ambivalence, and otherness. Nirenberg (2013) is careful to avoid making claims about Jewish people or Judaism for Jews, but Boyarin (2023) advocates for reintroducing real Jewish people into critical discourses of anti-Semitism. Some scholars claim that anti-Semitism operates independent of any positive attributes of actual Jewish people. Boyarin (2023), on the contrary, suggests that anti-Semites take issue with some positive attributes of the Jews and Jewishness. These features may include the prioritization of otherness and alterity, persistent questioning of identity, cohabitation, and the corporeal. But they may also include a controversial dual loyalty to Jewish people or "nation," often problematically conflated with dual loyalty to a nation-state apparatus. The belief in Jewish dual loyalty has been a chief rationale for violence and discrimination throughout modern history and one definitive criterion for anti-Semitism. And so, in fighting to erase anti-Semitism, Boyarin (2023) warns, something of this Jewishness may be in danger of being erased in the process.

Considerable attention has been paid to the idea that anti-Semitism is fueled by or defined by imagination, projection, and figuration, that is, that anti-Semitism is grounded on the projections of the anti-Semite and not primarily based on any particular characteristic of Jewish people or practices. This is the case across much of the literature on the subject. Boyarin's (2023) point, here, is to emphasize that there are, in fact, positive attributions that can be made about Jewish people and Jewish forms of life, features that are Jewish and that anti-Semites hate, and that anti-Semitism studies need to consider these features alongside the projections at the heart of anti-Semite's "logic." It seems that both are true: there are Jewish forms of life hated by anti-Semites and targeted by anti-Jewish practices *and* anti-Judaism and anti-Semitism are ways that the non-Jew organizes their world via forms of displacement and projection. The two seem to be intertwined and call for more rigorous thinking in the field of anti-Semitism studies.

Jonathan Judaken and Judeophobia

In the introduction to a collection of essays in a 2018 issue of the *American Historical Review*, Jonathan Judaken offers a state-of-the-field type overview of the critical theoretical scholarship on anti-Semitism. He implores his readers to think carefully about anti-Semitism, citing its rise in recent years and its under-theorization compared with other forms of prejudice, discrimination, and structural oppressions (see also Schraub, 2019). It is unclear whether under-theorization leads to anti-Semitism (as in the fact that anti-Semitism may be perpetuated by a lack of understanding of what anti-Semitism is and how to fight it), or whether anti-Semitism leads to under-theorization (as scholars may be hesitant to address anti-Semitism or may not prioritize its study). Theory is the segment of research across disciplines that deals with the foundations of those disciplines. Theory legitimates each discipline through justification of core concepts and assumptions, and it ties disparate facts together into explanations and understanding of the world. Judaken (2018) suggests that the under-theorization of anti-Semitism leaves scholars with a number of unanswered foundational questions about terminology, categorization, periodization, consistency across time and space, and motivation. Without thorough theoretical investigation, the study of anti-Semitism remains untethered in matters of persuasion, given weak theoretical foundations, and at worst instrumentalized to justify violence. I agree with Judaken's call for more theoretical thinking about anti-Semitism. That being said, I understand the persistence of these questions to be less related to the quality of scholarship or number of studies published than the difficulty in thinking about anti-Semitism in general. From my vantage point, this difficulty may even be a defining feature of anti-Semitism.

The study of anti-Semitism is contentious and leads to much nail biting by its scholars who face attacks from without and from within (see Lerman, 2022, for some contemporary examples). The anxiety surrounding scholarship on the subject is not an excuse to be any less rigorous or self-critical in our theorizing. In that spirit, Judaken (2013), in a review of Nirenberg's *Anti-Judaism* (2013), applauds his critical and deconstructive approach to the issue of anti-Judaism but also sees in it the persistence of a central unchanging principle that leads to what Arendt calls the myth of "eternal anti-Semitism."[7] Judaken (2013) leans heavily on Arendt's notion of eternalism to expose what he considers to be problematic thinking in contemporary scholarship. According to Judaken (2013), tracing—as Nirenberg (2013) does—the way anti-Judaism is used in various ever-changing and contradictory forms throughout Western civilization does not pay enough attention to the "social, technological, economic contexts" that determine how anti-Judaism was employed and in service of what power in each specific epoch (Judaken, 2013, np). This underemphasis, supposedly, doesn't just leave something out but brings too much attention to the *cohesion* of anti-Judaic themes between epochs; a cohesion that, for Judaken (2013), smacks of eternalism. For example, Nirenberg (2013) points out that Jews were seen as too carnal by the early Christian fathers *and* some enlightenment thinkers. This critique would apply to my analysis, here, as well.

Judaken (2013) acknowledges that Nirenberg's (2013) account gives convincing evidence for the influence of one epoch on another, as in the fact that the Nazis used the language and tropes of earlier Christian anti-Judaism. Still, without an emphasis on the historical and material practices of anti-Judaism, scholars may begin to reify concepts, seeing them as natural and unchanging, and in the worst cases eternalize and essentialize Jewish tropes (most obviously the trope of the ahistorical Jew) which can then be weaponized against real Jews. Nevertheless, I disagree with Judaken's (2013) assessment of Nirenberg (2013). Though Nirenberg (2013) points out the similarities in the representation of Judaism across epochs he also points out the contradictory accusations and ambivalences. For instance, the Jews are said to be too materialistic and "of the flesh" and at times over-spiritual and other-worldly. And more conclusively, Nirenberg's main thesis is that anti-Judaism (and if we follow Boyarin [2019], Judaism as well) was produced and continues to be produced by the specific material forces of each epoch *in irreconcilable ways.*

---

[7] The avoidance of eternal anti-Semitism is something like the cardinal rule in the contemporary study of anti-Semitism.

In my reading, Nirenberg (2013) refrains from focusing on the continuity across epochs even as they constellate in his narrative. Perhaps anticipating his critics, here is Nirenberg (2013) in his own words:

> My pages will treat anti-Judaism as mask, that is, as a *pedagogical fear* that gives enduring form to some of the key concepts and questions in the history of thought. But at the same time they will point to the constant change taking place behind the mask—that is, to the unceasing transformation of these concepts and questions, and of the figures of Judaism through which they were so often articulated. (Nirenberg, 2013, p. 10; my emphasis)

Nirenberg (2013) shows how the various changing components of anti-Jewish discourse are re-constellated in each epoch without ever remaining the same. I read "pedagogical fear" in the above-cited passage as something akin to proteophobia. Nirenberg (2013) focuses on the uncategorizability of Jewishness in every attempt to categorize it, and the fear that perpetuates the continued effort to categorize. He shows that the figure of the Jew functions like a mask or empty signifier that can be filled in by the social, technological, and historical material of each period—an abstract concept of Judaism which may be in precise contradistinction to the concrete Jewishness that Boyarin (2019) portrays.[8] The limitations of Nirenberg's account and my own are, indeed, limitations; more fine-grained socio-historical and material-economic scholarship is needed (see Cheyette, 2020, for one such example of this fine-grained analysis).[9]

Along with the need to resist eternalizing anti-Semitism, Judaken (2018) points out two other major roadblocks to rigorous theorizing about anti-Semitism: the Holocaust and the State of Israel. While it would be impossible to think about anti-Semitism without thinking

---

[8] According to Richard Wolin (2023):

As a "discourse" or "episteme," the ideology of anti-Semitism proved to be semantically diffuse and remarkably polyvalent. Thus, in portraying the "deformations" of political modernity, pejorative allusions to "capitalism," "commerce," "banking," "finance," "rootlessness," and "cosmopolitanism" consistently functioned as "stand-ins"—Lacanian *"points de capiton"* (quilting points)—for Jews and their disintegrative cultural influence. (p. 86)

[9] It is worth asking: How might the study of Jewishness—a form of life that changes over the course of history and yet still be called Jewish—help us to think about anti-Semitism beyond the critique of eternalism?

about the Holocaust and the State of Israel, difficulty in thinking about these two issues has historically led to a kind of "giving up on thinking in mid-thought" or a thinking instrumentally about anti-Semitism. Some scholars are accused of weaponizing anti-Semitism and the Holocaust in service of the Israeli government, whereas anti-Semitism is ignored or perpetrated by some scholars in service of Palestinian self-determination. Scholarship stalls on questions of the uniqueness of the Holocaust and the teleological thinking surrounding it. *Longue durèe* studies of anti-Semitism (as they are sometimes called) often tell a teleological (purpose-driven) story leading from the biblical Abraham to the gas-chambers. There are a number of logical fallacies that undermine the legitimacy of theoretical research into anti-Semitism, such as this teleological fallacy, and reasoning by authority or for the sake of political platforms (e.g., Zionism or anti-Zionism). Scholars who would otherwise be theoretically rigorous quickly slip into a questionable foundationalism, importing irrational assumptions through political allegiances or narratives of higher purpose in history's unfolding.

Judaken (2018, pp. 1124–1125) offers four methodological principles to protect against these problems and to guide future studies of "anti-Semitism:" (1) We must be careful with the terms we use in our analysis, especially the terms "anti-Semitism," "antisemitism," "Judeophobia," and "anti-Judaism." (2) The analysis must address the connections and intersections between the oppression of Jews and other oppressions (e.g., racism, sexism, homophobia, transphobia) in order to participate in a larger discussion about oppression, to find what is historically specific about anti-Semitism, and to refrain from fallacies such as exceptionalism and eternalism.[10] (3) Attention must be given to the "fundamental ambivalence" and the plasticity of Jewishness across time (p. 1125). (4) Attention must be given to the *theory* of anti-Semitism, including methodological questions (e.g., What is the concept being studied? How does one study it?). This theoretical (and thus generalizing) work must be developed in relation to concrete and historical specificity.

---

[10] Judaken (2018) challenges both the attempt to find a central transhistorical core of anti-Semitism (eternalism) and the attempt to reconcile the transhistorical and eternal notion with the culturally contextual reading of anti-Semitism like the one he finds in Marcus' "cyclical antisemitism."

Leading from these methodological principles, Judaken (2018) draws some helpful conceptual distinctions in the study of anti-Semitism: Stereotypes (generalizations beyond a particular instance) don't always imply prejudices (as emotional investments) based on those stereotypes. Prejudices don't always lead to discrimination, as enforced practices are based on prejudices. And discrimination need not be related to racial classifications or genocide. For Judaken (2018), using the term "anti-Semitism" to mean anything from stereotype to genocidal racism becomes a problem because anti-Jewish stereotypes do not necessarily infer genocidal hate.[11] To understand the shifting set of anti-Jewish practices across time, scholars must work to better understand the specific social, historical, and material conditions that make these practices possible in each period. He refers to this as a dynamic approach to anti-Semitism focusing on discontinuities rather than similarities. So, for instance, the Dreyfus Affair and alt-right conspiracies about George Soros (a wealthy Jewish Businessman and Holocaust survivor) share elements in common (e.g., a secret cabal, internationalism, hyperpower) but are mobilized for different, context specific ends; the Dreyfus Affair situated in a nationalist context and the Soros conspiracy within a globalized one.[12] One of Judaken's (2018) unique interventions is the use of the term "Judeophobia," which he says can encompass the five kinds of anti-Jewish practices without conflating them: Stereotypes, prejudices, discrimination, racialization, and murder. Judeophobia can, he contends, be analyzed within unique socio-historical coordinates.

Judaken (2018, p. 1132) also calls for a periodization into five epochs (ostensibly the five socio-historical coordinates that need their own analyses): (1) ancient Judeophobia of Egypt, Greece, and Rome; (2) early

---

[11] Some psychoanalytic accounts of ambivalence may also offer a challenge to the classificatory schema of anti-Jewish practices (stereotype, prejudice, discrimination, racism, genocide). In my reading of psychoanalysis, for example, the drive toward sameness which institutes generalization in the form of stereotypes is indeed a murderous one associated with the death drive (i.e., also the drive toward mastery); also, the process of typifying stereotypically (found first in the constitution of the imaginary egoic wholeness) is itself an ethical conundrum at the heart of society and subjective structure. The work of justice begins with reflecting critically on our projections and dealing with both ambivalence and the murderous response to that ambivalence.

[12] Though it can also be said that even in the earlier Dreyfus Affair, Jews represented a global conspiracy against nationalism.

Christian Judeophobia; (3) chimerical Christian Judeophobia centered around Medieval Europe; (4) modern racism following the Spanish Inquisition, the concurrent conquest of Americas, Enlightenment philosophy and science, and the rise of nationalism (the anti-Semitism period proper); and finally (5) post-Holocaust Judeophobia in the wake of globalization. Judaken posits that in using the term "Judeophobia," scholars will be able to knock down some roadblocks to the scholarship surrounding anti-Jewish practices (e.g., roadblocks such as the formula used in mainstream definitions of anti-Semitism that anti-Zionism is pretty much equal to anti-Semitism).

Finally, Judaken (2018, p. 1133) explains the use of the term "phobia" in Judeophobia. He justifies the use of this term in two steps: First, he links it to the psychoanalytic term "phobogenic objects," from revolutionary psychiatrist Frantz Fanon, which represents the *ambivalence* in the psychology of phobia (i.e., what one is afraid of because it is what one secretly enjoys). Second, he explains the operation of this ambivalence in anti-Jewish phobia through the work of Bryan Cheyette, who formalizes this ambivalence with conceptual resources found in Zygmunt Bauman's notion of proteophobia. For Bauman, according to Judaken (2018), there must be a new term for the root of anti-Semitism because of the persistent historical practice of setting Jews apart. For Bauman, anti-Semitism is not Jew-hatred but, rather, hatred of what is disruptive to established categories, the morphing figure of the Jew being put in this position *across epochs.*

Let me sum up what I have laid out so far. Judaken offers a state-of-the-field analysis for critical anti-Semitism studies and asserts some basic conceptual underpinnings to the field: five forms of anti-Jewish practices; five periods of Judeophobia; four scholarly guideposts (care with terms, intersections with other forms of oppression, fundamental ambivalence, theoretical investigation); two roadblocks (Israel and the Holocaust); and the adoption of the term "Judeophobia," which supposedly supports all of the above. Judaken's arguments are pressing, authoritative, and definitive. At the end of his introduction, he justifies the turn to the term "Judeophobia" through psychoanalysis of ambivalence *a la* Fanon and fear of ambivalence as proteophobia *a la* Bauman. I believe that he is

correct in doing so. Indeed, I also look to psychoanalysis and proteophobia to better understand the ambivalence associated with anti-Semitism.

I find the term "Judeophobia" to be helpful but limited since, for
instance, it seems to leave out those anti-Semitic practices which are less
related to the anxious fear of Jews than to joining a "ticket" or group that
has anti-Semitism as a plank in its platform, as Adorno (1948/2019b)
formulates it. Further still, proteophobia was coined in relation to
allosemitism which addresses the ambivalence within anti-Jewish practices of both Judeophobia and Judeophilia. Whereas Fanon's notion of a
phobogenic negrophobia is rooted in the racist's Manichean thinking
(binary opposites) (Hook, 2004, p. 128), proteophobia stems from the
fear of what problematizes that Manichean thinking.

In the end, Judaken (2018) unwittingly troubles his own neat framework. Let me explain. Bauman's proteophobia is based on an idea of the
Jews as set apart *across epochs*. Fanon's phobogenesis is historically contingent in content, yet constitutive of subjectivity *across epochs*. Both Bauman
and Fanon uncover something transhistorical or thus eternal-seeming in
form, though not natural or necessary; a contingent and empty signifier
similar to what Nirenberg (2013) calls the "mask" of anti-Judaism. These
performative contradictions in Judaken's (2018) schematic (for one, his
dismissal of similarities and his reliance on similarities) are all the more
evidence of the proteophobia Judaken (2018) points to.[13] In other words,
Judaken (2018) warns against essentialism and eternalism and criticizes
Nirenberg (2013) for developing a transhistorical theory, but then bases
his own framework on two theories that are similarly transhistorical, and
this itself evinces the difficulty in thinking anti-Semitism. Judaken's
thinking is a helpful warning and schematic, but it must be met with the
notion that we must try and fail and recognize the truth in our failure in
order to better understand and resist anti-Semitism or Judeophobia or
anti-Judaism.

In the rest of the chapter, I delve deeper into theoretical studies of anti-
Semitism, emphasizing how critical and psychoanalytic scholarship navi-
gates the intricate intersections of ambivalence, otherness, Jewishness,

---

[13] Instead of looking for discontinuities instead of similarities, perhaps we should look for discontinuities *within* similarities.

and anti-Semitism. This discussion serves as a precursor to the subsequent chapter on proteophobia, laying the groundwork for further exploration.

Critical and Psychoanalytic Theories of Anti-Semitism

Freud and Psychosocial Theory

Freud (1938/2001c) developed his psychoanalytic theory of anti-Semitism after his exile from Austria by the Nazis in 1938, although his exploration of the intersection between race and religion can be traced back to earlier works. Freud's experience of anti-Semitism in fin-de-siècle Vienna and its influence on psychoanalysis is well documented (Frosh, 2005). Freud developed a theory of anti-Semitism rooted in ancient and unconscious fantasies related in large part to Oedipal dynamics, fear of circumcision, and jealous rivalry over Jewish chosenness. He mobilized a sophisticated theory of cultural inheritance to better understand the dynamics and transmission of anti-Semitism. In what follows, I offer a brief introduction to this theory in order to give context to later psychoanalytic thinking around anti-Semitism and to situate the psychoanalytic interpretation of anti-Semitism in the complex dynamics between the individual and society.

In *Totem and Taboo* (1913/2001a), Freud proposes a theory of the human psyche developing in parallel with the progressive forms of social organization and knowledge. These stages are reduced to animism, religion, and science, and parallel mimetic attunement, oedipal prohibitions, and mature reasoning. The individual goes through a process of "civilization," through which the developing person progresses in stages to achieve a critical distance from impulses (a gap between impulse and activity) and a capacity to master these in conformity with social expectations; in effect, civilization refers to the sum total of these requirements and their achievement. Freud traces this development in the transition from external and culture-specific totems to the universal internalization of the incest taboo, and through the psyche's founding prohibition of the Oedipal complex. In like sequence, society develops from magic and myth to scientific reasoning.

Freud's theory of social and psychological development asserts that this development is propelled by a fundamental ambivalence, a fear of what is felt as ambivalence or could cause such ambivalent feelings (Freud, 1913/2001a). Freud recognizes this relation to ambivalence ("the dominance of opposing trends") in both a particular stage in social development (taboo) and in psychic development (obsessional neurosis) (Freud, 1913/2001a, p. 36). The Freudian unconscious can be understood as a concept closely associated or co-extensive with this ambivalence.[14] Freud speculates that ambivalence may be the fundamental experience of emotional life, but it could also be established later in relation to the parental or father complex, where the child experiences ambivalent feelings of love and hate for the parent and the temptation to transgress parental prohibitions (Freud, 1913/2001a).[15]

Looking to other cultures for "primitive" social and psychological developmental stages, Freud offers evidence for his psychoanalytic anthropology that is inaccurate and undeniably racist. Freud also couched this theory in the then popular language of ontogeny and phylogeny. In a literal interpretation of ontogeny and phylogeny, Freud is promoting a kind of neo-Lamarckian pseudoscience, where learned traits are inheritable. Yet, Freud seems to teeter-totter between a biological and a social reading of this idea of heritability of traits. For some of Freud's readers, this teeter-tottering between a so-called subjective (or hermeneutic) and objective (natural scientific) program may be a central contribution of psychoanalysis itself. Ricoeur (1965/1970) refers to this teeter-tottering as Freud's "mixed discourse," mixed but not reconciled, and as "the

---

[14] In this early work, Freud thought that ambivalence slowly diminishes in modern civilization and the social development of scientific reason, and that only the mentally ill still suffer from debilitating ambivalent obsessions. However, his later theory seems to show that this ambivalence persists.

[15] For Laplanche, the enigmatic message from the other establishes an ambivalence at the core of the psyche (Laplanche, 1999). Ambivalence comes from the Latin, *ambi*, as in "both" and, *vanetia*, as in "*strong*." Laplanche also suggests that this message may be pre-ambivalent, an uncanniness without any clear strong positions which might coincide or be confused. Proteophobia is not just fear of ambivalence, but also fear of what doesn't fit strongly into any clear-cut categories. It is slightly more conceptually proximate to the uncanny (Laplanche, 1999).

raison-d'etre of psychoanalysis" (Ricoeur, 1965/1970, p. 65). Freud failed to reconcile the two discourses, but his failure may be uniquely productive in the establishment of what Laplanche (2015) calls "psychical reality" which is something other than mere objective external or subjective internal realities.

Faced with the growing anti-Semitism in Europe, Freud continued the work he started in *Totem and Taboo* (1913/2001a) in his controversial final book, *Moses and Monotheism* (1939/2001d). Here, Freud reconstructs an origin story of Judaism (generally read as counterfactual, but influential nonetheless in postcolonial theory) while simultaneously developing on his earlier psychosocial theories, exploring the mechanisms and dynamics of the psyche as they run parallel to the development of religion and the law. Religion stems from the psyche, but the psyche is also influenced by historical elements that are not merely *inside* the individual psyche. Freud asks: What is the archaic inheritance or phylogenetic origin of constructions such as Jewishness or anti-Semitism, which do not arise from individual experience but play out in the psychic life of individuals? Early life traumas seem to have a meaning that is not learned from individual experience but comes from earlier generations.

Freud's theories are interpreted by a number of later authors. French psychoanalysts Jean Laplanche and Jean-Bertrand Pontalis (1968) encourage their readers to look past the pseudoscience of Freud's biological phylogenetic theory so as to explore and expand on the structure of Freud's observations about intergenerational transmission, emphasizing the linguistic nature of Freud's discovery. At its center, they write, "Freud finds it necessary to postulate an organization made of signifiers anteceding the effect of the event and the signified as a whole" (Laplanche & Pontalis, 1968, p. 324). In this reading, the organization made of signifiers (i.e., cultural myths and ideologies) precede the development of an individual's egoic faculties, and are passed down through early interactions with adult caregivers and inherited by the individual through the contingent implantation of enigmatic and untranslated messages that come to make up the individual's unconscious in moments of ambivalence. Freud (1939/2001d) argued that humans inherit the "universality of symbolism in language" (p. 98). According to Laplanche (1991), however, enigmatic signifiers are enigmatic precisely because those in the previous generation doing the implanting are not fully conscious of them either. Therefore, these historical sequences of signifiers (in the form of shared myths and ideologies) can be passed from generation to generation. The contents of the psychical apparatus, ego and unconscious id, are made up of particular instances of these shared forms. Freud (1939/2001d) writes that "The content of the unconscious, indeed, is in any case a collective, universal property of mankind" (p. 132).[16] Freud speculates that with these shared forms, we can treat the group as we do the individual neurotic, each with their own unconscious memory trace.

Loewenstein and Psychoanalytic Interpretations of Anti-Semitism[17]

Through this understanding of the connection between the individual and social forces—or the socially inherited contingent elements (mythical forms or complexes) and the individual meaning (historical instantiations of those forms)—Freud developed a theory of anti-Semitism in relation to psychoanalytic treatment and anthropology. The following is a summary of one such formulation told by second-generation psychoanalyst Rudolph Loewenstein (1898–1976), who trained under Eugen Bleuler (1857–1939) and Hanns Sachs (1881–1947), and who in 1951 wrote one of the first books focusing on anti-Semitism from a psychoanalytic perspective. Loewenstein analyzed Jacques Lacan (1901–1981) between 1933 and 1939 and, along with Ernst Kris and Heinz Hartmann,

---

[16] It is worth noting that Laplanche rejects this idea of a shared unconscious. For Laplanche, the unconscious is radically individual and made up of radically individual elements, even though it is given over by the other and constitutes an inner otherness or intimate exteriority. For Lacan, on the other hand, the unconscious is structured like a language and, at least in one reading, is made up of shared symbolic elements.

[17] The discussion in this section is drawn from limited number of first- and second-generation psychoanalysts, leaning heavily on Loewenstein (1951), what has been called ego psychology (with a focus on adaptation), and only a small slice of what Freud has to offer in terms of a theory of psychoanalysis. There are many strains of psychoanalysis, and I am not endorsing this one as the authoritative perspective. I am focusing my analysis on it here because of its historical influence and the explicit analysis of anti-Semitism found there. Later on, I will offer some brief discussion of Lacan and Laplanche, both of whom breathe new life into early psychoanalytic developments and offer compelling psychoanalytic models from which to study and practice.

was among the generation of European emigres credited with the development of Ego Psychology in the United States in the post-war era.

According to Loewenstein (1951), the psychoanalytic treatment consists in tracing the patient's symptoms to their psychological cause. Symptoms are caused by conflicts between opposing (ambivalent) emotional tendencies and are formed early in life in relation to primary caregivers. The child learns to be part of a social world through identifying with and separating from caregivers (not always in that order). Socialization is a demand from the caregivers to control aggressive and sexual drives through the postponement of gratifications. The form through which the child learns to control their drives becomes the pattern they continue to use to control drives in future situations where drives conflict with the requirements of the external world. These are psychological defense mechanisms and modes of displacement and substitution (e.g., repression, projection, splitting). Adult psychological disturbance, and the reason people come to psychoanalysis, constitute a breach in or failure of these defenses. The primary conflicts to be defended against are ambivalence and Oedipal dynamics. The child both loves and hates those who demand of them self-mastery and socialization. Usually one caregiver (the father figure, generally) plays the role of the lawgiver who prohibits the instant gratification offered through immediate access to the other caregiver (usually, the mother figure). Eventually, during the latency phase, the child internalizes the prohibitions through the development of a superego and the identification with the lawgiver. The patient relives their past and re-enacts these dynamics with the analyst through the transference. The patient's drive derivatives are evoked in the transference, and healthy defenses can be reestablished in response.[18]

Following this process, Freud formulates his theory of anti-Semitism (again, presented here in a consolidated form given by Rudolph Loewenstein in 1951): The conflict between Jews and Christians symbolizes the fundamental ambivalence and Oedipal complex. Jews are understood to have killed Christ just as the child murders the father in the Oedipal dynamic. Circumcision symbolizes the universality of castration

---

[18] According to Laplanche (2015), this story is psychoanalytic mythology or one way that patients have made sense of their experience.

anxiety that instantiates the paternal prohibition.[19] The Jews are identified via various formations of displacement and substitution with the
father of Christ. Christians are relieved of their guilt for this murder
through the worship of the sacrificed son. On a psychological level,
Christ-worship allows for the release from guilt related (through displacement and projection) to patricidal wishes in the Oedipal dynamic. The
imperfect Jewish father and his patricidal children are replaced by the
perfect Christian and godly son and his repentant flock. The Jews, as
non-believers, remain unrepentant killers in need of punishment. This
displacement is transmitted most effectively through religious education
during the latency period, the pivotal time when the superego is forming.
The child feels immense guilt and the persecutory superego paradoxically
becomes something to be defended against. The child fears punishment
for aggression and sexuality. The Jew becomes, then, the "symbols of bad
instincts" (Loewenstein, 1951, p. 40), and the representation of inner
ambivalences. This account of Christian anti-Semitism can be read as one
historical expression of a more universal problem of psychic ambivalence
within (and transmitted through) a historically specific form of life constituted structurally by Christian anti-Judaism.[20]

For Loewenstein (1951) building on Freud's theory, anti-Semitism is a
disorder reminiscent of both phobia and psychosis rooted in fear and
anxiety but not itself a psychological disease. It is a social configuration (a
historically specific pattern) through which psychological issues (ambivalence and otherness) are modeled, represented, instituted, and resisted.
The Jew has become a mythical figure (socially inherited and potentially

---

[19] In *The Jew's Body* (1991), Sandor Gilman examines the various ways that the Jewish body is made
visible throughout the history of Western modernity. He explores examples of Jewish physical features such as gates, eyes, noses, skin color, as well as aspects of the Jewish psyche, disease, and
gender. Gilman argues that Jewish racial identification is inscribed on the body and is seemingly
impossible to be fully erased. He also highlights how Christian anti-Semitism has been secularized
in scientific racism, where the rhetoric may have changed, but the underlying prejudices remain the
same. In the case of Freud, Gilman suggests that Jewish racial identity was transformed to make it
invisible and universal, resulting in a gendered structure. Gilman further argues that science and
enlightenment universalism did not eliminate prejudice in service of a universal goal, but rather, at
its core, the enlightenment is a project built on the logic of racism.

[20] Loewenstein (1951) suggests that though religious education seems to promote latent anti-
Semitism in the enactment of an Oedipal drama, it also provides the means for escaping the
Oedipal triangle through the acceptance of castration and socialization.

unconscious) on which individuals project their psychic conflicts. As such, anti-Semitic reactions are difficult to treat through reality testing alone. In other words, showing the anti-Semite that there are Jews who are not hyper-powerful and conspiring will not suffice to dislodge these projections. The ambivalent quality means that the anti-Semite, in this example, can always claim that the powerless Jew is indeed powerful in their powerlessness (echoing Nietzsche), requiring provisions from non-Jewish social institutions. Since psychoanalysis is, by definition, a treatment of individuals who are constituted by socially inherited myths, psychoanalysts may be capable of treating some kinds of anti-Semitism. At least that is Loewenstein's (1951) wager.

Loewenstein (1951) claims that his patients enact anti-Semitism through the transference as a matter of course for productive psycho-analysis. Either the analyst is Jewish, or they identify the analyst with Freud as the iconic Jew. In these cases, the Jew represents the father and an aspect of the self as a universal figure of ambivalence (Loewenstein, 1951, p. 31). Certain figures are displaced, and inner drives are projected onto the analyst. The Jew becomes the scapegoat of the patient's desires (Loewenstein, 1951, p. 34).[21] Loewenstein claims that the position of the analyst is the position of the Jew, given the specific historical context in which the progenitor of psychoanalysis was Jewish; the analyst's position mimics Freud's own.

Modern anti-Semitism has also been analyzed in terms of Freud's theory of mental contagion and group psychology. Mental contagion is tied to superstition where Jews are given the mythological status of being evil, cursed, taboo, and untouchable. The whole group (the Jews) becomes personified in this mythological thinking (as in conspiracy theories), where psychological forces are projected out into the world (Loewenstein, 1951, p. 46). Mythical thinking is defined by the process of generalization (as in xenophobia) that erases the particularity of individual people and historical moments. Psychological disorder and psychological ambivalence seem impossible to resolve and so are replaced by concrete and historically specific social ambivalences (e.g., minority rights) which are shared between people and seem easier to bear (Loewenstein, 1951, p. 49).

---

[21] According to Loewenstein (1951), Jews may also have some of this anti-Jewish transference.

It follows that the "inner enemy" of a whole nation becomes the inner enemy of the individuals composing it. Thus the Jews came to personify Evil, and all the ignominious defeats man suffers in his struggle against his instincts could be blamed on them (Loewenstein, 1951, p. 57).

The anti-Semite replaces the real Jew and social complexities with the mythical Jew as a social problem that *can* (supposedly) be solved; an unconscious wish that the psychic pressure of ambivalence can be relieved in a displaced and social form. Yet the unresolvability of psychic ambivalence is projected onto the figure of the Jew and at times Jewish people. Anti-Semites becomes convinced that their problems would dissolve if only Jewish people were out of the picture.

The neurotic, more generally, displaces complex psychic ambivalences with fantasies and rigid defenses. All neurotics project this inner life out into the social world, and in analysis onto the person of the analyst. According to this psychoanalytic theory, anti-Semitism may be structural to modern civilization (just as neurosis may be). We need to find healthier ways to cope with our ambivalence such that it does not become violent:

It is impossible to eradicate from our culture the fundamental traditional elements which form the historical basis for modern anti-Semitism. But we hope that it will not always be impossible to prevent these potentialities from being translated into violent collective outbreaks (Loewenstein, 1951, p. 202).

Loewenstein is ahead of his time in formulating a structural form of racism. He is suggesting that anti-Semitism is baked into "Judeo-Christian" forms of life. Freud suggests that the goal of psychoanalysis is to transform suffering into everyday unhappiness; and in such a formulation, there is an acknowledgment that the dissatisfaction of psychic ambivalence is constitutive of the psychical subject. Hope for the future, then, may be found not in getting rid of that subject but in facing that dissatisfaction.

Early psychoanalysts formulated a theory of anti-Semitism rooted in the essential psychic ambivalence mimicked in Christian mythology. As

Freud acknowledged, cultural myths seem to take the shape of psychic processes, but psychic processes also seem to take the shape of cultural myths. Of course, both Freud and Loewenstein were working in a period of history rife with explicit anti-Jewish tensions. Much of the theory above relies on the anti-Jewish forces at work in the structure of "Judeo-Christian" society, and it may seem that we are no longer in a religious society. Adorno (1948/2019b) suggests that there was a qualitative break between Christian anti-Semitism (what he refers to as "Sunday school anti-Semitism") and fascist anti-Semitism. Recent violence linked to Christian, Islamic, and Jewish fundamentalism and nationalism may indicate that these "Judeo-Christian" ideas are still relevant in understanding contemporary anti-Semitism. More to the point, Nirenberg (2013) and Frosh (2005) show that anti-Judaism takes the *form* of ambivalence even if the *content* of Christianity has been displaced or secularized as nationalism, racism, or the liberal social order. As we will see, critical theorists and later psychoanalytic thinkers will recontextualize anti-Semitism as it is perpetuated in a (supposedly) secular society without losing its association with ambivalence and displacement.

Critical Theory and Anti-Semitism

Faced with growing oppression, many Jewish critical theorists and psychoanalysts took refuge in the United States where they formed scholarly circles and shared ideas across disciplines, especially in relation to the rise of fascism and anti-Semitism. Max Horkheimer, head of the Institute for Social Research also known as the Frankfurt School, emigrated to the United States in 1934 as the threat to Jewish intellectuals became imminent in Hitler's Germany. Adorno joined in 1938 at the behest of Horkheimer and was offered a position in music studies at the Princeton Office of Radio Research as well as a small position at Columbia University with Horkheimer. In the early 1940s, Adorno conducted a study with the help of Leo Löwenthal (1900–1993) on the right-wing authoritarianism of Martin Luther Thomas, a California radio announcer. This led to the publication of *Prophets of Deceit* (1949/2021) where Löwenthal and Norbert Guterman (1900–1984) psychoanalyzed public speeches and propaganda of fascist-style demagogues. This, in turn, was followed by Adorno's concentrated metapsychological study "Freudian Theory and the Pattern of Fascist Propaganda" (1951). These projects on the authoritarian roots of anti-Semitism also led to the famous volume *The Authoritarian Personality* (1950/2019).[22,23]

In *Behemoth* (1942/2009), one of the first Frankfurt School texts to focus on anti-Semitism, Franz Neumann (1900–1954) differentiates between totalitarian forms of anti-Semitism rooted in magical thinking "beyond discussion" (the Jew as evil incarnate) and non-totalitarian varieties that are connected to problems with rationality (religious, economic, political, and social) (p. 122).[24] According to historian Martin Jay (1980), the Frankfurt School broke with Neumann's totalitarian/non-totalitarian schema during the war since following from it, only the rational form of anti-Semitism could be analyzed by critical theorists, whose methods up to that point were focused on rationality. In the *Dialectic of Enlightenment* (1947/2004), Horkheimer and Adorno turned to psychoanalysis to deal with the magical and mythical thinking involved in both totalitarian and non-totalitarian forms of anti-Semitism (Jay, 1980, p. 140).[25]

---

[22] Most of this work that followed the move to the United States was premised on the dialectical, social, and psychoanalytic thesis, inspired by Walter Benjamin (among others), developed by Adorno and Horkheimer during the war, and documented in 1944 in the unpublished "Philosophical Fragments" that would later be published as the *Dialectic of Enlightenment* (1947/2004). Historian Rolf Wiggershaus (1994) suggests that Horkheimer's *Eclipse of Reason* (1947/2004), Marcuse's *Eros and Civilization* (1955), and Adorno's *Minima Moralia* (1951/2005) and late *Negative Dialectics* (1967/2004) were all continuations to this dialectic project.

[23] Susan Buck-Morss suggests that many of these themes were already there in Adorno's work as early as 1931 (Jay, 1984, p. 244).

[24] It should be noted that *Behemoth* (1942) was written before the end of the war and therefore before the extent of the genocide was revealed.

[25] Questions of psychology and psychoanalysis played a role in Horkheimer and Adorno's thinking well before the war. Adorno and Horkheimer had been studying and debating psychology and psychoanalysis together since the early 1920s (Wiggershaus, 1994, p. 46). Adorno's retracted 1926–1927 dissertation was entitled "The Concept of the Unconscious in the Transcendental Theory of Mind." According to Brandon Bloch (2019), Adorno's dialectic of psyche and social can be traced back to this work where Adorno looks to Freud's unconscious for the part of the human that is *both* social and psychological. Adorno considered other nineteenth-century versions of the unconscious insufficient on this precise issue. The dissertation focused on a dialectic of conscious and unconscious in order to critique irrationalism, inaugurating a perennial project for the institute (Abromeit, 2011, p. 199). In 1929, Horkheimer met Erich Fromm, who became an instructor at

In the *Dialectic of Enlightenment* (1947/2004), Horkheimer and Adorno complicate a progressive reading of Freud's psychosocial theory as a linear development from animism to reason. The scholars show how history is not a narrative of progressive development from barbarism to enlightenment civilization. They use anti-Semitism as an example of how what can be read as progress (civilization) can also be understood as regress (producing the means for systematic and catastrophic barbarism). They draw inspiration from Freud (1930/2001b) who, in his later theory, recognizes the ambivalence that persists in so-called healthy psychic and social development, where "the price we pay for our advance in civilization is a loss of happiness through the heightening of the sense of guilt" (p. 134).

For Horkheimer and Adorno (1947/2004), anti-Semitism could be understood as a historically specific expression of a more general hate for the negative principle in thought, or that which resists categorization. Jay (1980) frames it accordingly:

> For Horkheimer and Adorno, then, perhaps the ultimate source of anti-Semitism and its functional equivalents is the rage against the non-identical that characterizes the totalistic dominating impulse of western civilization. (p. 148)

For the anti-Semite, then, the Jew is the non-identical that is unassimilable into categorical schemas, and holds society back from becoming totally ordered, administered, or understood clearly. In Adorno's work, the concept of the non-identical is used to represent that which is excluded or erased in the process of categorical identification in human rationality. This process of categorization is totalized and no longer reasonable. If the process of reasoning becomes unreasonable and civilization is found to be barbarous, it may be traced back to the totalizing force of reasoning that has become instrumentalized and has lost the critical negativity required

---

the institute the following year. Fromm played a crucial role in advancing the reading of Freud and Marx together, a new and fruitful endeavor at the time (Jay, 1996, p. 88). He also had a major influence on Horkheimer's thinking and the institute's approach to empirical social research. Both Adorno and Horkheimer continued to develop their conception of psychoanalysis in an opposite direction from Fromm (Jay, 1996, p. 89).

to expose what in identification is untrue and non-identical. This may seem like a pessimistic perspective, or one without hope. Yet, Horkheimer and Adorno (1947/2004) offer a glimmer of hope in a process of critical reasoning which prioritizes the negative principle or non-identity expunged by the anti-Semite. In psychoanalysis, Horkheimer and Adorno (1947/2004) find a form of critical thinking capable of resisting such a totalizing force.

Methodologically, Horkheimer and Adorno (1947/2004) use an experimental and performative form of writing that mimics both psycho-analytic free-association, and the complex and multi-form nature of the matter-at-hand.

> No attempt was made to weigh the relative significance of each "element" in the compound that was anti-Semitism, nor were the causal links among them fully delineated. Instead, Horkheimer and Adorno offered what might be called a decentered constellation of factors juxtaposed in unmedi-ated fashion. (Jay, 1980, p. 145)

Horkheimer and Adorno (1947/2004) recognized that the investiga-tion of social phenomena was also to participate in social processes, and therefore the method and style must match the object of study. Scholars who attempt to read Horkheimer and Adorno (1947/2004) systemati-cally in the manner of previous philosophical texts, especially their chap-ter on anti-Semitism, may be perplexed by the lack of center, consistency, or completion (e.g., Lapidot, 2021). Where anti-Semitism is concerned, the attempt to create clear and definitive categories and identities to bet-ter predict and control could too easily participate in the rigid style of thinking and the attempted elimination of negation traced to anti-Semitism.

> In [Horkheimer's] mind, and perhaps in that of certain of his collaborators, the Jews became the metaphoric equivalent of that remnant of society pre-serving negation and the non-identical. [...] The Critical Theorist was understood as 'the Jew' of the administered society. And conversely, anti-Semitism became a model of the totalistic liquidation of non-identity in the one-dimensional world. (Jay, 1980, pp. 148–149)

Much like how Loewenstein (1951) described how the analyst becomes a figure of the Jew in relation to the analytic patient, Horkheimer positions the critical theorists as the Jew and as the "no" in relation to social order.

Adorno and *The Authoritarian Personality* Study

The Authoritarian Personality (1950/2019) was an attempt to explore the hypotheses developed in these earlier theoretical works. The study was commissioned by the American Jewish Committee in the early 1940s along with several other studies. The study was ambitious in its aims: to better understand the interaction of psychology with authoritarianism, totalitarianism, fascism, and racism; to offer a psychological analysis that avoids reducing social phenomena to mere psychological explanations; and to develop a distinctive psychometric approach, all while incorporating psychoanalytic principles. In *The Authoritarian Personality* (1950/2019), Adorno and his American colleagues developed the Fascist Scale (F-Scale) as part of a larger empirical, psychological study of fascism and anti-Semitism in post-war America. The study was not an attempt to understand an anti-Semitic personality, since for Adorno (1948/2019b), the study was asking who was willing to join a movement that had anti-Semitism as a plank in its platform and not merely who hated Jews or was going to attack Jews spontaneously.

Still, individuals who scored high on the F-Scale are more likely to hold anti-Semitic attitudes toward Jews and to be sympathetic to social institutions that espouse anti-Semitism as a principle. In reflecting on these findings, Adorno (1948/2019b) expanded his psychoanalytic theory where socio-economic and psychological forces are in dynamic relation. The individuals who participated in the study seemed to use anti-Semitism as a defense against the social alienation inherent to capitalism. The psychology of each individual could not be explained as social forces alone, but it could be explained in relation to the *failure* of those forces. Adorno theorized that the psyche is not forged *in* the cauldron of a supposedly rational socio-economic order but in what bubbles over the edge.

People are inevitably as irrational as the world in which they live. Thus, psychology— i.e., the realm of irrational determination of attitudes and behavior—is not so much opposed to economic causation as it is the outcome of economic irrationality which is itself an intrinsic element of the socio-economic totality in which we live. (Adorno, 1948/2019b, p.lii)

Psychological attitudes are tied to economic ones but are irreconcilable with them. Take the psychological attitude of envy. The anti-Semite is said to be envious of Jews. Adorno (1948/2019b) states that

[…] people are not anti-Semitic because they are envious of the Jews. They are envious as such because of constant social pressure and the blatant contradiction between today's economic potentialities and their own deeply unsatisfactory existence. Eventually, their envy is directed against the Jews, or any other suitable minority group, following the line of least resistance. (p. lii)

The envy is itself caused by social forces that are then experienced psychologically as ambivalence and projected out onto a target that conforms to the shape of that ambivalence. Nirenberg's (2013) study of the ways ambivalence has been projected across epochs can be read as an explanation for the continued use of the figure of the Jew as the "line of least resistance" given the use of that figure's form in relation to different specific historical contexts.

Since the anti-Semite does not need to actually hold prejudicial views to join an anti-Semitic movement, "psychological prejudice" may not be the best term to describe what is being studied. But is anti-Semitism merely sociology and economics? No. Yet, even if it could be argued that people are not motivated directly by economic forces such as markets, money, or profit, they defend against the social alienation caused by the economic system as a totality through the logic of exchangeability and commodity fetishism. The logic of exchangeability refers to the way singular and nonexchangeable things are made to fit into categories in being made equivalent through social processes so as to be exchangeable.

For Adorno (1948/2019b), the categories of analysis required for both sociological and psychological approaches are found to be inadequate, though he makes a case for sticking to psychology in *The Authoritarian Personality* study despite the failure of psychological categories to explain anti-Semitism. The process by which someone defends against social alienation and participates in anti-Semitism is not merely psychological or merely sociological or, however, merely some neat pairing or reconciliation of the two into a unified whole (Adorno, 1967-8). Instead, the process is only grasped in the very failure of each side of the social and psychological binary. The larger totality is also maintained by its own failure. Adorno notes that "The essence of this totality is to maintain itself through the self-interest of those it comprises, but to simultaneously hamper and endanger this self-interest constantly and incessantly" (Adorno, 1948/2019b). In other words, discrimination is not found in the socio-economic system but the contradiction at the very heart of that system which is a failure to make good on social and psychological promises. By promise, here, I mean the promise of categories to be self-consistent and self-identical. The failure of these alienated categories (e.g., the branches of social science) reflects the broader social alienation produced in a totalized society. Social totality maintains psychological self-interest by producing the very alienation that the psychological subject must defend against. This is akin to the contradictory formula developed in the *Dialectic of Enlightenment* (1947/2004): self-preservation equals self-destruction. Anti-Semitism is suicidal. The anti-Semitic solution to this alienation is a compulsive repetition of the problem—making everything the same, exchangeable, and categorizable—and the insistence that the totalizing force makes good on its promise by erasing contradiction, alienation, and social and psychological ambivalences. The Final Solution to the Jewish Question was a suicidal attempt to make good on the promises of social totality.

Though it was a psychological study, *The Authoritarian Personality* (1950/2019) did not provide a psychological explanation for anti-Semitism. Instead, the authors sought to understand the relationship *between* the social and psychological patterns inherent to modern anti-Semitism from the perspective of psychology. Adorno's interpretation of the study emphasizes what Horkheimer already recognized: the autonomous psychological subject undermines itself through anti-Semitism (Jay, 1980, pp. 141–142). For Adorno, this is not a shortcoming of the study, or a proposal to stop thinking psychologically, but the very fruits of psychological investigations into anti-Semitism (Strosberg, 2022a, 2022b). This theory was not published in *The Authoritarian Personality* (aside from the sentiment that there is no psychology of anti-Semitism) since, it seems, it ran counter to mainstream American academic ideas. This critical theory is foundational to my understanding of contemporary anti-Semitism, and I will return to Adorno and his colleagues for a more detailed analysis in Chaps. 5 and 6.

Langmuir and Chimerical Antisemitism

In his widely cited study, Gavin Langmuir (1996) situates his notion of "chimerical" anti-Semitism as a response to these early social and psychological theories, and purports to offer a psychoanalytic method of investigation. Langmuir (1996) does not offer a detailed psychoanalytic account, but in focusing on language and rhetoric, he builds a bridge to psychoanalysis. The study is a historical investigation, an attempt at periodization, and a discursive analysis of anti-Semitic assertions. Though I don't fully agree with his conclusions, Langmuir (1996) synthesizes much of the previous literature and offers persuasive historical evidence for the role of ambivalence in contemporary anti-Semitism.

As Judaken (2018) will echo over 20 years later, Langmuir (1996) laments the continued use of the term "anti-Semitism" for anti-Jewish prejudice and xenophobic phenomena since such usage tends to reify pseudo-scientific notions of a "Semitic" race. However, Langmuir (1996) also defends the term, as it captures the genocidal violence perpetrated in its name, since no general term (e.g., racism, prejudice, xenophobia) would do justice to the historical specificity of the Shoah. Therefore, he removes the hyphen in anti-Semitism, leaving a new signifier, "antisemitism," signaling the inseparability of the term "Semitic" from racist discourse. This new signifier is now in standard usage. Ultimately, he defines antisemitism in relation to historically situated forms of anti-Jewish practices that are characterized by their "chimerical" quality and divorced from rationality. On the one hand, I believe Langmuir is correct in his assessment of antisemitism as historically specific and qualitatively distinct from other forms of prejudice. On the other hand, rationality must be understood as capable of being instrumentalized irrationally and perhaps even nonrationally. Even chimerical assertions find their pulse in a logic of equivalences at the heart of human rationality and all language practices. This later idea, inspired by critical theory and psychoanalysis, is a challenge to Langmuir's (1996) analysis and draws further attention to the seemingly uncategorizable aspects of antisemitism, while opening the door to the possibility of interpreting both rational and nonrational anti-Jewish assertions. I unpack these assertions in more detail below.

Langmuir (1996) criticizes the idea, stemming from social psychology and sociology, that antisemitism is merely a historically distinct form of a single basic process of ethnic prejudice such that there is merely a difference in degree between the hatred of Jews by Nazis and prejudice found between ethno-national groups like the French and Germans (p. 317). This conflation forecloses the possible qualitative distinctions between prejudice that leads to workplace discrimination and a prejudice that leads to antisemitism, conspiracy theories, dehumanization, or genocide.

According to Langmuir (1996), early theories defined prejudice as a "faulty and inflexible generalization" (Allport, 1979, cited in Langmuir, 1996, p. 317). Langmuir points to some issues that arise from this definition: What criteria are used to judge the truth of a generalization? Since all judgment is prejudgment and all language a form of generalization, what is the line that differentiates realistic generalizations from overgeneralization and unreality? And are there qualitative differences between them or just matters of degree? At first, social scientists were forced to rely on their own culturally relative and biased criteria. This lacked scientific rigor, for obvious reasons. Later, scientists emphasized the *rigidity of belief* to measure problematic prejudices. Normal prejudice can be untaught, they assumed, but abnormal prejudice resists learning and reality testing. In Langmuir's (1996) view, the emphasis on rigidity leads to a reductionist fallacy which claims to determine the reality of a statement based on the rigidity of belief. To use the criteria of rigidity, it seemed, a researcher would need to conflate the falsity of a statement with rigidity or continue to import the criteria for rational assertions from social biases.[26] Neither of these approaches satisfies Langmuir's criteria for a study of anti-Jewish practices that explains the historical specificity of antisemitism leading to the Shoah, and I will continue to address Langmuir's (1996) argument on its own terms.

Langmuir (1996) seems unclear about the place of *The Authoritarian Personality* (1950/2019) within this framework. He claims that the study is, indeed, based on the reductionist fallacy inherent in the turn to rigidity, but also that the authors may offer a solution to the reductionist fallacy by looking to the *structure* of rigid thinking rather than the *content* of a rigid thought.[27] This structural solution has its own problems. As Langmuir (1996) points out, someone can be rigid in one domain and flexible in another; the Calvinists, for instance, were economically flexible though theologically rigid. Langmuir (1996) contends that the equivocation of dangerous prejudice with rigidity ignores the differences between "nonrational" and "irrational" thinking, or in other words, a thought process that is not based on a logical process versus one that is logical but false. This distinction between the nonrational and the irrational is essential to what he considers a more viable solution to the question of the definition of antisemitism.

Like Judaken (2018), Langmuir (1996) rejects any formulation of antisemitism as eternal or unchanging over time. He acknowledges that, of course, various forms of anti-Jewish practices can be analyzed through the persistent and complex dynamics between Jewish people and non-Jews. However, "antisemitism" as mobilized by the Nazis cannot be so analyzed merely through the dynamics of what social psychologists would call "intergroup relations." Instead, antisemitism must be explored

---

[26] Adorno suggests that rigidity signifies the false, as it stifles open and critical thought. This theme pervades his work, evident in his use of dialectic and rejection of synthesis. Rigidity, more a social structure than a psychological trait, manifests in discourse as a barrier between individuals. It fractures when faced with the object's lack of rigidity and its resistance to predefined concepts and categories. A connection between psychic structure and rigidity emerges in neurosis's rigid character (Shapiro, 1984) and language's rigidity in psychosis (Bateson, 1972). In *The Location of Culture* (1994), Homi Bhabha frames colonial discourse through the lens of ambivalence and rigid categorical distinctions inherent in colonialism.

[27] Though Langmuir (1996) acknowledges that the emphasis on rigid structure rather than rigid content may be true, he rejects the strategy because it seems impracticably broad.

through the figure of the Jew or what the Jew symbolizes for the non-Jew, and how that symbol functions in a social system (with or without proximity to Jewish people); in other words, *what the articulation of such a socially instituted signifier does for the psychological subject who uses that signifier to communicate within that social system*. To do this, Langmuir (1996) borrows from discourse (psycho)analytic methodology and analyzes anti-Jewish statements through which practices are justified or carried out. He finds three distinct discursive forms—realistic, xenophobic, and chimerical—each with its own function and tactic of persuasion corresponding to rationality, irrationality, and nonrationality.

According to Langmuir, realistic assertions are employed to rationally justify hostility after objective analysis of an outgroup is conducted (rudimentary or complex). Supposedly, the person making such assertions is trying their best, using rational thinking, and coming to a logical conclusion, inaccurate as it might be. Realistic assertions are still prejudgments in that they do not hold true in each case, though they allow for rational prediction and therefore control of the environment where the appropriate information is available. To pick some low-hanging fruit, prejudice against someone who runs at you with a knife screaming "I'm going to kill you" seems realistic and rational even if it turns out that the running and screaming person turns out to be an actor pulling a prank.

According to Langmuir (1996), xenophobic assertions lack the "genuineness" of the realistic assertion.[28] Some examples may include assertions such as Muslims are terrorists, Jews control the banks, Russians are warmongers, homosexuals corrupt children, and Palestinians will oppress Jews if they are given political representation. Not all the available information is used, and abstract qualities are emphasized. Instead of a

---

[28] The concept of xenophobia was developed in the field of anthropology after the First World War to describe hostility toward strangers. According to Langmuir (1996) the concept of ethnic prejudice was developed by John Dollard in 1939, reading Freudian theory together with the social science of intergroup hostility to better understand race relations in the United States. With the rise of Nazi anti-Semitism, these resources were put to work to think about anti-Jewish practices. Much of that work, as I've already noted, relied on Freud's oedipal theory. According to Langmuir, this too often led to the psychologization of anti-Semitism and racism (e.g., the anti-Semite is sick or has a personality disorder). It should be noted that Adorno was careful not to do this. Langmuir also notes that after 1954, when research turned to the pervasiveness of anti-Black racism, they stopped thinking in terms of pathology and started to see it as, again, a problem of learning.

statistically realistic stereotype of an outgroup (e.g., there is a higher percentage of Jewish people in the movie industry compared to other groups), xenophobic assertions take as their subject a felt social menace (e.g., Jews control the media).[29] Further still, xenophobic assertions are often contradictory (e.g., the Jews are weak, and the Jews are powerful). Langmuir offers two explanations for xenophobia: Someone feels unable to solve a social problem and points to concrete aspects of the world to gain a better grasp of it, or they refuse to take a realistic look at all the facts. This type of assertion may be made to relieve built-up social tension—felt psychologically—through the necessity of immediate action or to obscure and manipulate others. The persistence of ambivalences in psychic and social life may lead to certain self-preservation tactics that function in some ways as self-fulfilling prophecies on the part of antisemites (e.g., the Jews are dirty and isolated, let's force them into ghettos).[30] Eventually, the original xenophobic assertions became naturalized and ever more rational and realistic.

According to this model, chimerical assertions are what differentiates ancient antisemitism from modern and Nazi antisemitism. Langmuir (1996) claims that these "chimerical assertions have no 'kernel of truth'" (p. 334). "The Jews perform ritual murder" is an example of this type of assertion. Langmuir does make room for what he calls "weak" forms of chimerical assertions that have a vague kernel of truth. Take, for example, a Jew held responsible for the death of a Christian in a small Polish town without evidence. Since there have been some historical cases where Jews have indeed killed Christians, there is a "kernel of truth" in the assertion "Jews kill Christians" even though there is no evidence that *this* Jew killed *this* Christian. What makes it chimerical, then, is the (automatic) move from the particularity of the one situation to a generalization (e.g., all

---

[29] Here is an example of this xenophobic assertion: As a Ukrainian civilian amidst a war with Russia, encountering a Russian civilian triggers fear that they may harm me because of the conflict. Despite recognizing that some Russians oppose the war, I can't shake the suspicion that this individual harbors hostile intentions, mirroring the violence inflicted by Russian soldiers on Ukrainians. The signifier "Russian" becomes synonymous with the realistic social threat, detached from any real person. This fear may persist even if I've never personally encountered a Russian citizen and long after the end of the war.

[30] A similar case of self-fulfilling prophecies can be made about xenophobic assertions that Palestinians are terrorists or that they hate Jews.

unsolved murders must be the work of Jews, or all Jews kill Christians), and generally for the sake of immediate action. Implicit in this chimerical assertion is the ambivalence of signification that allows for "Jews kill Christians" to mean both "some Jews kill Christians" and "All Jews kill Christians," but also the rearrangement into "Jews are Christian Killers." For Langmuir (1996), the term "antisemitism" should be reserved for chimerical assertions about Jews. This is in line with the idea—also found in Adorno et al. (1950/2019) and Sartre (1946/1965)—that the anti-Semite may not even believe in what they are asserting since the assertion is evacuated of critical reason in the adoption of a social or political platform. I read this as a return to a theory of rigidity in an altered form. The structure of rigid belief in a conspiratorial platform takes the place of rational thinking and only appears to be a form of thinking; it is, to borrow an idea from Critical Theory, purely instrumental.

Langmuir (1996) gives a psychoanalytic-like explanation for these chimerical assertions; they stem from an "interior conflict as a social problem" (p. 338) or an individual anxious phobia which leads to the collapse of the individual into society from which they are alienated.

> The initial or originating function of chimerical assertions would seem to be to express the awareness of individual members of the ingroup of a menace within themselves, their awareness at some psychic level that there are threatening cracks in their personality between their imagination or impulses and the social values they have internalized, their feeling that they are not comfortably integrated either with their society or within themselves. (Langmuir, 1996, p. 338)

In other words, the ambivalence leading to unbearable psychic anxiety—in the face of the socio-economic forces that seem uncontrollable or changes and contradictions in the organization of life (e.g., between religious and secular authorities or in new forms of urban life)—leads to (phobic) substitution by social signifiers that allow for sense-making (e.g., the Jews are the problem). The call for immediate action is an attempt at psychic relief from psychic ambivalence through actions aiming at social order:

[...] the symbolization refers to the menace syntactically to manipulate, concrete, external agents, it can serve to release tension temporarily by inciting immediate, if inappropriate, action, and it can distract attention from the real, internal, and more threatening causes and thereby reduce consciousness of their internality. (Langmuir, 1996, p. 338)

Langmuir (1996) seems to be suggesting, here, that the call for immediate action found in both xenophobic and chimerical assertions is a distraction from the real internal threat *and* a reduction of consciousness of internality, perhaps a reduction of internality itself—a position reminiscent of Horkheimer and Adorno's (1947/2004) assessment of anti-Semitism undermining the autonomy of psychological individuals and an assessment I take up in greater length in Chaps. 5 and 6.

There are several problems that emerge with Langmuir's (1996) study. Judaken (2018), for instance, suggests that this theory of chimerical antisemitism may explain why antisemitism led to Auschwitz, but not why other forms of prejudice and oppression *did not* lead to Auschwitz. Langmuir (1996) seems mistaken in attributing chimera solely to antisemitism or to the figure of the Jew. Some scholars suggest that chimerical antisemitism existed before the Middle Ages (Peter Schäfer, 1997), and Langmuir (1996) admits that chimerical assertions have been directed at Black people. Other groups and figures of thought—such as women, Arabs, witches, and gay, lesbian, and trans people—have been similarly accused of nonrealistic and nonrational charges, and we can imagine that these charges were also mobilized to defend against material forces of alienation.

Moreover, Langmuir (1996) aptly contends that any prejudiced assertion rooted in the biology of a group have no kernel of truth, given that human groups are inherently dynamic and mutable, rendering such claims chimerical. Yet, despite this understanding, many individuals persist in essentializing race as a biologically significant and scientifically meaningful construct. Karen and Barbara Fields (2012) argue convincingly that many purportedly realistic claims about race are, in fact, chimerical. They propose that one day, society may come to recognize the absurdity of ubiquitous racial checkboxes on scientific and medical documents, much like how we now perceive the irrationality of the American witch trials. This is not to suggest that race holds no significance, but rather that its meaning is invariably entangled with racist discourse, even when invoked in pursuits such as affirmative action or combating sickle cell anemia. Race emerges through the entrails of racism.

Nevertheless, Langmuir makes a good argument that material realities of the Middle Ages made possible new forms of nonrational assertions that took on a conspiratorial and delusional form of anti-Jewish practices, or at least the dominance of these forms. In the final analysis, though, his explanation for antisemitism is remarkably like the psychoanalytic one described above. The internal ambivalence that challenges individual integration within a social order, when faced with a problem of prediction and control, is projected outward to maintain psychic equilibrium. This process of integration ultimately fails, because ambivalence (and otherness) is constitutive of subjectivity, as I have mentioned above and will develop further with the work of Stephen Frosh (2005) in the following section. The Jew comes to represent this psychic position of failure of integration because of their historical position as the figure of ambivalence in association with material realities relative to Christianity, Diaspora, modernity, Israel, etc.

Langmuir is hoping to determine why chimerical antisemitism led to the Shoah whereas other forms of anti-Judaism and racism did not. I think this may be the wrong question to ask or perhaps just a little misleading, and one that exceptionalizes the Shoah beyond its historical specificity, placing it outside of world history. Obviously, nothing else could have led to the Shoah because the Shoah is a unique historical event. On the other hand, other forms of prejudice have led to other unique atrocities (e.g., the Armenian Genocide, the Vietnam War, the atomic bombings of Nagasaki and Hiroshima, the systematic oppression of Palestinians, the Trans-Atlantic Slave Trade, the systematic oppression of African Americans). The potential for catastrophe is already there in modernity, where humans are classified systematically, as if ready to be eliminated. I agree that chimera is involved, and so is proteophobia (fear of the uncategorizable). In fact, the term "chimera" comes from the mythical Greek creature that is multi-form and uncategorizable.

I have spent so much time on Langmuir's (1996) work because, flawed as it is, it brings the critical and psychoanalytic theories of antisemitism into the conversation and offers a bridge to the psychoanalytic theory of antisemitism rooted in the projection of psychic ambivalence. I don't think that Langmuir succeeds in his attempt to organize antisemitic prejudice into a clear definition, even though he does exceptional work of describing it. The boundaries are found to be somewhat arbitrary, and the categories are mixed, especially with the introduction of "weak chimera." That being said, Langmuir is admirably modest, acknowledging that the work is incomplete, and that he is working "towards" a definition that has not yet been given. When considered in terms of proteophobia, then, the flaws in Langmuir (1996) can be read as illuminating feature of the work.

Following Langmuir's (1996) study of chimerical forms of antisemitism and its critique, an analysis must account for the irrational and non-rational facets of antisemitism that lead to conspiracy theories and violent anti-Jewish practices, as well as those aspects of seemingly rational assertions that slip between the rational, irrational, and nonrational. Psychoanalysis and critical theory offer a robust theoretical framework for this project. I have already introduced the Frankfurt School. I will now turn to clinical psychologist, Stephen Frosh (2005), for a contemporary and critical psychoanalytic approach.

Frosh and Otherness

Stephen Frosh (2005) offers a thorough survey of psychoanalytic theories of anti-Semitism. If I understand him correctly, he argues that anti-Semitism is best understood in terms of ambivalence and otherness, which are intrinsic to the constitution of subjectivity. By analyzing various theoretical perspectives, Frosh concludes that anti-Semitism represents a historical expression of hostility toward otherness, and when viewed from a psychoanalytic standpoint, this hostility toward otherness arises in conjunction with issues of ambivalence and psychic conflict. Even though his earlier work offered an appreciation of Adorno, recognizing in *The Authoritarian Personality* (1950/2019) study that "the individual's personality structure is socially constructed during development" (Frosh, 1989, p. 233), Frosh (2005) suggests that the psychosocial understanding of otherness was not available to the early critical and psychoanalytic thinkers (e.g., Adorno) who addressed the issue of anti-Semitism primarily via the language of projection.

Frosh (2005) makes a set of unsettling assertions: "All otherness in the West is Jewish, including that inner otherness that is unconscious desire" (p. 215), and "the social inheritance of anti-Semitism is so powerful that it serves as one of the building blocks upon which western subjectivity is built" (p. 160). He maintains these claims despite what seems like the declining influence of Christianity and religious anti-Semitism. According to Frosh (2005), "anti-Semitism is not 'hard-wired' into the psyche, but rather is the culturally available vehicle for the expression of certain psychic conflicts that are themselves more likely to occur under some social circumstances [...] than others" (p. 194). In other words, if all otherness in the West is Jewish, it is because economic and material conditions led to rigid cultural fantasies, myths, and ideologies.

Frosh (2005) makes an appeal to the complex dynamic between society and a psychoanalytic subject decentered by the unconscious. He gives historical nuance to psychoanalytic thinking around this dynamic in relation to anti-Semitism through an analysis of the historical specificity of psychoanalytic thinking as developed in relation to Jewish questions which, themselves, revolve around complex social dynamics; namely, Diaspora, the status of Judaism for Christianity, minority rights, socio-biological thinking, modern nationalism, and globalism. In my interpretation, Nirenberg's (2013) study of anti-Judaism provides further support for Frosh's (2005) thought-provoking assertions, by demonstrating how deeply anti-Judaism is embedded within a Western social-symbolic system and situated within particular socio-historical contexts. Frosh (2005) shows how the language of psychoanalysis was (and perhaps continues to be) rooted in Jewish forms of life and in proximity to anti-Semitism at the time Freud and his colleagues were developing its rudiments (see also Sandor Gilman, 1991). Similar to Loewenstein's (1951) understanding, psychoanalysis, modern Jewishness, and anti-Semitism have become inseparable. With this in mind, Frosh (2005, 2023) shows that psychoanalysis is uniquely equipped to unpack the complex dynamics involved in anti-Semitism.

As previously discussed, psychoanalytic investigations into anti-Semitism explore several interrelated psychological themes (see also,

Ackerman & Jahoda, 1950; Fenichel, 1948; Ostow, 1995; Simmel, 1946). Frosh (2005) cites clinical psychologist Danielle Knafo (1999), who presents a comprehensive list of such themes, which include,

> [...] displacement, projection, scapegoating, castration anxiety (as linked to circumcision), latent homosexuality, sibling rivalry, intolerance of small differences, rejection of dark pigmentation because of its association with feces, Jewish disavowal of the murder of the father, Jewish masochism, psychopathy, paranoia, and envy of the Chosen People. (Frosh, 2005, p. 153)

Although Freud and his initial followers were animated by an interest in and lived experiences with anti-Semitism, psychoanalysts at the time were limited in their ability to study anti-Semitism as a social phenomenon; given its roots in medical practice, psychoanalysis was initially concerned with individual psychology. Most of those psychoanalysts recognized that anti-Semitism was a social phenomenon, contingent on culture and society, if *expressed* psychologically, yet they seemed to lack the language to talk about the relation between individual psychology and society. Accordingly, Frosh (2005) notes, there were few psychoanalytic explanations of anti-Semitism, and even fewer after 1960.

Frosh (2005) looks to later psychoanalytic thinkers who formulated, more thoroughly, the idea that the psychological individual is a product of society and contains an otherness at its very core, against which its identity is forged. Faced with this constitutive otherness, the subject experiences a deep ambivalence. As a productive tension—between identity and non-identity, love and hate, passivity and activity, inner and outer—this ambivalence constitutes subjectivity but is also felt as anxiety. The psychoanalytic subject, then, is born through a reaction to the social otherness embedded at the center of itself. Autonomy of the psychological subject is always already premised on a pre-established heteronomy. To maintain internal psychic integration and boundaries between the self and what is not the self, the subject continues to defend against this ambivalence and otherness—even while it is being constituted by it. Ethnocentrism and xenophobia, Frosh (2005) contends, are related to the preservation of these boundaries. Due to specific historical contexts, the Jew represents (or becomes the phobic substitute for) the foreignness within the subject that threatens the subject with disintegration. For everything to have its place in the psychic order, the (constitutive) otherness must be expelled, in the hopes of relieving dis-integrating anxiety. Again, due to our historical specificity, the Jews become the perfect target (object, idea, signifier, whatever you want to call it) for attempts to relieve this anxiety. The Jew is, in the social imaginary, "comfortable in difference" and "offer[s] a suitable container for negativity" (Ackerman & Jahoda, 1950, cited in Frosh, 2005, p. 188).

This container or figure of difference and negativity—the Jew—is experienced as a threat to both social and psychical order. "Hatred of the Jew," Frosh (2005) notes, "is hatred of otherness, of anything that threatens to disrupt the hard-fought-for unity of the psyche; the other, the stranger, the outsider all introduce difference and potential conflict, all remind the anti-Semite of uncontrollable elements in the unconscious, and all, therefore, are to be opposed" (p. 194). According to Frosh (2005), early psychoanalytic theories didn't have the language to grapple with this otherness as it is both an aspect of the unconscious and a principle of social organization. But Frosh's (2005) psychosocial psychoanalysis helps us understand how—with any attempt to annihilate the otherness, difference, and negativity through the annihilation of Jews—the anti-Semite becomes suicidal through the annihilation of a subjectivity constituted by that otherness and difference. And so, yet another ambivalence is established.

Frosh (2005) traces the theory of psychic ambivalence through guilt in Christian society and formulates anti-Semitism as a failure to tolerate this ambivalence. Take, for instance, these ineradicable contradictions: The Jew is a representation of the father (the castrater, mind) and yet also a representation of the feminine (the castrated, the body). Melanie Klein can be read as a psychoanalytic thinker who formulated new methods for tolerating, rather than denying, this ambivalence:

> [Kleinian analysis] allows for gradual integration of the psyche without denial of negativity; that is, it makes tolerance of ambivalence possible, with an accompanying capacity to feel more deeply, for example to experience guilt and loss and form intimate relationships. (Frosh, 2005, p. 170)

Tolerance for the negativity is linked, here, with tolerance of ambivalence. Frosh (2005) suggests that fascist anti-Semitism was rooted in not just the fear of ambivalence—and the establishment of a "bulwark" against it—but also "anything threatening the fantasy of purity, anything, that is, with the stamp of complex reality upon it" (p. 178).

Frosh (2005) formulates this as a fear of complex reality (not only as fear of ambivalence) and of the other as the mask of otherness, difference, negativity, and ultimately what is unresolvable, indeed uncategorizable. Anti-Semitism is a violent response to an otherness posed to the subject by the unconscious, and Jewish forms of life. Toward the end of his book, Frosh (2005) offers a succinct formulation of this understanding of anti-Semitism. It is worth quoting at length:

> What seems to be both desired and feared is the 'other'. For psychoanalysts, this is primarily the other of the unconscious, but what is becoming increasingly clear from recent psychoanalytic theorizing is that this inner other is itself an emblem of external otherness. To this point, this realisation seems mostly to be expressed in the form of an analogy (the unconscious is like the stranger, the alien) [...] The key issue here is that the other is not some pragmatically constructed and convenient carrier of personal disturbance, but an absolutely central element in social life. Whether this has always to be the case is a moot point, but it is clear that historically and culturally, otherness and the sense of the alien is deeply embedded in Western society. Whilst there are several forms that this takes, including vicious modes of anti-Black and other colour racism, anti-Semitism has been and remains a potent signifier of the underside of Western culture. The Jew is a principle of otherness for the West, articulating (through contrast) what is safe and unitary by embodying difference. The two-thousand year history of Christian anti-Semitism has created a figure that is more than a symbol of the splits in Western society; the Jew is rather the kernel of otherness, that which is always found everywhere, yet is never to be allowed in. Inchoate fantasies of purity opposed by Jewish corruption, of secret societies and conspiracies, of trickery and poison... show that the Jew is the materialization of that otherness which is most feared and least understood. 'In' the unconscious, this means that otherness itself has a 'Jewish' feel to it; the hidden recesses of sex and aggression are easily identified with anti-Semitic paradigms. It is not, then, that the Jew is just a

convenient scapegoat upon whom these inner urges can be projected; it is rather that just as psychoanalysis is 'Jewish' in important ways, so is the unconscious that it has discovered and invented. All otherness in the West is Jewish, including that inner otherness that is unconscious desire. (Frosh, 2005, pp. 214–215).

With this statement, Frosh (2005) lays the groundwork for a new critical psychoanalytic study of anti-Semitism as a fear of otherness that is uncategorizable, or what I have been calling proteophobia. Frosh (2005) accomplishes this by constellating the simultaneous internality and externality of the unconscious with uncategorizability of Jewishness and the centrality of Jewishness to both Western thinking and psychoanalysis. He suggests that anti-Semitism is the fear of the other, who, for historically specific reasons, comes to embody an ambivalence, not only internal to the psyche but also between the psyche and society.

There are a set of questions that remain. For instance, what is the difference between fear of the other, fear of difference, fear of the stranger, fear of the foreigner, and fear of otherness? An important distinction is the Jew as other in terms of difference and the Jew as *otherness* in terms of what doesn't fit into clear categories. It is unclear whether the Jew can even fit into the category of "the different" since Judaism is so internal to the Western thought; that is, if the Jew is the perennially "different," is the Jew not *integral* to—and therefore assimilable in—Western thought?

In addition to these questions, I wonder whether Frosh's exploration of later psychoanalytic theorists—notably Klein, Lacan, Laplanche—overlooks insights that are already available in the work of early critical theorists, especially Adorno. Frosh seems to be extending the work of the Frankfurt School's theory of anti-Semitism through an appeal to later psychoanalytic thinkers who recognize the deeply social kernel of the unconscious. To my mind, this reading, important as it is, omits much of Adorno's psychoanalytic thinking. Generally, it seems that Frosh (2005) considers Adorno's psychoanalytic work to remain too psychological, and that the emphasis on the intrapsychic operation of projection is unfit to address robust social processes (pp. 195–196; see Frosh, 1989, for more forgiving read). He acknowledges that the critical theorists were first and foremost social thinkers but considers their conclusions to betray this social theory because of their overreliance on intrapsychic operations and commitment to Freudian orthodoxy. I have an alternative reading of Adorno's work that I detail in Chaps. 5 and 6. Nevertheless, I appreciate Frosh's focus on the psychoanalytic theories of Klein, Lacan, and Laplanche, as they offer new foundations for psychoanalysis that are rooted in the concepts of otherness and ambivalence (see especially Lacan, 1966/2006; and Laplanche, 1991, 2007, 2015).

* * *

In this chapter, I set out to provide an overview of the study of anti-Semitism. I acknowledge that my treatment may have been too brief. Throughout the history of its study, the understanding of anti-Semitism has proven to be difficult, even among its most theoretically rigorous scholars. I traced a non-linear path from early psychoanalytic interpretations and critical theories to contemporary issues surrounding the definition of anti-Semitism. Some scholars have identified elements of anti-Judaism and anti-Semitism deeply ingrained in "Western" thought. As I see it, the uncategorizable (also associated with negativity, non-identity, otherness, ambivalence, the unconscious, enigma, and the uncanny) serves as a mask or an empty core around which both the history and study of anti-Semitism revolve, exhibiting historically changing and elliptical movements. The examination and theoretical categorization of this phenomenon of anti-Semitism is intertwined with its production, necessitating scholars to reflect on their own involvement in the subject matter. Bauman's (1995) notion of proteophobia, which denotes the anxious fear of the uncategorizable, proves useful in this context. Thus it is to proteophobia we turn in the next chapter.

References

Abromeit, J. (2011). *Max Horkheimer and the foundations of the Frankfurt School*. Cambridge University Press.

Ackerman, N. W., & Jahoda, M. (1950). *Anti-Semitism and emotional disorder: A Psychoanalytic interpretation*. Harper.

Adorno, T. W. (1967-8). Sociology and psychology (i & ii). *New Left Review 46*, 67–80; *47*, 79–97.

Adorno, T.W. (2004). *Negative dialectic* (E. B. Ashton, Trans.). Routledge. (Original work published 1967)

Adorno, T. W. (2005). *Minima moralia: Reflections from damaged life.* Verso. (Original work published in 1951)

Adorno, T. W. (2019a). *Notes on literature* (R. Tiedemann, Ed. & S. E. Nicolson, Trans.). Columbia University Press. (Original work published 1958)

Adorno, T. W. (2019b). Remarks on the authoritarian personality. In T. W. Adorno, E. Frenkel-Brunswik, D. J. Levinson, & R. N. Sanford (Authors), *The authoritarian personality* (pp. xli-lxvi). Verso. (Original work drafted 1948)

Adorno, T. W., Frenkel-Brunswik, E., Levinson, D. J., & Sanford, R. N. (2019). *The authoritarian personality.* Verso. (Original work published 1950)

Allport, G. W. (1979). *The nature of prejudice.* Addison-Wesley. (Original work published 1954)

Anidjar, G. (2007). *Semites.* Stanford University Press.

Badiou, A., Hazan, E., & Segrè, I. (2013). *Reflections on anti-Semitism.* Verso.

Bahbah, H. (1994). *The location of culture.* Routledge.

Bateson, G. (1972). *Steps to an ecology of mind: Collected essays in anthropology, psychiatry, evolution, and epistemology.* University of Chicago Press.

Bauman, Z. (1995). *Life in fragments. Essays in postmodern morality.* Basil Blackwell.

Bloch, B. (2019). The origins of Adorno's psycho-social dialectic: Psychoanalysis and neo Kantianism in the young Adorno. *Modern Intellectual History, 16*(2), 501–529. https://doi.org/10.1017/S147924431700049X

Boyarin, D. (2019). *Judaism: The genealogy of a modern notion.* Rutgers University Press.

Boyarin, D. (2023). *The no-state solution: A Jewish manifesto.* Yale University Press.

Butler, J. (2013). *Parting ways: Jewishness and the critique of Zionism.* Columbia University Press.

Cheyette, B. (2020). *The ghetto: A very short introduction.* Oxford University Press.

Cohen, S. J. D. (1999). *The beginnings of Jewishness: Boundaries, varieties, uncertainties.* University of California Press.

Derrida, J. (1992). Force of law: The "mystical foundation of authority". In D. Cornell, M. Rosenfeld, & D. G. Carlson (Eds.), *Deconstruction and the possibility of justice* (pp. 3–67). Taylor and Francis.

Fenichel, O. (1948). Elements of a psychoanalytic theory of anti-Semitism. In E. Simmel (Ed.), *Anti-Semitism: A social disease* (pp. 11–32). International Universities Press.

Fields, B. J. & Fields, K. E. (2012). *Racecraft: The soul of inequality in American life.* Verso.

Freud, S. (2001a). Totem and taboo. In J. Strachey (Ed. & Trans.), *The standard edition of the complete psychological works of Sigmund Freud, volume XIII (1912–1913).* Vintage Books. (Original work published 1913)

Freud, S. (2001b). Civilization and its discontents. In J. Strachey (Ed. & Trans.), *The standard edition of the complete psychological works of Sigmund Freud, volume XXI. The future of an illusion, civilization and its discontents and other works (1927–1931)* (pp. 57–145.) Vintage Books. (Original work published 1930)

Freud, S. (2001c). A comment on anti-Semitism. In J. Strachey (Ed. & Trans.) *The standard edition of the complete psychological works of Sigmund Freud, volume XXIII (1937–1939): Moses and monotheism, an outline of psychoanalysis and other works* (pp. 289–293). Vintage Books. (Original work published 1938)

Freud, S. (2001d). Moses and monotheism. In J. Strachey (Ed. & Trans.), *The standard edition of the complete psychological works of Sigmund Freud, volume XXIII: Moses and monotheism, an outline of psycho-analysis and other works.* Vintage Books. (Original work published 1939)

Frosh, S. (1989). *Psychoanalysis and psychology: Minding the gap.* Macmillan.

Frosh, S. (2005). *Hate and the 'Jewish Science': Anti-Semitism, Nazism and psychoanalysis.* Palgrave Macmillan.

Frosh, S. (2023). *Antisemitism and racism: Ethical challenges for psychoanalysis.* Bloomsbury.

Gilman, S. L. (1991). *The Jew's body.* Routledge.

Hirsh, D. (2018). *Contemporary left antisemitism.* Routledge.

Hook, D. (2004). Fanon and the psychoanalysis of racism. In D. Hook (Ed.), *Critical psychology* (pp. 114–137). Juta Academic Publishing.

Horkheimer, M. (2004). *Eclipse of reason.* Continuum. (Original work published 1947)

Horkheimer, M., & Adorno, T. W. (2004). *Dialectic of enlightenment: Philosophical fragments* (G. S. Noerr, Ed. & E. Jephcott, Trans.). Stanford. (Original work published 1947)

Jay, M. (1980). The Jews and the Frankfurt School: Critical theory's analysis of anti-Semitism. *New German Critique, 19,* 137–149. https://doi.org/10.2307/487976

Jay, M. (1984). *Marxism and totality: The adventures of a concept from Lukacs to Habermas*. University of California Press.

Jay, M. (1996). *The dialectical imagination: A history of the Frankfurt School and the Institute of Social Research, 1923–1950*. University of California Press. (Original work published 1976)

Judaken, J. (2013). Deconstructing anti-Semitism and eternal anti-Judaism: Jonathan Judaken on David Nirenberg's *Anti-Judaism: The Western Tradition*. *Marginalia*. Retrieved December 28, 2022, from https://themarginaliareview.com/deconstructing-anti-semitism-and-eternal-anti-judaism/

Judaken, J. (2018). Introduction. *The American Historical Review, 123*(4), 1122–1138. https://doi.org/10.1093/ahr/rhy024

Knafo, D. (1999). Anti-Semitism in the clinical setting: Transference and countertransference dimensions. *Journal of the American Psychoanalytic Association, 47*(1), 35–63. https://doi.org/10.1177/00030651990470010801

Lacan, J. (2006). *Écrits: The first complete edition in English* (J. A. Miller, Ed. & B. Fink, Trans.). W.W. Norton & Co. (Original work published 1966)

Langmuir, G. (1996). *Towards a definition of antisemitism*. University of California Press.

Lapidot, E. (2021). *Jews out of the question: A critique of anti-anti-Semitism*. SUNY Press.

Laplanche, J. (1991). *New foundations for psychoanalysis*. Basil Blackwell.

Laplanche, J. (1999). *Essays on otherness*. Routledge.

Laplanche, J. (2007). Gender, sex, and the sexual (S. Fairfield, Trans.). *Studies in Gender and Sexuality, 8*(2), 201–219. https://doi.org/10.1080/15240650701225567

Laplanche, J. (2015). *Between seduction and inspiration: Man* (J. Mehlman, Trans.). The Unconscious in Translation.

Laplanche, J., & Pontalis, J. B. (1968). Fantasy and the origins of sexuality. *The International Journal of Psychoanalysis, 49*(1), 1–18.

Lerman, A. (2022). *Whatever happened to antisemitism?: Redefinition and the myth of the 'collective Jew'*. Pluto Press.

Loewenstein, R. (1951). *Christians and Jews: A psychoanalytic study*. International Universities Press.

Lowenthal, L. & Guterman, N. (2021). *Prophets of deceit: A study of the techniques of the American agitator*. Verso. (Originally published 1949)

Lyotard, J-F. (1990). *Heidegger and "the Jews"* (A. Michel & M. S. Roberts, Trans.). University of Minnesota Press.

Marcus, K. (2015). *The definition of antisemitism*. Oxford University Press.

Marcuse, H. (1955). *Eros and civilization: A philosophical inquiry into Freud.* Beacon Press.

Marx. K. (1994). Thesis on Feuerbach. In L. H. Simon (Ed.). *Marx: Selected writings.* Hackett. (Original work published 1888)

Memmi, A. (1962). *Portrait of a Jew.* Penguin.

Neumann, F. (2009). *Behemoth: The structure and practice of National Socialism, 1933–1944.* Rowman. (Originally published 1942)

Nietzsche, F. W. (2005). The anti-Christ. In A. Ridley & J. Norman (Eds.). *Nietzsche: The anti-Christ, ecce homo, twilight of the idols: And other writings* (J. Norman, Trans.). Cambridge University Press. (Original work published 1895)

Nirenberg, D. (2013). *Anti-Judaism: A Western tradition.* Norton.

Ostow, M. (1995). *Myth and madness: The psychodynamics of anti-Semitism.* Transaction Publishers.

Ricoeur, P. (1970). *Freud and philosophy: An essay on interpretation.* Yale University Press. (Originally published 1965)

Samuels, M. (2016). *The right to difference: French universalism and the Jews.* University of Chicago Press.

Sartre, J. P. (1965). *Anti-Semite and Jew: An exploration of the etiology of hate.* Schocken. (Original work published 1946)

Schäfer, P. (1997). *Judeophobia: Attitudes toward the Jews in the Ancient World.* Cambridge University Press.

Schraub, D. (2019). White Jews: An intersectional approach. *AJS Review, 43*(2), 379–407. https://doi.org/10.1017/S0364009419000461

Shapiro, D. (1984). *Autonomy and rigid character.* Basic books.

Simmel, E. (Ed.). (1946). *Anti-Semitism, a social disease.* International Universities Press.

Strosberg, B.B. (2022a). Reading Lacan *as* or *with* phenomenology: Implications for psychosis. *Psychoanalysis, Culture and Society, 3*(27), 235–249. https://doi.org/10.1057/s41282-022-00283-3

Strosberg, B. B. (2022b). Critical theory of anti-Semitism: Implications for politics, education, and psychoanalysis. In D. Burston & J. Mills (Eds.), *Critical theory and psychoanalysis.* Routledge.

Weiss, B. (2019). *How to fight anti-semitism.* Penguin.

Wiggershaus, R. (1994). *The Frankfurt School: Its history, theories, and political significance.* MIT Press.

Wolin, R. (2023). *Heidegger in ruins: Between philosophy and ideology.* Yale University Press.

4

Proteophobia

Zygmunt Bauman's Sketch of Proteophobia

To my understanding, Bryan Cheyette is responsible for the rehabilitation of Zygmunt Bauman's work in recent scholarship surrounding anti-Semitism. Cheyette refers to Bauman's term "proteophobia" in *Diasporas of the Mind: Jewish and Postcolonial Writing and the Nightmare of History* (2013) and later discusses the concept in an interview with Michael Rothberg and Felix Axster (2019). The uncategorizability of the Jewish is figural in Cheyette's work at least as early as 1994 with the publication of *Constructions of 'the Jew' in English Literature and Society: Racial Representations, 1875–1945*. While the term doesn't get much airtime in his 2013 book, the examples invoked in the book illustrate important aspects of the uncategorizable and multi-form figure of the Jew.

In *Life in Fragments* (1995), Bauman formulates proteophobia as the anxious fear of the form-changing, multi-form, or uncategorizable signifier, idea, or object. The term "proteophobia" refers to the protean and comes from Greek mythology where Proteus is the shapeshifting sea god and the eldest son of Poseidon. The term "protean" is used as an adjective

B. B. Strosberg, *Anti-Semitism at the Limit*, Studies in the Psychosocial, https://doi.org/10.1007/978-3-031-72025-3_4

for "mutability." Here is a passage from Bauman (1995) on proteophobia:

> The confused, ambivalent sentiments aroused by the presence of strangers—those under-defined, under-determined others, neither neighbours nor aliens, yet potentially (incongruously) both—I propose to describe as proteophobia. The term refers to the apprehension aroused by the presence of multiform, allotropic phenomena which stubbornly elide assignment and sap the familiar classificatory grids. This apprehension is akin to the anxiety of misunderstanding, which—after Wittgenstein—can be explicated as 'not knowing how to go on'. Proteophobia refers therefore to the dislike of situations in which one feels lost, confused, disempowered. Obviously, such situations are the productive waste of social spacing: we do not know how to go on in certain situations because the rules of conduct that define for us the meaning of 'knowing how to go on' do not cover them. We set apart such anxiety-arousing situations, therefore, precisely because there has already been some social spacing done, and so we have mastered some rules which regiment conduct within the ordered space—and yet in some cases it is not clear which of these rules apply. (Bauman, 1995, p. 181)

These so-called strangers—and they are not really that—evoke the feeling of anxious ambivalence, which as we have seen is related to an unassimilable otherness. The ambivalence is rooted in the way that some phenomena—for example, shapeshifting or that posited as waste in the historical and dialectical process—trouble categorical schemas which are bound up with the totalizing rules of social (and historical-material) ordering and processes of understanding, both of which help the subject make sense of what is happening to them. It is not just that it threatens to trouble the rules—since breaking rules can be quite enjoyable—but also that it troubles the very rules for following rules and thus provokes destabilizing anxiety for the individual.

Proteophobia, here, is found to be related to the anxious fear of the stranger but is not synonymous with xenophobia. It is not the fear of the stranger as the external alien other. Such a classification of the stranger would be too ordered to provoke the kind of anxiety Bauman (1995) is associating with proteophobia. The proteophobic object cannot be included *or excluded*—that is, included as strangers becoming neighbors *or* excluded as strangers and/or alien others. Pre-established "classificatory grids" such as familiar/strange no longer apply or are found to be in conflict with one another and within and across each side of the binary. The concept of the stranger is too limiting in its association with externality. In this sense, the "stranger" of proteophobia is closer to the uncanny or *unheimlich* (Freud, 1919/2001).[1] The object in proteophobia is not just strange but also difficult to clearly categorize as strange, being so familiar as it is. Thus proteophobia is evoked in the presence of strangers precisely in the ambivalent moment when the stranger arouses the sense of the strange that is simultaneously so familiar.

Bauman (1995) makes three preliminary points about thinking of anti-Semitism in terms of proteophobia. These points are consistent with most if not all of the above-mentioned critical frameworks: First, anti-Semitism as "hate directed at Jews" is far too limited a definition. Most scholars agree on this point. Second, xenophobia (fear of the foreigner or stranger) and heterophobia (fear of the different or other) are not accurate enough to do justice to anti-Semitism. The Jew was the clearest example of "the stranger" in modern Europe, for most of its history, and thus xenophobia may seem to apply to anti-Semitism. Yet, modernity is at least in part defined by universal freedom (of thought and movement) and thus was full of, if not defined by, such strangers in the streets. Heterophobia, on the other hand, requires the recognition of the other *as other* so defined. Jews are not fully included in the ingroup, nor are they fully excluded. They cannot be so easily defined as wholly other, indeed, "they explode the very categories meant to service the defining business" (Bauman, 1995, p. 208). In other words, xenophobia and heterophobia are grounded in the acceptance of a binary opposition, whereas proteophobia is the anxiety of what doesn't fit into that logic. Third, anti-Jewish practices have existed for over two millennia and are complex and multifaceted phenomena that require nuanced study. Anti-Semitism cannot be fully understood in isolation but should be examined in relation to larger transformations in society. The ever-changing constellation of

---

[1] See Strosberg et al. (2023) for more on the negative dialectic of the uncanny in the Lacanian concept of "extimacy" or the "intimate exteriority."

anti-Semitic phenomena must be seen as part of world history and not treated as an independent issue or primordial archetype.

Bauman (1995) knowingly employs a somewhat paradoxical expression when he asserts that "the Jew is ambivalence incarnate" (p. 211). This ambivalence disrupts social order by frustrating traditional logical laws of contradiction and the excluded middle, especially in modernity. Ambivalence is identified through what the thinker feels (anxious fear) when faced with the uncategorizable, hence Bauman (1995) proposes the term *proteophobia*. Even the fear of the multi-form changes as the structures and material coordinates of society change. In other words, scholars must track the changing forms of the fear of the form-changing.

Bauman (1995) speculates that, historically, Judaism came to "incarnate" ambivalence because Jews saw themselves as the center of the G-d's world despite being small in number and relatively powerless. Jews have historically lacked military force but maintained a myth of election (as *Hashem's* chosen people) that allowed them to survive as a people without the civilization being wiped out like most other ancient civilizations that did have military force. Bauman also speculates that the Jews remained a figure of ambivalence in their position as a limit case for Christianity. The Jews occupy a unique position within the Christian order of the universe, acting as both uncanny doppelgangers (the "new Jews") and "resistors" (Christian universalism supersedes Jewish particularism). It was the Christian Church that conceptualized the notion of the Jew in an abstract sense, with the Jew representing what is unassimilable within this framework.

Modern life is defined by the order and rational clarity of categorization used to defend against the experience of ambivalence. But as with all categorizations, something leftover remains an enigma—what Bauman (1995) refers to as "a thick file labeled 'miscellaneous' that pokes fun at the serious business of filing" (p. 213). The Jew is not merely what is unwelcomed into the social order (national, religious, racial, gendered) as the other of that order. The figure of ambivalence does not just not fit into the social order as inside or outside; *it troubles that order and disturbs binary oppositions.*[2] And order in society is the positive dialectical process by which the left-out are either incorporated or destroyed, excluded, or at the very least, branded (Bauman, 1995, p. 214).

Bauman (1998) argues that with the arrival of modernity—and new national, scientific, religious, and economic ordering of peoples—the Jews were among the peoples that did not quite fit anywhere. "There was no door shut on the way to modernity," he quips, "in which the Jews did not put their fingers" (Bauman, 1995, p. 219). In postmodernity, late modernity, or what Bauman (2000) calls "liquid modernity," humans are still driven to order, but there is no positive global order through which to identify. The Jew is the reminder of the pre-modern world where the stranger was excluded, the modern world where the Jew is included as exclusion, and as protean and sea-changing, Jews become the representatives of the disturbing liquid modernity.[3]

Psychoanalytic Concepts of Phobia and Ambivalence

As I noted in the first chapter, most of the contemporary work on anti-Semitism comes from fields neighboring psychology and psychoanalysis (e.g., history, sociology, Jewish studies), perhaps owing to its designation as a social phenomenon. However, scholars in these fields continue to build theories around concepts that seem unmistakably psychological (phobia, paranoia, ambivalence). It is my task, here, to explore the concept of phobia and ambivalence and to better understand the implications of proteophobia, but also to problematize the relationship between these seemingly psychological concepts and social theory.

---

[2] One could think of this binary logic as a phallic/masculine logic troubled by the diasporic/feminine logic of Jewishness (see Osserman, 2022).

[3] Identification seems to be undergoing decentralization, with anti-immigration laws serving as attempts to safeguard aspects of modernity and ethno-nationalist identity that remain significant. Bauman (1995) suggests that the current order involves the privatization of identity production, leading to identities being constructed in opposition to each other. Within this framework, Jewish identity often receives inadequate attention and is excluded from intersectional analysis.

Lacan (2021) describes the phenomenology of phobia as "the total ambiguity of what is desired and what is feared" (p. 305).[4] In *Black Skin, White Masks*, Fanon (1952/2008) defines phobia in the context of anti-Black racism and colonialism as an anxious fear of something outside the individual that invokes an ambivalence of revulsion—simultaneous fear and attraction. Ambivalence gives rise to phobia, which serves as the central symptom or cornerstone of neurosis (See Laplanche & Pontalis, 1967/1988, p. 37). The phobic process, in this understanding, is experienced by individuals who are themselves constituted as subjects by the ambivalence of early child/parent dynamics (e.g., attachment, individuation, separation, *nom-du-père*, language acquisition, regulation of affect, Oedipus complex, castration). In phobia, affect seeks out a substitute signifier, idea, or object via association, and each of these phobias can be traced back to a compromise—perhaps always ambivalent[5]—and a substitution of one idea for another (perhaps an existentially annihilating one). "Displacement onto the phobic object," Laplanche and Pontalis (1967/1988) write, "permits the objectivation, localisation and containment of anxiety" (p. 123).

It is important to note that phobia, as I am formulating it here, following Freud and more contemporary psychoanalytic thinkers, does not

---

[4] Lacan (2021) reminds us that the object of phobia is not identical to anxiety or the actual source of fear but serves the function of keeping fear at a distance and indicating something itself that must be avoided. Laplanche, too, argues that phobia is not merely a displacement of an unbearable fear onto a more manageable fear, as in the displacement of Little Hans' real fear of his father (and castration) onto the fear of horses. Instead, the symptom of phobia, Laplanche (2002) writes, "is a realization of desire and not an allegorical scene of fear" (p. 204). Lacan (2021) describes the phobic object as composed of "double-edged signifier elements," embodying the true essence of ambivalence, invoking both anxiety and desire (p. 351). He suggests that the phobic substitution process commences with the introduction of the symbolic and the fear of castration, as the child's sexual existence becomes an enigma necessitating resolution (Lacan, 1966/2006, p. 432). The phobic signifier assumes a role that is simultaneously ambivalent and symbolically structuring, akin to the function of the *nom-du-père* (name of the father) in the absence of the latter. Phobia coalesces around a central mythical framework, which for some individuals remains a steadfast organizing principle, while for others, it is subject to displacement by other signifiers, leading to a range of fluctuating anxieties and desires. Evans (1996) likens phobia's structural role in individual obsessional neurosis to myth's role in Claude Lèvi-Strauss' anthropology.

[5] Auchincloss and Samberg (2012) note that ambivalence is central to processes of separation and individuation, though it is sometimes used indiscriminately such that it loses some of its psychoanalytic specificity. This specificity is related to love and hate for the same object (and the like) and not merely the conflict between wish and defense.

enjoy the status of what Freud called an independent pathological process; that is, phobia emerges, in effect, as an answer to the problems that pathological processes present.[6] For example, in the condition most closely associated with phobia, phobic neurosis/anxiety hysteria (the two are different but not meaningfully so, here), phobia emerges in order to confront the anxiety that arises when "pathogenic material"—the true, or at least motivating source of psychic disturbance or enigma—is repressed, leaving the affect effectively active but unattached to its initial context. This affect is localized and contained (made meaningful and avoidable) through the displacement and fixation onto the phobic substitute. Fixation can be understood "as a name for the mode of inscription of certain ideational contents (experiences, imagos, phantasies) which persist in the unconscious in unchanging fashion and to which the instinct remains bound" (Laplanche & Pontalis, 1967/1988, p. 162). In phobia, anxious fear, desire, and aggression are displaced and fixated onto a central signifier, an idea or object localizable within a specific symbolic system along the path of least resistance (via primary processes of association, metaphor and metonymy, translation and transposition).[7]

In the context of racism, Fanon (1952/2008) formulates negrophobia as a socially sanctioned phobic fixation on an organizing principle of binarism. It is socially sanctioned by society's Manichean splitting into Black/White as an attempt at a solution to ambivalence. "[T]his kind of [binary] logic sustains racism," writes Derek Hook (2004), "because it suggests that two such groups are effectively unbridgeable, so radically different to one another, so mutually opposed, that no reconciliation, or mutual understanding would ever be possible" (p. 128). If, in anti-Black racism, phobia can be attributed to a Manichean binarism or splitting, what is the status of anti-Semitism within this phobic framework? One difference is that anti-Black racism involves the conviction—however fantastical—that the Manichean binary can be upheld (as well as socially

---

[6] It is worth noting that phobia does not have a separate entry in many psychoanalytic dictionaries and encyclopedias, but instead is covered under anxiety, neurosis, hysteria, and displacement (e.g., Auchincloss & Samberg, 2012; Erwin, 2002; Laplanche & Pontalis, 1967/1988).

[7] Lacan (1966/2006) refers to the signifier as the "motor force" of phobia (p. 374). Laplanche (1991) might call this particular signifier a "designified signifier" because it functions as an unlinkable "thing-representation" in the psychical apparatus.

sanctioned and sustained via spurious but vigorous efforts, e.g., race science, segregation); whereas the figure of the Jew—perennially an outsider among "us," uncertainly identifiable according to morphological features or other classificatory schemas—appears to undermine any attempt to erect and enforce this binary on which the logic of anti-Black racism depends.[8] So, when Bauman (1995) refers to Jews as "ambivalence incarnate" and uses the concept of proteophobia, he is gesturing to the perpetual failure of such splitting operations and the anxious return of ambivalence that it provokes. This may account for the fantasy of the erasure of Jews in the Nazi Final Solution rather than merely a "splitting" off of Jews as in the enforcement of affixed visible and symbolic identifiers (Jewish stars, identification cards) or segregation.

In phobia, the binding and fixation of affect to a localizable and seemingly external object allow for the binary ordering against the anxiety of ambivalence.[9] This anxiety of ambivalence seems to demand such a solution. For early analysts like Karl Abraham, psychical maturity is characterized by an overcoming of ambivalence (Erwin, 2002, p. 3), or a kind of genital fixity, sublimation, or socially valuable forms of defensive compromise. However, in the form of anti-Black racism and anti-Semitism we can recognize dangerous and pathological forms of "socially valuable" defense. For Melanie Klein, contra Abraham (her contemporary and

---

[8] Blackness does not conform to the binary either—negrophilia, the flip side of negrophobia, is also a form of racism—but in the racist fantasy, it does. The splitting is an attempt to finally solve ambivalence, but it is always a failure because the phobia is still related to ambivalence in that the phobic object is also an object of desire (see also studies on the subject of racism and jouissance in Hook, 2017, 2018; George & Hook, 2021).

[9] According to Laplanche and Pontalis (1967/1988), analysts should use the term *ambivalence* only where there is a "non-dialectical opposition" by which they mean the process where, for example, love and hate are inseparable without each engendering the other or resolving into a higher order (p. 28). It seems that dialectical opposition is used, here, to refer to an interactive binary opposition and its resolution, as in the case of desire and prohibition, for instance. It should be noted, however, that ambivalence proceeds—it is not merely a static simultaneity; being must "go-on being"—yet without synthesis or reconciliation, and should in this sense be considered negatively dialectical as "the motor of any dialectic" (Laplanche & Pontalis, 1967/1988, p. 295).

onetime analyst), the aim of analysis is to achieve a greater tolerance for ambivalence, rather than seeking its resolution or erasure.[10]

Ambivalence may need to be tolerated, perhaps promoted, and not resolved, but is proteophobia best understood merely as a phobic reaction against ambivalence? Frosh (2005) contends, in his engagement with anti-Semitism, fascism goes beyond a mere fear of ambivalence, and proteophobia is more than that too; it extends to the fear of what is excluded from classificatory schemas (or produced as "waste" in such categorizing operations) and what changes form. Frosh (2005) emphasizes that it is not solely ambivalence that evokes this anxious fear, but also anything that challenges the fantasy of purity or bears the imprint of "complex reality" (p. 178).[11]

---

[10] Another way of approaching this issue is to recognize the ego as a form of defense, a signifier, a symptom, indeed, a phobic symptom. The ego, too, is a product of a defense against ambivalence, yet ambivalence persists *for* the egoic subject. Ambivalence seems to persist beyond its supposed overcoming, so wrapped up as it is, in the maintenance of psychic interiority. The ego, taken as the psychological subject of conscious interiority in much of psychological and psychoanalytic discourse (but not all), is itself a product of continued splitting, what Melanie Klein recognized as the most primitive defense against anxiety in the face of fundamentally ambivalent instincts. Laplanche and Pontalis (1967/1988) explain that "[…] the ego is well and truly the agent of defense, but in so far as it cannot defend itself without splitting itself off from that which threatens it, it relinquishes the incompatible idea to a type of process over which it has no control" (p. 134). The ego is itself a product of a kind of Manichean split in response to the ambivalence of internal/external. The ego is what is registered as internal whereas everything else becomes external (including the unconscious over which the ego has no control).

The ego blinds us with its rigid classifications of internal/external, but for Laplanche (1991), the internality of the ego is formed by the external other leading to a primary ambivalence rooted in this otherness. Something always resists the fixity of classification and is deposited as waste in the ego's formation. This waste becomes unconscious. As we have seen, the Jew comes to represent this figure of ambivalence, of this internal otherness, of the unconscious, but also what is deposited as waste in classificatory schemas (race, religion, nation).

[11] Horkheimer and Adorno (1947/2004) use the language of paranoid projection in their analysis of anti-Semitism. As Horkheimer and Adorno (1947/2004) contend,

If the psychic energy of paranoia stems from the libidinal dynamic laid bare by psychoanalysis, its objective impregnability is founded on the ambiguity inseparable from the objectifying act; indeed, the latter's hallucinatory power will have been originally decisive. To clarify, it can be said in the language of natural selection theory that during the formative period of the human sensorium those individuals survived in whom the power of the projective mechanisms extended most deeply into their rudimentary logical faculties, or was least moderated by the premature onset of reflection. [...] Paranoia is the shadow of cognition. (p. 161)

For these thinkers, paranoia is a part of thinking, and is pathological, not in its lack of rationality, but in its pathological form of rationality; individual paranoia can be defended against by way of a

I believe that Laplanche (1991) can help us think about ambivalence in relation to this complex reality, specifically in terms of an otherness and a sociality that persists structurally at the core of subjectivity, and perhaps even that otherness that Frosh (2005) links with Jewishness and the Jewish target of anti-Semitism. Laplanche is radical in his approach to ambivalence, promoting it as an alternative to the oppressive binary logic of phallocentrism in "the modern occidental world" (1996, p. 9), and calling for "models of symbolization that are more flexible, more multiple, more ambivalent" (2007, p. 218). Ambivalence here is not merely what is feared in proteophobia but also what could help to uproot it.[12]

Across his innovative work developing "new foundations for psychoanalysis," Laplanche (1991) develops a general theory of seduction and the enigmatic message, which provides valuable insights for comprehending proteophobia and the intricate nature of psychical reality, particularly in the context of the subject's connection to the unsettling concept of "*ètrangèté*" or "strangerness" (see also Laplanche, 1996, 1999, 2007, 2015). Laplanche's neologism "strangerness" encapsulates the uncanny

---

socially sanctioned logic. As Fanon put it, the phobic (or projective paranoiac) person is governed by "the laws of rational prelogic and effective prelogic" but a logic nonetheless (1952/2008, p. 155).

What do we make of paranoia, here, in relation to phobia? Paranoia is often an example of psychosis (Lacan, 1997) the way that phobia is the central symptom of neurosis. Both phobia and paranoia facilitate the transition between the imaginary and the symbolic system. Anti-Semitism and anti-Black racism seem to blur such clear categorical delineations between phobia and projection. The projection involved in paranoia and the displacement involved in phobia occur across diagnostic categories. If the racist is paranoid and projects aggression outside onto a phobic object, would it be accurate to call this psychosis? As a socially sanctioned phobia, might that sociality undermine the psychotic dimension which is also usually refined by the foreclosure of the social link (Lacan, 1997)? In Lacanian terms, would we not say that the Jew becomes a *nom-du-père* of some sorts? Projection is "the defense whereby forbidden or intolerable thoughts and feelings are attributed to others" (Auchincloss & Samberg, 2012, p. 186).

[12] This is not unlike Homi Bhabha's (1994) idea of ambivalence offering a kind of hybridity as a social transformation. This hybridity is established in the process of mimicry described by Lacan (1966/2006). For Bhabha (1994), the hybrid object is one that is not fixed and is established as what disrupts what has been fixed. The hybrid object is another word for the object of proteophobic anxiety:

The paranoid threat from the hybrid is finally uncontainable because it breaks down the symmetry and duality of self/other, inside/outside. In the productivity of power, the boundaries of authority—its reality effects—are always besieged by 'the other scene' of fixations and phantoms. (Bhabha, 1994, p. 116)

I will note the oddity that Bhabha doesn't discuss Jews more in his *The Location of Culture* (1994) since we are iconic figures of hybridity.

quality of the unconscious, amalgamating the notions of strange and foreign. This framework helps us move beyond the xenophobic fear of what is deemed strange or the heterophobic fear of what is classified as other, offering a deeper understanding of proteophobia and complex reality. Proteophobia, the anxious fear of what doesn't fit into our classificatory schemas, can here be understood, with Laplanche, in terms of an enigmatic message that establishes a foundational ambivalence and uncategorizability of a psychical subject constituted "through the entrails" of the other (to return to Nirenberg's [2013] turn of phrase).[13]

---

[13] Laplanche (2015) argues that the infant is faced with (and inherits) adult mythico-symbolic codes that are cultural and ideological in origin, transmitted in the messages of adults who are engaging with the child. These myths are those on the order of race, nation, religion, capital, etc. These myths are in relation to what Lèvi-Strauss calls the "exigency of order" (cited in Laplanche, 2015, p. 239). This idea of an exigency of ordering (categorization), which is "at the root of all thought" (Levi-Strauss cited in Laplanche, 2015, p. 239), is a form of binding and translation triggered by the confrontation with an existential and sexual anxiety aroused by enigmatic elements which were not able to be translated (and incorporated into the ego's lived experience) and resist the transmission of ordering logic (exchange, binary, etc.). In the principal messages, the existential and sexual enigmas are "figured" as "anomaly, contradiction, or scandal" (Levi-Strauss cited in Laplanche, 2015, p. 239). I will add to this list the figures of ambivalence and "strangerness."

To reiterate, these complex realities (e.g., ambivalences) evoke the existential anxiety, necessitating an order which requires a certain kind of translation found within the adult world of mythico-symbolic culture (race, religion, nation, gender, capital). This is a binary or phallic order of the world rooted in what Lacan would call "castration" or a symbolic figure/name/no of the father that institutes this binary ordering of categorization. Sometimes that father figure and subsequent (symbolic) order does not take hold and requires a paranoid fantasy or phobic object substitute to bring the child (to bridge the gap) from an infantile prelinguistic imaginary register to the symbolic order. This jargon of castration and binary is just one way of putting it. Laplanche emphasizes the contingency of the particular myths/codes/ideologies, and that there is something that is pushed into the unconscious which is not of this binary phallic logic, the name-of-the-father, phobia, etc. For Laplanche and contrary to Lacanian theory, the symbolic order, as ordered, is on par with his conception of ego and binding, and not the unconscious.

The enigma (and the ambivalences, anomalies, contradictions, and scandals), concomitant with this ordering (at the root of all ego and thought) disrupts the binary opposition and the ego's classificatory grid. As we are beginning to see, the figure of the Jew elicits a mythical and ideological thought process, *and* an enigma. These culturally inherited myths are, for Laplanche (2015), purely mythical and therefore can be replaced by other myths.

This unconscious, for Laplanche, is not another ego, another consciousness, another language, or a set of myths—even as it comes from an other. It is made up of elements, yes, but not narrative chains of signification. For Laplanche, this is how psychoanalysts need to orient (or disorient) themselves. And importantly, for Laplanche, analysis is the process of unbinding these ideologies (individual and social) but at the level of the individual, not at the level of the social ideology itself. Clinical work, for Laplanche (2015), is some amalgam of therapy and analysis, that is, binding and unbinding.

The formulation of the subject through the other's messages, as discussed in Laplanche's work (though not elaborated here), takes us a step closer to an understanding of social structures and provides valuable tools for understanding the transmission of discourse and cultural messages such as myths and ideologies. Moreover, proteophobia marks a disruption in the classificatory schemas that govern the rules of social ordering and subjective understanding. However, it is important to note that this analysis does not yet reach the level of comprehensive examination of social totalities. All this seems a little too psychological to account for such a social process as anti-Semitism, no? Hook (2004) writes that this is the challenge but also the promise of critical psychological approaches, which require,

> [...] not just an ability to conceptualise how *politics impacts on psychology but an awareness also of how the psychological repeats, reiterates and reinforces the political.* So, racism, like denigrating images of blackness, are [sic] in no way natural, ahistorical, predisposed 'qualities of cerebral matter', although they do, in racist or colonial environments, feature powerfully in the unconscious minds of individuals and of the society, just as they do circulate within its psychical phenomena. The conclusion we may draw from this state of affairs is that we need strong psychological accounts of racism if such forms of prejudice are to be adequately confronted and redressed. Such an account of racism finds its place as one component part of an awareness and contestation of forms of racism and prejudice, even if it alone is not sufficient. Racism no doubt exists at levels of social structure, of social meaning and discourse, as well as at the level of individual psychology. All such dimensions of racism need to be confronted. (p. 135)

I agree with Hook's (2004) appeal to the study of racism at both the levels of psychology and social structure. Anti-Semitism and racism can be understood in terms of myths, ideologies, and discourses, and socially sanctioned and libidinally laden phobic and paranoid displacements and fixations, projections, and introjections. The theory of negative psychology uncovered in the study of anti-Semitism and elaborated in the following chapters, contributes to Hook's (2004) problematic of critical psychology.

Much like Laplanche's theory of otherness, what I term "negative psychology" blurs the boundaries between interior and exterior, projection and perception, psychical and social reality, thereby complicating the conceptual clarity within each domain. In other words, psychological and social factors don't simply coexist or interact dialectically with one another; rather, they are internally contradictory and necessitate immanent critique. Sartre (1965) referred to anti-Semitism as "a basic fear of oneself and of truth [...] that thing of indefinite approximation" (p. 12). The psychological domain is internally fractured, and anti-Semitism seems to be a self-destructive attempt at an adhesive solution. I delve into negative psychology in the next chapter, exploring the theoretical underpinnings and practical implications of Adorno's critical theory of anti-Semitism, and how the dialectical logic of negative psychology can be mobilized to resist proteophobia. But first, I take a brief digression to address a metaphorical issue posed in stating that anti-Semitism is "a basic fear of oneself" (Sartre) or that "the Jew is ambivalence incarnate" (Bauman).

Rhetorical Constructions and Proteophobia

Psychoanalysis, like critical theory, lends itself to the study of anti-Semitism as proteophobia in its capacity for critical reflection on basic assumptions, but also in its attention to what is left out of classificatory schemas (and totalities like the ego and society) *as left out*. Frosh's (2005) work, at the intersection of critical theory and psychoanalysis, demonstrates that the methodology and theory of the psychoanalytic unconscious cannot be divorced from the otherness that is inherent to discourse surrounding Jewishness and anti-Semitism. What's more, the ways in which psychoanalysis approaches subjectivity and the concept of the unconscious are shaped by the historical context of Freud and his followers (and detractors), including the tradition of Jewish thought and the experience of anti-Semitism. As we have seen, Jewishness has been thought in terms of this otherness and ambivalence, and otherness and ambivalence have been thought in terms of the Jewish. Indeed, Frosh (2005) suggests that "all otherness in the West is Jewish" (p. 215), in much the same way that Bauman (1995) states that "the Jew is ambivalence incarnate" (p. 211).[14]

The previous rhetorical statements employ metaphors (the Jew is X, and X is Jewish), which as metaphors do, require the capacity to recognize similarities in dissimilarities. Historically, the figure of the Jew has held significant importance as a rhetorical tool, among Jews and non-Jews alike, enabling metaphorical constructions with diverse and often contradictory meanings. This is demonstrated by the wide ranging facets of society denounced by anti-Semites as "Jewish" but also the numerous scholarly examples in which the Jew has been used as a metaphor: The analyst is the Jew (Loewenstein); the critical theorist is the Jew (Horkheimer); ambivalence is Jewish (Bauman); modernity is Jewish; technology and the Holocaust are Jewish (Heidegger); slave-morality is Jewish (Nietzsche); race is essentially Jewish (Žižek); the unconscious is Jewish (Frosh); the negative principle is Jewish (Horkheimer and Adorno); Fanon is a *luftmenschen* Jew (Cheyette); Sebald writes Jewish (Mendelsohn); Said is the last Jew (Said). The Jew is uncategorizable, but then, also, the uncategorizable is Jewish. And last but not least, I am Jewish (Me).

Universalizing the Jew as a figure of thought to fit these various metaphorical constructions can pose the risk of erasing the particular context and experience of Jewish history and embodiment. Inversely, some scholars have argued that thinking in terms of this Jewishness may lead to the marginalization or relativization of other contemporaneous struggles such as those faced by Black, Queer, or Palestinian communities. In the process of metaphorical thinking, there is a danger of defensive over-categorization, of making everything the same or similar, and through analogy, of doing so to make potentially dubious arguments. Bryan Cheyette (2013) addresses these risks involved in metaphorical thinking

---

[14] For Laplanche, there are two levels of theory in psychoanalysis. At one level are theories of sexuality, unconscious, and repression, and these are used to account for the experience of psychoanalysis in practice. These are within the domain of science and require falsification. The other level of theory is made up of myths and ideologies of the subject. They are not theories applied to patients (or should not be, at least) but expressed by the patients in therapy. These are used by the patient to soothe intellectual and sexual anxieties (Laplanche, 2021, p. 154). Perhaps both the Oedipus complex and anti-Semitism are of this latter variety.

which lead to an "anxiety of appropriation" (p. xiv).[15] He highlights the risk of metaphorical thinking in racial discourse that flattens historical and particular oppressed peoples into figures of thought (Jews, Blacks) without always fleshing them back out again.

So why do it? Cheyette (2013) cautions that the opposite is also true. Refusing to recognize similarities can result in the siloing of disciplines, ideas, struggles, and people, when in fact, these realms are already intersecting and interacting, interconnected metaphorically if not materially. For instance, Jewish and Palestinian communities and struggles are *already* intertwined through the history of Orientalism, cohabitation, oppression, resistance, exile, etc. This anxiety of appropriation, Cheyette (2013) shows, can lead to the concealment of these ambivalent and multi-form connections. When discussing Jewish struggles in tandem with postcolonial struggles, there is an anxiety of appropriation due to the inherent ambivalences surrounding Jews, particularly the ambivalent relation between both Jews and anti-Semitism and Jews and Israel. In this context, postcolonial theory borrows from Jewish forms of identity, suffering, and resistance, and simultaneously represses their influence.

Cheyette's work focuses on a number of these ambivalences and connection. In *Diasporas of the Mind* (2013) he traces the figure of the Jew as *luftmensch* in Jewish and postcolonial theory and literature. *Luftmensch* is a Yiddish term meaning free-floating and disembodied "air-person"; a term later stolen by the Nazis to characterize the nationless, parasitic Jew. It is also associated with the term *"rootless cosmopolitan,"* an anti-Semitic epithet, referring to Jews who lacked national allegiance, often in the context of Soviet Russia. According to Cheyette (2013), anti-Semitism and colonialism collide in the "proteophobic anxiety of being a *luftmensch*" (p. 40), by which he seems to mean the anxiety of diasporic thinking or thinking untethered from singular allegiances and clearly

---

[15] Here is more from Cheyette (2013) on the anxiety of appropriation:

There is always a risk in engaging in metaphorical thinking, which I have called the anxiety of appropriation, especially in relation to histories of racial victimization. There is an understandable fear that the objects of racial discourse, who were mere figurative beings in relation to this discourse, might once again descend into metaphor. But the alternative to such metaphorical thinking is a sense of disciplinary uniqueness, outside such imaginative connectedness, which results in an inability to embrace the dissimilar. (p. xiv)

delineated identity positions. Such diasporic thinking crosses boundaries and seems to demand intersectionality in the face of contradiction and ambivalence.

In postcolonial theory, for instance, Cheyette (2013) finds that Fanon becomes "an empty signifier or *luftmensch*" and gets taken up in contradictory and polarized ways by various scholars (p. 45).[16] Cheyette (2013) explores the productive use made of the figure of diaspora and *luftmensch* in the development of postcolonial theory. He also recognizes the risk of erasing Jewish particularity and embodiment in universalizing these figures. As Cheyette notes, "the line between universalizing Jewish history and superseding it can be quite thin" (p. 30).

In a frequently cited article, Grillo and Wildman (1991) show that in the process of analogical comparison, one of the terms is dominant and other effectively erased (often race when compared with Jewishness), leading to competition between oppressed groups who are vying for resources and for what seems like a limited quanta of memory and public attention. Still, in refusing to explore these comparisons, something else is silenced. Against this anxiety of appropriation and competitive logic, Michael Rothberg (2009) proposes the idea of multidirectional memory, arguing that "memory is not a zero-sum game" (p. 11). Cheyette (2013) and Rothberg (2009, 2019) both emphasize in their analyses of anti-Semitism, colonialism, and racism that we are always already working within mixed, multidirectional, implicated, and intersecting fields.[17] The boundaries and directions become blurred, troubling the neat ordering or categorization of various groups, struggles, disciplines, and so on. This ambivalence exposes anxieties and necessitates more careful approaches to investigation, but it also offers the potential for resisting oppressive categorical schemas and the force of proteophobia.

In an interview following the events of October 7, 2023, Michael Rothberg (Rothberg & Lenz, 2024) presents an ethics of comparison. His ethic serves as a framework for comparative thinking that embraces ongoing ambivalence and complexity. According to Rothberg, when

---

[16] It goes without saying that Fanon is hardly unique in being taken up in contradictory ways.

[17] Most if not all words and concepts are the product of metaphorical constructions of some kind which have been naturalized over the course of history.

juxtaposing events such as anti-Black racism and anti-Semitism, Gaza and the Warsaw Ghetto, or Israel and Nazi Germany, our ethical responsibility is to inquire: Does the comparison exacerbate conflict and violence, or does it foster solidarity among victimized groups? Rothberg advocates for striving toward solidarity. When engaging in comparative analysis, is it to reinforce a predetermined conclusion, or does it encourage exploration of complexity, generation of new questions, formation of innovative connections, and cultivation of critical thought?

Comparison and metaphorical rhetoric surrounding Jews, anti-Semitism, and the Holocaust can be utilized to connect struggles or sow division; at the same time, it can be used to illustrate a historical pattern or an exception to a rule. There has been extensive scholarship aimed at recontextualizing the history of anti-Semitism, and especially the Holocaust, to avoid exceptionalizing Jewish suffering. Exceptionalizing Jewish suffering appears to dehistoricize anti-Semitism by divorcing it from its socio-economic historical context. While this contextualizing endeavor is valuable, it sometimes inadvertently perpetuates its own form of proteophobia. In the endeavor to resist exceptionalizing Jewish suffering—often accompanied by the caveat: "I say this in no way to diminish its horror, of course, but rather to deny its *singularity*" (Mills, 2019, p. 103)—scholars unintentionally perpetuate Jewish exceptionalism "out of their own entrails." Stripped of its singularity, Jewish history comes to embody universally exchangeable signifiers: from the Diaspora to diasporas, the Holocaust to holocausts, from anti-Semitism to anti-Semitisms. The Jewish, then, functions as a master (or floating or empty or rootless) signifier stripped of its historical specificity. The Jewish is both a figure of particularity *and* the destroyer of particularity. The history of Jewish suffering is indeed singular in its particularity, yet in *this* regard, it is not singular.

Cheyette (2013) argues for more comparative and metaphorical thinking, but I am hesitant to endorse this call, outright, without a more robust theory of proteophobia that can temper the moment of metaphorical condensations where new rigid categories are established, and something is potentially repressed. How might we perpetuate the *ambivalence* of metaphorical creations rather than silencing either side of the multi-form figures?

I will end this chapter by pointing to one possibility found in psycho-analysis, that of exploring these rhetorical operations as functions of thinking or primary linguistic and "psychological" processes. Rhetorical tropes of metaphor and metonymy are central concepts for French psychoanalytic thinkers such as Lacan and Laplanche (after Roman Jakobson), for which these terms describe the constitution of the unconscious (e.g., condensation, displacement, contiguity, similarity).[18] Indeed, phobia may be one such rhetorical process, rigid and mechanical as that process might be.[19] It is through attention to these processes that many psychoanalysts make room for the unconscious and offer the patient relief from suffering through playfully creative openness where there had been a rigid repetition of patterns and metaphors.

Metaphors can help us gain a deeper self-understanding, but as Thomas Ogden (1989) suggests, psychoanalysis is not centered on making new metaphors or interpretations but liberating patients from previous frameworks of organized experience (whether conscious or unconscious) thus enabling them to endure not knowing and embrace the possibility of a transformative future. He writes:

---

[18] Lacan and Laplanche held differing views on the relationship between the unconscious and rhetorical tropes. Lacan posited that the unconscious is structured akin to linguistic terms, while Laplanche argued that the unconscious is not organized or structured, rather it is produced as a byproduct of linguistic processes.

[19] Phobia functions according to metaphorical process which Lacan (2021) defines as "a matter of a substitution [e.g., displacement] which at the same time maintains what it is substituting" (p. 369). For Lacan, this process of substation is the very structure of the unconscious and neurotic desire. For Laplanche (1991), on the other hand, these rhetorical tropes are related to the binding operation of translation and not primary processes *of* the untranslated unconscious (the unconscious is a not-structured like a language). Laplanche (1991) writes of the binding into ego by Eros (what he calls the life sexual drives):

It seems to me that it is therefore more likely to undergo a metaphoric displacement rather than a metonymic displacement, for the very simple reason that only structures which display a certain totality and a certain internal articulation can lend themselves to the analogy which produces metaphoric substitution; analogies are only possible between units that display certain structurations and certain formal similarities at the level of their totality. (p. 147)

In *Minima Moralia* (1951/2005), Adorno wrote that "Love is the power to see similarity in the dissimilar" (p. 191). This love is what Laplanche is referring to as the binding process of eros. And this power is also one of domination and oppression. We must also cultivate the negatively dialectical ability to recognize the dissimilar in the similar, to follow the unconscious.

The value of developing new ways of knowing lies not simply in the greater self-understanding one might achieve, but as importantly in the possibility that a wider range of thoughts, feelings, and sensations might be brought into being. Each insight, however valuable, immediately constitutes the next resistance in that the new knowledge is already part of the static known and must be overcome in the process of freshly knowing. (Ogden, 1989, p. 1)

We know psychoanalysis is going well, Ogden (1989) notes, when the patient complains that they understand less than when they started. By tolerating the not-knowing, patients and therapists alike make room for change. Metaphor, comparison, and interpretation can be used to harden meanings and to give preformed answers, but they can also be used to challenge and suspend previous ways of understanding, leaving the door ajar.

References

Adorno, T. W. (2005). *Minima moralia: Reflections from damaged life.* Verso. (Original work published in 1951)

Auchincloss, E. L., & Samberg, E. (Eds.). (2012). *Psychoanalytic terms and concepts.* Yale University Press. https://doi.org/10.2307/j.ctv6jm9bp

Bahbah, H. (1994). *The location of culture.* Routledge.

Bauman, Z. (1995). *Life in fragments. Essays in postmodern morality.* Basil Blackwell.

Bauman, Z. (1998). Allosemitism: Premodern, modern, postmodern. In B. Cheyette & L. Marcus (Eds.), *Modernity, culture, and "the Jew".* Polity Press.

Bauman, Z. (2000). *Liquid modernity.* Polity Press.

Cheyette, B. (2013). *Diasporas of the mind: Jewish and postcolonial writing and the nightmare of history.* Yale University Press.

Cheyette, B., Rothberg, M., & Axster, F. (2019). Relational Thinking: A Dialogue on the Theory and Politics of Research on Antisemitism and Racism. *Lernen Aus De Geschichte.* https://lernen-aus-der-geschichte.de/Lernenund-Lehren/content/14651 (accessed August 10, 2023)

Erwin, E. (Ed.). (2002). *The Freud encyclopedia: Theory, therapy, and culture.* Routledge.

Evans, D. (1996). *An introductory dictionary of Lacanian psychoanalysis.* Routledge. https://doi.org/10.4324/9780203135570

Fanon, F. (2008). *Black skin white masks* (C. L. Markmann, Trans.). Pluto Press. (Original work published 1952)

Freud, S. (2001). The 'uncanny'. In J. Strachey (Ed. & Trans.), *The standard edition of the complete psychological works of Sigmund Freud, volume XVII (1917–1919): An infantile neurosis and other works* (pp. 217–256). Vintage Books. (Original work published 1919)

Frosh, S. (2005). *Hate and the 'Jewish Science': Anti-Semitism, Nazism and psychoanalysis.* Palgrave Macmillan.

George, S., & Hook, D. (2021). *Lacan and race: Racism, identity, and psychoanalytic theory.* Routledge.

Grillo, T., & Wildman, S. M. (1991). Obscuring the importance of race: The implication of making comparisons between racism and sexism (or other -isms). *Duke Law Journal, 1991*(2), 397–412. https://doi.org/10.2307/1372732

Hook, D. (2004). Fanon and the psychoanalysis of racism. In D. Hook (Ed.), *Critical psychology* (pp. 114–137). Juta Academic Publishing.

Hook, D. (2017). What is "enjoyment as a political factor"? *Political Psychology, 38*(4), 605–620. https://www.jstor.org/stable/45094377

Hook, D. (2018). Racism and jouissance: Evaluating the 'racism as (the theft of) enjoyment' hypothesis. *Psychoanalysis, Culture and Society, 23*(3), 244–266.

Horkheimer, M., & Adorno, T. W. (2004). *Dialectic of enlightenment: Philosophical fragments* (G. S. Noerr, Ed. & E. Jephcott, Trans.). Stanford. (Original work published 1947)

Lacan, J. (1997) *The seminars of Jacques Lacan book III: The psychosis* (R. Grigg, Trans.). W.W. Norton.

Lacan, J. (2006). *Écrits: The first complete edition in English* (J. A. Miller, Ed. & B. Fink, Trans.). W.W. Norton & Co. (Original work published 1966)

Lacan, J. (2021). *The object relation: The seminar of Jacques Lacan, book IV* (J. A. Miller, Ed. & A. Price, Trans.). Polity.

Lapidot, E. (2021). *Jews out of the question: A critique of anti-anti-Semitism.* SUNY Press.

Laplanche, J. (1991). *New foundations for psychoanalysis.* Basil Blackwell.

Laplanche, J. (1996). Psychoanalysis as anti-hermeneutics (L. Thurston, Trans.). *Radical Philosophy, 79*(12), 7–12. https://www.radicalphilosophy.com/article/psychoanalysis-as-anti-hermeneutics

Laplanche, J. (1999). *Essays on otherness.* Routledge.

Laplanche, J. (2002). *The unfinished Copernican revolution* (L. Thurston, Trans.). The Unconscious in Translation.

Laplanche, J. (2007). Gender, sex, and the sexual (S. Fairfield, Trans.). *Studies in Gender and Sexuality, 8*(2), 201–219. https://doi.org/10.1080/15240650701225567

Laplanche, J. (2015). *Between seduction and inspiration: Man* (J. Mehlman, Trans.). The Unconscious in Translation.

Laplanche, J., & Pontalis, J. B. (1988). *The language of psychoanalysis.* Karnac. (Original work published 1967)

Mills, C. (2019). *The racial contract.* Cornell University Press. (Original work published 1997)

Nirenberg, D. (2013). *Anti-Judaism: A Western tradition.* Norton.

Ogden, T. (1989). *The primitive edge of experience.* Jason Aronson.

Osserman, J. (2022). *Circumcision on the couch: The cultural, psychological, and gendered dimensions of the world's oldest surgery.* Bloomsbury.

Rothberg, M. (2009). *Multidirectional memory: Remembering the holocaust in the age of decolonization.* Stanford University Press.

Rothberg, M. (2019). *The implicated subject: Beyond victims and perpetrators.* Stanford University Press.

Rothberg, M., & Lenz, R. (2024). We need an ethics of comparison. *Medico International.* Retrieved March 14, 2024, from https://www.medico.de/en/we-need-an-ethics-of-comparison-19392

Sartre, J. P. (1965). *Anti-Semite and Jew: An exploration of the etiology of hate.* Schocken. (Original work published 1946)

Strosberg, B. B., Hook, D., & Leadem, S. (2023). Uncanny teletherapy: Working with extimacy. *Journal of the American Psychoanalytic Association, 71*(2), 237–258. https://doi.org/10.1177/00030651231170561

5

Excursus on Adorno's Negative Psychology

Revisiting Adorno's Contribution to Psychology[1]

Following the Second World War, Adorno et al.'s *The Authoritarian Personality* (1950/2019) became the most influential engagement between Frankfurt School critical theorists and the field of psychology—1000 pages on the psychology of prejudice and oppression which, always salient, is of pressing interest in light of the recent rise of anti-Semitism and authoritarian regimes across the world. And, as is the case with influential engagements, a standard reading of the study has sedimented in commentaries on the topic. The recent publication of Theodor W. Adorno's retracted "Remarks on *The Authoritarian Personality*" (1948/2019) provides a timely impetus to reexamine and challenge certain long-held ideas about Adorno's contribution to psychology—for instance that *The Authoritarian Personality* reduces complex social phenomena (like anti-Semitism) to individual motivation and

---

[1] Part of Chap. 5 was first published in 2021 as "Adorno's Negative Psychology" in *Social and Personality Psychology Compass*, *15*(2). It is reproduced with permission of the publisher, John Wiley and Sons.

personality (e.g., Tajfel & Turner, 2004). Adorno's *Remarks* provide an alternative approach to the usual reading of *The Authoritarian Personality*; one where the psychology of authoritarianism and anti-Semitism is likened to "the end of psychology itself" (Adorno, 1948/2019, p. lxiv), aligning the study with Adorno's more critical and dialectical theory.

In this chapter, I respond to both the surprising dearth of commentary on his work in recent psychological scholarship and some past problematic interpretations. To accomplish these tasks, I clarify the psychoanalytic concepts employed by Adorno as both a dialectical psychology and heralding an end of psychology. Taken together, I label this Adorno's *negative psychology*, since for Adorno there must be a psychology after the concept of psychology is critiqued from within psychology. Reframed in this way, Adorno can continue to serve as a crucial site of critical engagement for psychologists studying anti-Semitism. Although Adorno's theory is often criticized for reducing anti-Semitism to mere psychological projection, his negative psychology demonstrates that this is not an accurate depiction. Negative psychology provides a critical model for understanding the impact of anti-Semitic and proteophobic thinking on the psychological subject as well as offer a means of studying anti-Semitism that avoids psychological reductionism or falling into proteophobia's trap. In what follows, I focus primarily on *The Authoritarian Personality* (1950/2019) which addresses anti-Semitism as well as authoritarianism, and in the next chapter I use these ideas to analyze anti-Semitism more specifically.

The Authoritarian Personality and Critical Psychology

The Authoritarian Personality

The Authoritarian Personality (1950/2019) found that certain character traits of Americans following World War II (e.g., conventionalism, submission, projectivity, superstition, aggression) predicted a susceptibility to anti-democratic propaganda and possibly to fascism, accordingly. The study developed the famous F-Scale which correlates high scores with authoritarian personality (the fascist character), as well as with ethnic prejudice and anti-Semitism. Although the study is Adorno's best-known work in the field of psychology, he engaged with psychology throughout his life: from his early withdrawn 1926–1927 habilitation in psychology, where he first explored the potential for the Freudian unconscious to trouble the social and psychological (Bloch, 2019), to his mid-career *Minima Moralia* (1951/2005) and his late *Negative Dialectics* (1967/2004). As Hullot-Kentor (2006) notes,

> [Adorno's] early appropriation of Freud was so complete and formative of every aspect of his thinking that during his years in the United States, mostly the 1940s, in spite of the fact that he had no clinical training in the field, he credibly presented himself as psychologist—then meaning a psychoanalytic researcher—in letters of introduction and in his participation on research projects [...] (p. 10).

Despite his consistent engagement with psychoanalytic psychology and research in the field, Adorno is most often considered by psychologists solely in relation to his work on *The Authoritarian Personality* (1950/2019), if he is considered at all. Even critical psychology, a subdiscipline of psychology defined (at least in part) by a dialogue with critical theory, is inconsistent vis-à-vis Adorno. Some critical psychology volumes barely engage with Adorno (e.g., Gough, 2017; Walkerdine, 2002), some oversimplify his contribution (e.g., Rogers, 2003), while in others his various works abound (e.g., Teo, 2014; Parker, 2015). Where authors do take up the influence of Adorno's dialectical approach to psychology in general (e.g., Ibáñez & Íñguez, 1997; Morss, 1995; Sloan, 1995), it is rarely in relation to *The Authoritarian Personality.*

Even among critical psychologists, Adorno's work on *The Authoritarian Personality* is approached in this misleading manner, as a psychological explanation for social problems:

> One example of social reductionism comes from the study by Adorno, Frenkel-Brunswik, Levinson and Sanford [...], who attempted to explain the strong anti-Semitic feelings that were prevalent in Nazi Germany. The

authors of this work suggested that social prejudice could be accounted for in terms of authoritarianism, which came about as a result of having strict parents who were harsh disciplinarians. While it is possible that personality traits such as authoritarianism may explain some part of prejudice, such reductionistic accounts place the final responsibility for such social problems within a narrow and individualistic perspective, while ignoring the impact of wider cultural, social and political forces. Locating responsibility within the individual carries with it political implications that typically underplay the impact of social influences.[2] (Tuffin, 2005, p. 51)

Tuffin (2005) later concedes that his characterization of Adorno et al.'s project is simplified, following up his critique with a brief proviso that the link made in the study between individual development and social processes may not be causal (p. 112). Despite such concessions, *The Authoritarian Personality* is generally still thought of as psychologizing.

Some psychologists explicitly position their work against an individualist approach attributed to Adorno and his colleagues: "Much of the work on the social psychology of intergroup relations," these critics suggest, "has focused on patterns of individual prejudice and discrimination and on the motivational sequences of interpersonal interaction," of which *The Authoritarian Personality* is read as the "outstanding example" (Tajfel & Turner, 2004, p. 276). Tajfel and Turner insinuate that what is stressed in *The Authoritarian Personality* is an individual and interpersonal psychology under the influence of *external* social forces. Likewise, Michael Billig (1991) accuses Adorno of over-psychologizing in the study, yet he recognizes that it is inconsistent with Adorno's other work (p. 126). Condor (1997) suggests that while Adorno et al.'s approach is critical in attempting to use research "as a powerful platform for political

---

[2] It is worth noting that Tuffin's (2005) interpretation of the study is misleading in a number of ways beyond the reduction of social phenomena to individual and interpersonal psychology. Adorno et al. (1950/2019) are primarily concerned with anti-Semitism in the United States where the study was conducted, certainly not an explanation of anti-Semitism in Nazi Germany as Tuffin (2005) suggests. Further, Adorno et al. are not, as is stated, looking to account for prejudice by way of authoritarianism. It would be more appropriate to say that they were trying to account for authoritarianism by way of prejudice, but even that would be an exaggeration. Brunner (1994) points out that the F-Scale (the primary measure of authoritarian personality) is related to authoritarianism through a series of correlations: prejudice and fascism, fascism and anti-democratic sentiment, and anti-democratic sentiment with authoritarianism (p. 635).

intervention," they succumb to the uncritical role as expert authorities from within the discipline of psychology (p. 112). To this, she opposes contemporary critical psychology's attempt to "point to (social) psychology's ideological grounding and its role in social regulation (Condor, 1997, p. 112).

The concerns raised in critical assessments of Adorno et al.'s study are important but impotent: They take the act of conducting research as political and even constitutive of social reality, and they question the nature of psychological and social phenomena. Yet, these are concerns that Adorno also shares, and I will show how he addressed them throughout his work. One notable exception to this trend in the scholarship comes from Frosh (1989) who gives a generous reading of Adorno et al. (1950/2019) and Adorno's contributions to psychology and psychoanalysis more generally:

> What *The Authoritarian Personality* achieves in an unsurpassed way, is to convey the intimacy of the link between those social processes that make modernity such an unnerving experience, and the viciously defensive enclosure that is the racist response. (Frosh, 1989, p. 236)

I have attempted to develop proteophobia as a framework along the lines of this defensive enclosure.

Dialectic of The Authoritarian Personality

Adorno was openly discontented with the empirico-psychological research methods employed in *The Authoritarian Personality* and the very concept of individual personality as an explanatory construction. However, his critical reflections, "Remarks on *The Authoritarian Personality*," were not published in the original version of the study, as Adorno had intended them to be. Some mystery surrounds this retraction, but it is not hard to imagine that the *Remarks* may have threatened the philosophical foundations of psychology employed in the study, as others have similarly speculated (see Gordon, 2019, p. xxxiv). Assuming that Adorno's co-authors, all professional psychologists, were implicated in denying Adorno (a philosopher above all else) this chapter, we can certainly account for some of the typical readings of *The Authoritarian Personality* as arising from the inner tensions between the authors and the subsequent absence of Adorno's own discussion of the findings only now widely available in his *Remarks*. In this section, I look to Adorno's *Remarks* in order to re-situate *The Authoritarian Personality* in the midst of his more critical and negatively dialectical projects.

Adorno's negative dialectic stands in resistance to the dialectical processes of system-building philosophies. Adorno maintains that opposing forces, contradicting concepts, and contradictions within concepts cannot be reconciled into a higher synthesis without becoming untrue. Adorno shows that the persistence of the non-identical moment of opposing tendencies haunts every moment of identity; hence, the irrational impurity that haunts rationality, and as I will explain below, the identity of psychology haunted by the non-identity of negative psychology.

Adorno is well aware that *The Authoritarian Personality*, as a psychological study, seems to neglect his Marxist commitments—it is not looking at the economic or historical factors but only what Adorno (1948/2019) calls the "subjective aspect" (p. xlii; see also Adorno et al., 1950/2019, p. 972). "Psychology in its proper sense," for Frankfurt School theorists like Adorno, "is always psychology of the individual" (Horkheimer, as cited in Jay, 1996, p. 102). *The Authoritarian Personality* sets out to "analyze the type of person…whose general psychological disposition makes him a potential follower of totalitarian movements and bigoted ideologies" (Adorno, 1948/2019, p. xliv). Yet, the sources of authoritarianism, according to Adorno, are not themselves psychological but social. Therefore, he considers the study to be simply "in the realm of 'reaction,' not of stimuli" (Adorno, 1948/2019, p. xlii). *The Authoritarian Personality* cannot *explain* authoritarianism or anti-Semitism psychologically, despite being read as attempting to do just that (e.g., Tuffin, 2005).

What, then, is the study doing? It is looking for the *subject* of authoritarianism. And, according to Adorno, the psychological subject is ineliminable from, but not the answer to, questions of social process, especially where the concept of the psychological contradicts itself and reaches a limit. For instance, individuals who score high in the measure for authoritarian personality are found to be, disturbingly, better adjusted to the status quo of American individualism due in part to those very authoritarian characteristics (e.g., submission to outside power and homogeneity) than lower-scoring individuals (Adorno 1948/2019, p. xlii). According to Adorno's own interpretation, *The Authoritarian Personality* finds that "high-scoring subjects do not seem to behave as autonomous units whose decisions are important for their own fate as well as that of society, but rather as submissive centers of reaction" (Adorno, 1948/2019, p. xlii). He finds a contradiction inherent in the concept of psychology as the "subjective aspect," inching his readers toward an immanent critique—a critique of a concept from within the logic of that same concept. American individualism, exemplified by the logic of psychology as the unit of autonomous choice and freedom, is contradicted by the findings which show that heteronomy (i.e., subjection to an outside authority) is experienced as psychological autonomy.

Adorno et al. (1950/2019) conclude the study clearly stating that they are "strictly limited to psychological aspects of the more general problem of prejudice" not an explanation for social phenomena (p. 972). They offer some psychological coordinates of a subject susceptible to joining a fascist movement. But psychological factors must be seen as surface manifestations of processes *yet to be explored*; in Adorno's thinking, they must be explained socially. Anti-Semitism, for instance, is due in part to social and economic factors. Envy may "cause" anti-Semitism, but it is not envy of the Jewish person, per se. Jewishness replaces the object in the larger social processes. The envy translated as prejudice toward Jews is not a psychological factor that is "inside" the anti-Semite, rather, "it is the realm of ideology in which unconscious psychological processes seem to transform objective and therefore opaque, 'unconscious' economic laws into individual patterns of behavior" (Adorno, 1948/2019, p. liii).[3]

---

[3] Anti-Semitism is beyond an individual's conscious animosity toward Jews *regardless* of whether this hostility is conscious or not. Ideological and unconscious factors have a hold on the anti-Semite, regardless of the reality of Jewish characteristics or conscious animosity. The figure of the Jew becomes, as Žižek (1992/2009) puts it, "a way to stitch up the inconsistency of our own ideological system" (p. 49), and I would add, an inconsistency tied to a proteophobic reaction. Anti-Semitism, in this light, functions in a symbolic system above and beyond Judeophobia or prejudice. There would be less cognitive dissonance if there is an alignment of conscious and unconscious anti-Semitism, anti-Semitism and Judeophobia, or accuracy in anti-Semitic stereotypes, but such

Ultimately, social factors may be felt psychologically without being psychological factors; and that is precisely what *The Authoritarian Personality* uncovers reflexively. In fact, Adorno (1948/2019) considers a psychology of anything like anti-Semitism to be impossible (p. lxii). He suggests that "the psychology of the contemporary anti-Semite in a way presupposes *the end of psychology itself;* for this reason it cannot be adequately described psychologically" (Adorno, 1948/2019, p. lxiv; my italics). But an inadequate psychological description speaks its own truth in failing. Josè Esteban Muñoz (2019) refers to this as "failure worth knowing" (p. 16). And for Adorno, psychoanalytic theory was uniquely poised to expose this insight. He explicitly states that the study is "in full harmony" with orthodox Freudian psychoanalysis (Adorno, 1948/2019, p. xliv). The authors of *The Authoritarian Personality*, according to Adorno (1948/2019), reject any attempt to reconcile the social and the psychological, "to 'sociologize' psychoanalysis through the softening of basic concepts, e.g., the unconscious, infantile sexuality, the psychological dynamism of the monad, by looking for environmental influences which would have to be registered in terms of the ego rather than the unconscious" (p. xlvi).

The rise of authoritarianism demonstrates the disintegration of individuality itself and thus "psychology" as a unified concept. Following developments in psychoanalytic theory, Adorno contends that the ego itself can no longer be seen as capable of any sort of purity or viewed as distinct from the unconscious. If anything, he makes it clear in his *Remarks* that the authoritarian personality amounts to the "failure of individuation" and the foreclosure of what he calls "the individual's own psychological household (Adorno, 1948/2019, p. lxiii). Psychology is marked by its own failure, an immanent critique of psychology that

---

an alignment is hardly necessary for anti-Semitism to function in the symbolic system. As Žižek (1992/2009) notes, an anti-Semite faced with disconfirming evidence or reality testing might say:

'You see how dangerous they really are? It is difficult to recognize their real nature. They hide it behind the mask of everyday appearance—and it is exactly this hiding of one's real nature, this duplicity, that is a basic feature of the Jewish nature.' An ideology really succeeds when even the facts which at first sight contradict it start to function as arguments in its favour. (p. 50)

In other words, there may be a correspondence between what some Jews are like and what anti-Semites fear, or between psychological factors like envy and social ideology, but there could be no correspondence at all. The envy is not *caused* by Jews even if the anti-Semite does envy Jews.

corresponds to a *negative psychology*.[4] In this instance, the qualifier "negative" does not intend that there is nothing to be said in the field of psychology or to be gleaned from *The Authoritarian Personality*. It is after all, *a failure worth knowing*. For Adorno, the most important insight might be just that: The identification with and internalization of a powerful authority mimics the process by which the individual subject comes into being, renouncing instinctual pleasures to enter into a socio-linguistic community—"the mechanisms to which individuals are incessantly subject from without, are to be found in the depth of these same individuals" (Adorno, 1948/2019, p. lxv). The loss of autonomy at the core of authoritarianism mimics the process of individuation or rather its perpetual failure.

Psychoanalysis and the Ends of Psychology

The Ends of Psychology

The following section introduces some psychoanalytic themes and highlights the way that psychoanalysis manifests the negative psychology evoked in Adorno's *Remarks*. However, please note that this is merely a sampling and not a comprehensive survey or account of any of these psychoanalytic themes. In "Freudian Theory and the Pattern of Fascist Propaganda" (1951/1982), Adorno continues the exploration of psychoanalysis where his *Remarks* left off. Adorno analyzes the theory of identification from Freud's *Group Psychology and Analysis of the Ego* (1921/2001a), where contemporary forms of authoritarianism seem to be anticipated. It is here that Adorno makes his most consequential formulations for a negative psychology.

Adorno (1951/1982) finds in Freud's text a theory of the psychological impact of socio-economic factors associated with "the decline of the

---

[4] Hullot-Kentor (2006) refers to this as antipsychological: "[…]what is antipsychological in Adorno's thinking is, paradoxically, not only opposed to psychological reality but also affirms it" (p. 12). I prefer the term "negative psychology" because I think it fits better with the paradox of a failed psychology that affirms the need for psychological study. In *The Melancholy Science*, Gillian Rose (1979) also used the term "negative psychology" with reference to Adorno (p. 106).

individual and his subsequent weakness" amplified in authoritarianism (p. 120). Although Freud wasn't interested in the political causes, per se, he saw that this weakness led to a "willingness to yield unquestioningly to powerful outside, collective agencies" (Adorno, 1951/1982, p. 120). Adorno asks how members of industrial societies, where humans are raised to value rugged individuality above all else, are seduced by the heteronomy of authoritarianism. For Freud, this seduction is tied to an archaic libidinal bond. "Libido" is Freud's term for the pleasure-seeking impulse—much like hunger; however, libido is the quantum of excitation that keeps the baby suckling at the beast long after the baby has satisfied its bodily hunger, and this libidinal surplus (suckling beyond need) led Freud to characterize libido as sexual. Surrender of individuality can, as libidinal, be pleasurable and sexual. It is not that groups revert to an archaic state of nature, but that they bring out libidinal and excessive aspects. Adorno (1951/1982) adds that this aspect is "not simply the re-occurrence of the archaic but its reproduction in and by civilization itself," at once constituting and rebelling against civilization (p. 122). And importantly for Adorno, the id is not alone in its service to the libido; the ego too—that traditionally conscious and transparent psychological mechanism—itself serves the unconscious against the individual and social order. What Adorno is referring to here is the process by which the ego, the rational faculty which promotes self-preservation through the reality principle, is rooted in unconscious libidinal processes which become self-destructive in the embrace of authoritarianism and anti-Semitism. Potential heteronomy is not triggered by an existential alienation of a more genuine humanness (as it might be for Erich Fromm, 1941/1994); it is a byproduct of the sexual process of individuation—a side effect of *becoming* human.

Following Adorno, authoritarianism mobilizes the libidinal processes of identification (complicit in individuation) by way of love that is never at the level of consciousness, produced, one could say, by the perpetual failure of human sexuality to be solely satisfied by its physiological aims. Identification—and the ambivalence involved in identification—is "the *earliest* expression of an emotional tie" (Freud, as cited in Adorno, 1951/1982, p. 125). Narcissistic love for oneself is replaced by the identification with the "great little man" embodied by the leader who is "one of the folks" (Adorno, 1951/1982, p. 127). The likeness that the leader shares with the members of the group leads to this identification, and "the leader image gratifies the follower's twofold wish to submit to authority and to be the authority himself" (Adorno, 1951/1982, p. 127). The authoritarian personality "falls, as it were, negatively in love" (Adorno et al., 1950/2019, p. 611). This archaic mimetic process of imitation explains how heteronomy can appear as autonomy; mimesis, implied by primary identification and exploited by authoritarianism, is both to lose oneself in imitation and also to find oneself in the other's image.

The process amounts to a semblance of the individual. "To be sure, this process has a psychological dimension," Adorno (1951/1982) admits, "but it also indicates a growing tendency toward the abolition of psychological motivation in the old, liberalistic sense" (pp. 135–136).

> When the leaders become conscious of mass psychology and take it into their own hands, [psychology] ceases to exist in a certain sense. This potentiality is contained in the basic construct of psychoanalysis inasmuch as for Freud the concept of psychology is essentially a negative one. He defines the realm of psychology by the supremacy of the unconscious and postulates that what is id should become ego. The emancipation of man from the heteronomous rule of his unconscious would be tantamount to the abolition of his "psychology." (Adorno, 1951/1982, p. 136)

This contradiction in Freudian psychoanalysis, that the "ends" of psychology (e.g., an ego unburdened by repression) are also the "end" of psychology (e.g., the elimination of the very defenses that institute a psychological subject), is not one, according to Adorno, that can or should be reconciled. It is internal to the psyche—the matter-at-hand. Here, Adorno's negative dialectic surfaces: the concept of a psychological subject is always the "bondage of the individual" but it is also the "autonomy of the individual" (Adorno, 1951/1982, p. 136); hence, I offer the term "negative psychology," which conveys a need for psychology even as it, as the concept, becomes non-identical with itself.

Adorno's Negative Dialectics

In the previous sections, I explored problems with relegating *The Authoritarian Personality* to reductionistic psychology and looked to Adorno's own interpretation of the findings to discover a more dialectical psychology that I have, here and there, labeled "negative" following Adorno's reading of psychoanalysis. I suggested that for Adorno, the psychological subject as the egoic agent of reasoning is compromised, and with it the prospect of a psychology that can fully justify its singular province. Yet, Adorno does not conclude that humans are wholly bereft of agency and autonomy. This section binds Adorno's thinking around psychoanalysis to his conception of negative dialectics—an analysis of the contradiction that constitutes the thing conceived. Concepts contain an excess that undermines their own consistency and authority but are necessary for thinking. This becomes a double bind inescapable through the logic, which Adorno associates with "identity thinking" and "the untrue," underlying most conceptions of psychology. Much like the hope for change offered in the psychoanalytic clinic, Adorno's negative dialectics offers hope for resistance to the *status quo* at the level of thought's relationship to the thing conceived.

Dialectics, for Adorno (1967/2004), is a manifestation of the matter-at-hand immanent to the process of thinking and not "a method to be slapped on outwardly" (p. 4).

> The name dialectics says no more, to begin with, than that objects do not go into their concepts without leaving a remainder, that they come to contradict the traditional norm of adequacy. Contradiction […] indicates the untruth of identity. (Adorno, 1967/2004 p. 5)

And yet, he continues, "to think is to identify (Adorno, 1967/2004, p. 5). Therefore, to do justice to the thing conceived, be it the psyche or society, the thinker must think of both the truth and the untruth contained in the concept without reconciliation into a higher synthesis or identity. Adorno does this very thing in his analysis of *The Authoritarian Personality* (1950/2019).

Much like the example of psychology used earlier, society too should be understood in virtue of contradiction, not in spite of it. Society is constituted by the failure immanent to communication, the indeterminacy inherent in language, and by those very things that lead to its destruction (e.g., the sale of weapons, wage labor, etc.) (Adorno, 1965–1966/2008, p. 9). Contradiction is found not just between two concepts (e.g., society and psyche) but also within and immanent to each concept.

Research is itself justified by generally implicit philosophical commitments and ways of thinking. Even philosophy—traditionally regarded as a search for, and study of, first things or apodictic (i.e., proven by the certainty of philosophical logic) foundations—is in peril in the face of unquestioned commitments to begin and end with non-contradiction and identity, as a rule. "If philosophy is still necessary," Adorno (1998) insists, "it is so only […] as critique, as resistance to the expanding heteronomy, if only as thought's powerless attempt to remain its own master and to convict of untruth" (p. 10). Given Adorno's philosophical commitments, anathema to the past and present American empirical research paradigm, it is perfectly contradictory that he is remembered chiefly for his contribution to that paradigm through *The Authoritarian Personality*. Yet, rather than merely comparing Adorno's psychological works with his more sociological ones as some have done (e.g., Billig, 1991), Adorno implores his readers to find constitutive contradictions and ambivalences immanent to each which trouble clear-cut categorizations. Negative dialectics helps us think of negative psychology and against proteophobia. The moral force, as one could put it, of negative dialectics is in withstanding the "consistent sense of nonidentity" (Adorno, 1967/2004, p. 5). Proteophobia, as I have been formulating it in the context of anti-Semitism, is a fear of the sense of this non-identity associated with the Jews.

The Authority of Psychology

In this last section before more practical concluding remarks, I turn to Adorno and Horkheimer's *Dialectic of Enlightenment* (1947/2004). This theoretically sophisticated text acts as a model of sorts for the "negative" approach I am advocating to be taken up by critical psychologists in analyzing anti-Semitism and one that is present in the dialectical aspects of Adorno's work on *The Authoritarian Personality* read through his *Remarks*. It models a way of approaching the matter-at-hand that attempts to do justice to what might be concealed in any investigation—the inevitable unconsciousness of research. One of the main thrusts of the text is the failure of progress narratives. And while this may seem dark and pessimistic, to shy away from it is itself an injustice. This is of particular importance for the science of psychology which still seems to experience itself as a neutral and progressive program.

In the *Dialectic of Enlightenment*, Horkheimer and Adorno (1947/2004) find that there is no escape from the irrationality implicit in the processes of language where an object is subsumed by its concept—the mastery referred to in these opening lines of the book and leading to "triumphant calamity" (p. 1). This mastery, the legacy of enlightenment thinking, is complicit in contemporary authoritarianism and anti-Semitism.

Domination and oppression, as in authoritarianism and anti-Semitism, are intrinsically bound up with reason and rationality. "The mind," Horkheimer and Adorno (1947/2004) insist, "and all that is good in its origins and existence, is hopelessly implicated in this horror" (p. 185). Our rational faculty has given us a weapon to fight violent nature—self-preserving but a weapon, nonetheless. Reason's "ruse consists in making humans into beasts with an ever-wider reach" (Horkheimer & Adorno, 1947/2004, p. 185). Further, the otherness of nature we are armed against is also there in the human. This attempt to dominate and control the otherness of nature is the drive to organize the world with reason's concepts and categories, the adaptive repression of our drive impulses, and the oppression of the powerless.

Authoritarianism is a return of that repressed nature (Horkheimer & Adorno, 1947/2004, p. 218)—what I earlier referred to as the archaic libidinal bond. The more thought is instrumentalized to serve human progressive goals without acknowledgment of its complicity in its opposite (regression), and the more we commit to non-dialectical rationality, the more that rationality becomes domination. "We owe the serum which the doctor administers to the sick child," Horkheimer and Adorno (1947/2004) warn, "to the attack on defenseless creatures" (p. 185). And since this concept, "defenseless creature," like all concepts, contains more than it means, and in this case contains us humans as well, self-preservation is found to be self-destruction, suicidal.

Nature, for civilization, becomes the ultimate danger. Prediction and control of nature through logical enterprise begins with the categorical identification of danger. Yet, in this relation to nature, "without which mind does not exist, enslavement to nature persists" (Horkheimer & Adorno, 1947/2004, p. 31). The progressive striving for self-preservation leads to the return of nature as "crisis and war," the very humanness is inhumanity (Horkheimer & Adorno, 1947/2004, p. 23). Progressive narratives of science and technology (with their totalizing classificatory grids) promise the liberation from violent nature only if we commit to categorizing away irrationality as the ultimate sin (Horkheimer & Adorno, 1947/2004, p. 24). Positivist science and philosophy become a systematic mapping only possible with a non-dialectical approach to irrationality where rationality is identical with itself, and equivocations can be settled apodictically. Domination of nature is the presupposition for the mind and for the reality principle. Horkheimer and Adorno (1947/2004) maintain that "the self's hostility to sacrifice," which gave us the possibility to dominate nature and each other, "included a sacrifice of the self" (p. 42); again, the end(s) of psychology. But Adorno does not advocate for the embrace of an inevitable irrationality. Rather, he advocates for a form of thinking that turns back on itself—negative dialectics and immanent critique.

Jessica Benjamin and Joel Whitebook, both psychoanalysts informed by critical theory, see flaws in Adorno's reading of psychoanalysis worth considering. Benjamin (1977) suggests that Adorno lacks a robust theory of intersubjectivity that would overcome his supposed subject-object dualism (p. 137). Whitebook (1996) rejects Adorno's formulation of the ego and uses the concept of sublimation as a way to "conceptualize nonviolent forms of ego synthesis" (p. 14). These concerns deserve further engagement beyond the scope of this investigation. But in brief, these critiques fail to grasp the rhetorical nature of Adorno's ethics; one where expressions like "the end of psychology" function like an interpretation in the clinic as Lacan (1998) points out, "directed not so much at the meaning as towards reducing the non-meaning" (p. 212) and "to isolate in the subject a kernel…of *non-sense*" (p. 250). We should also note that some theorists reject Adorno's thinking as pessimistic and politically sterile. How, these critics ask, does one fight authoritarianism or anti-Semitism, let alone mental disorder, if the very fight against it may be complicit in it?

Whitebook (2004) contends that negative dialectical commitments undermine all utopian projects, and Adorno and Horkheimer become "imprisoned in a theoretical impasse from which they would never escape" (p. 79). It is true that Adorno's ethical commitment to truth sought through critical reasoning's ability to explore the failure of a concept to subsume its object prevails over his commitment to "the good" which, he would say, must take its mission from the present and oppressive state. This may look like a logical or ethical flaw in Adorno's thinking, but it is precisely what makes it radical—committed to a future impossible to imagine, be it justice for the oppressed or mental health. An alternative taken by Adorno's student Jürgen Habermas, for instance, is to build a philosophical system on a proto-political one based on discursive communication, but one that may inevitably rely on unquestioned axiomatic foundations and normative principles about the possibility of undistorted communication (Whitebook, 2004, p. 91). Instead, Adorno offers resistance to untruth as the hope for humanity, even in the face of "the calamity which reason alone cannot avert" (Horkheimer & Adorno, 1947/2004, p. 187).

Adorno, Psychoanalysis, and the Study of Anti-Semitism

Adorno's under-acknowledged contribution to psychology is a unique way of grappling with difficult issues—issues that still haunt psychology. Yet, it is understandable why these phantoms remain. Adorno's interpretation of the well-known *The Authoritarian Personality* was only available as an unpublished typewritten manuscript until recently, his negative psychology seems to go against our most basic structures of thinking, and it can seem hopelessly pessimistic. But Adorno is not illogical, he insists on taking logic at its word and to its "end." We continue to face crises and contradictions within psychology and from without, of which anti-Semitism is but one, and we need all the help we can get. It may be time to think negatively in psychology.

Nevertheless, some thinkers continue to insist that Adorno's dialectical project leads to conservatism (e.g., Whitebook, 2004, p. 79). It may be true that negative dialectics is not progressively searching for a higher synthesis, but it is certainly not conservative. The commitment to the non-identical is not just a prophylactic but also, what Adorno (1967/2004) calls, a "logic of disintegration" (pp. 144–145). And while Whitebook (2004) may be right to demand that "nothing else will do" but for critical theory to return to psychoanalysis in contemporary struggles against domination (p. 97), what is radical in psychoanalysis is the commitments it shares with negative dialectics (e.g., the non-identical, nonconceptual, unimaginable, uncategorizable), the very things that may, for him, lead to quietism. And although Adorno (1967/2004) was critical of (mainly American) clinical psychoanalysis that receives its "view of normalcy from the existing society" (p. 273; see also Mariotti, 2009), certain spheres of clinical psychoanalysis can be considered negatively dialectical, committed to the ethics of the non-identical in the concept of the unconscious. As we saw in Chap. 3, Stephen Frosh (2005) points to Klein, Lacan, and Laplanche for three examples of such psychoanalytic projects. I expanded on this in Chap. 4.

In Lacanian psychoanalysis, the process of free-association and interpretation are not aimed at understanding or producing meaningful syntheses, as they are elsewhere in psychoanalysis. Rather, they expose the analysand to the untruth of identifying with the ego's narratives. The patient's speech is returned by the analyst in an "inverted form" that exposes the non-identity of speech with its meaning, not unlike the concept with its object; "I am deceiving you" could be returned as "you are telling the truth" (Lacan, 1998, pp. 139–140), or indeed with a punctuating silence. In this form, one that might have altered Adorno's view of clinical psychoanalysis (at least a little) if he was properly exposed, psychoanalytic technique follows the unconscious excess—the non-identity—contained in the patient's speech, which alone holds the prospect of something new or unimaginable appearing. Translation of the analysand's speech or dream material into something understandable, Laplanche (1996) formulates "is always at the same time the failure of translation—that is, repression, the constitution of the unconscious from what translation deposits as waste" (p. 11). Although the ethical effect of interpretation may isolate the analysand's *non-sense*, interpretation is not itself nonsense (Lacan, 1998, p. 250), and likewise, negative psychology may isolate the kernel of non-sense, non-identity, and non-categorizable in the psychological subject, as Adorno discovered, without reducing psychology to something positive or to nonsense.

Further, as an impossible profession (Freud, 1937/2001b, p. 248), psychoanalysis may offer a model for change that contends with issues raised by negative psychology. Yet, Whitebook (2004) is not quite right to only emphasize the need for psychoanalysis. Freud recognizes that education and governing are also impossible professions. Lacan later added scientific research to that list (Zwart, 2018, p. 21). Adorno takes up a rhetorical approach to education and research where he can inspire critical thinking that is not cut off from the nonconceptual; an impossible task, but one we might, as a field, learn from. It is the impossibility in each of those professions, perhaps the constitutive failure of each, that offers hope for a future yet to be imagined or conceptualized. In my clinical practice, I am often guided by the idea that we cannot imagine what change will look like, it might even be impossible, but the impossible can be actualized in the very interminable resistance to untruth.

Negative psychology can be read as a way of constellating the psychoanalytic approaches to otherness gestured toward by Stephen Frosh

(2005) as a requirement for a psychoanalytic theory capable of thinking rigorously about anti-Semitism; one that is not merely psychological or merely sociological or a combination of the two. We have seen that Adorno's psychoanalysis as negative psychology is precisely that, prefigures later developments in psychoanalysis, and is developed in relation to anti-Semitism, no less. In the next chapter, I expand on Adorno's theory of anti-Semitism, returning to the *Dialectic of Enlightenment* and reflecting on the implications of that theory for psychoanalysis, politics, and education.

References

Adorno, T. W. (1982). Freudian theory and the pattern of fascist propaganda. In A. Arato & E. Gephardt (Eds.), *The essential Frankfurt School reader* (pp. 118–137). Continuum. (Original work published 1951)

Adorno, T. W. (1998). *Critical models* (H. W. Pickford, Trans.). Columbia University Press.

Adorno, T.W. (2004). *Negative dialectic* (E. B. Ashton, Trans.). Routledge. (Original work published 1967)

Adorno, T. W. (2005). *Minima moralia: Reflections from damaged life.* Verso. (Original work published in 1951)

Adorno, T. W. (2008). *Lectures on negative dialectics: Fragments of a lecture course 1965/1966* (R. Tiedemann, Ed. & R. Livingston, Trans.). Polity.

Adorno, T. W. (2019). Remarks on the authoritarian personality. In T. W. Adorno, E. Frenkel-Brunswik, D. J. Levinson, & R. N. Sanford (Authors), *The authoritarian personality* (pp. xli-lxvi). Verso. (Original work drafted 1948)

Adorno, T. W., Frenkel-Brunswik, E., Levinson, D. J., & Sanford, R. N. (2019). *The authoritarian personality.* Verso. (Original work published 1950)

Benjamin, J. (1977). The end of internalization: Adorno's social psychology. *Telos, 32*, 42–64. https://doi.org/10.3817/0677032042

Billig, M. (1991). *Ideology and opinions: Studies in rhetorical psychology.* Sage Publications.

Bloch, B. (2019). The origins of Adorno's psycho-social dialectic: Psychoanalysis and neo Kantianism in the young Adorno. *Modern Intellectual History, 16*(2), 501–529. https://doi.org/10.1017/S147924431700049X

Brunner, J. (1994). Looking into the heart of the workers, or: How Erich Fromm turned critical theory into empirical research. *Political Psychology, 15*(4), 631–654. https://doi.org/10.2307/3791624

Condor, S. (1997). And so say all of us?: Some thoughts on 'experiential democratization' as an aim for critical social psychologists. In T. Ibáñez & L. Íñiguez (Eds.), *Critical social psychology* (pp. 111–146). Sage. https://doi.org/10.4135/9781446279199.n8

Freud, S. (2001a). Group psychology and the analysis of the ego. In J. Strachey (Ed. & Trans.), *The standard edition of the complete psychological works of Sigmund Freud, volume XVIII (1920–1922)* (pp. 65–143). Vintage. (Original work published 1921)

Freud, S. (2001b). Analysis terminable and interminable. In Strachey, J. (Ed. & Trans.) *The standard edition of the complete psychological works of Sigmund Freud: Volume XXIII (1937–1939)* (pp. 209–253). Vintage Books. (Original work published 1937)

Fromm, E. (1994). *Escape from freedom.* Holt. (Original work published 1941)

Frosh, S. (1989). *Psychoanalysis and psychology: Minding the gap.* Macmillan.

Frosh, S. (2005). *Hate and the 'Jewish Science': Anti-Semitism, Nazism and psychoanalysis.* Palgrave Macmillan.

Gordon, P. E. (2019). Introduction by Peter E. Gordon. In T. W. Adorno, E. Frenkel-Brunswik, D. J. Levinson, & N. Sanford (Authors), *The authoritarian personality* (pp. xiii–xl). Verso.

Gough, B. (Ed.). (2017). *The Palgrave handbook of critical social psychology.* Palgrave Macmillan. https://doi.org/10.1057/978-1-137-51018-1

Horkheimer, M., & Adorno, T. W. (2004). *Dialectic of enlightenment: Philosophical fragments* (G. S. Noerr, Ed. & E. Jephcott, Trans.). Stanford. (Original work published 1947)

Hullot-Kentor, R. (2006). *Things beyond resemblance: Collected essays on Theodor W. Adorno.* Columbia University Press.

Ibáñez, T., & Íñiguez, L. (Eds.). (1997). *Critical social psychology.* Sage. https://doi.org/10.4135/9781446279199

Jay, M. (1996). *The dialectical imagination: A history of the Frankfurt School and the Institute of Social Research, 1923–1950.* University of California Press. (Original work published 1976)

Lacan, J. (1998). *The seminars of Jacques Lacan book XI: The four fundamental concepts of psychoanalysis* (J. A. Miller, Ed. & A. Sheridan, Trans.). Norton.

Laplanche, J. (1996). Psychoanalysis as anti-hermeneutics (L. Thurston, Trans.). *Radical Philosophy, 79*(12), 7–12. https://www.radicalphilosophy.com/article/psychoanalysis-as-anti-hermeneutics

Mariotti, S. (2009). Damaged life as exuberant vitality in America: Adorno, alienation, and the psychic economy. *Telos, 149*, 169–190. https://doi.org/10.3817/1209149169

Morss, J. R. (1995). *Growing critical: Alternatives to developmental psychology.* Routledge. https://doi.org/10.4324/9780203130797

Parker, I. (Ed.). (2015). *Handbook of critical psychology.* Routledge.

Rogers, W. S. (2003). *Social psychology: Experimental and critical approaches.* Open University Press.

Rose, G. (1979). *The melancholy science.* Verso.

Sloan, T. (1995). *Damaged life: The crisis of the modern psyche.* Routledge. https://doi.org/10.4324/9780203407295

Tajfel, H., & Turner, J. C. (2004). The social identity theory of inter-group behavior. In J. T. Jost & J. Sidanius (Eds.), *Political psychology: Key readings* (pp. 276–293). Psychology Press. https://doi.org/10.4324/9780203505984-16

Teo, T. (Ed.). (2014). *Encyclopedia of critical psychology.* Springer.

Tuffin, K. (2005). *Understanding critical social psychology.* Sage. https://doi.org/10.4135/9781446217566

Walkerdine, V. (Ed.). (2002). *Challenging subjects: Critical psychology for a new millennium.* Palgrave.

Whitebook, J. (1996). *Perversion and utopia: A study psychoanalysis and critical theory.* MIT Press.

Whitebook, J. (2004). The marriage of Marx and Freud: Critical theory and psychoanalysis. In F. Rush (Ed.), *The Cambridge companion to critical theory* (pp. 74–102). Cambridge University Press. https://doi.org/10.1017/CCOL0521816602

Žižek, S. (2009). *Sublime object of Ideology.* Verso. (Original work published 1992)

Zwart, H. (2018). *Tales of research misconduct: A Lacanian diagnostics of integrity challenges in science novels.* Springer Open. https://doi.org/10.1007/978-3-319-65554-3

6

A Critical Theory of Anti-Semitism

Horkheimer and Adorno's Analysis of Anti-Semitism[1]

In the *Dialectic of Enlightenment* (1947/2004), Horkheimer and Adorno articulated a renewed critical project for theory; one meant to contend with a crisis in the social world resulting from contradictions in science and philosophy. They trace this crisis to the instrumentalization of reason, as exemplified by the totalizing social forces that turn the autonomous and reasoning individual against itself (Stalinism, late capitalism, anti-Semitism, etc.). The last chapter in the *Dialectic of Enlightenment*, entitled "Elements of Anti-Semitism: Limit of Enlightenment," is a psychoanalytic examination of this crisis as it relates to the logic of anti-Semitism. Paradoxically, the irrationalism that permeates modern anti-Semitism is deemed to be consistent with enlightenment rationality, formulated as the mastery of the unknown through exchangeability and categorization leading to ever more accurate prediction and control.

---

[1] Part of Chap. 6 was first published in 2022 as "Critical theory of anti-Semitism: Implications for politics, education, and Psychoanalysis." In D. Burston & J. Mills (Eds.). *Critical Theory and Psychoanalysis*. Routledge. It is reproduced with permission of the licensor through PLSclear.

© The Author(s), under exclusive license to Springer Nature Switzerland AG 2024
B. B. Strosberg, *Anti-Semitism at the Limit*, Studies in the Psychosocial,
https://doi.org/10.1007/978-3-031-72025-3_6

Ostensible solutions to the problem of anti-Semitism which appeal to that logic (e.g., assimilation, nationalism, reality testing) either fail abjectly or even seem to make the problem worse. Horkheimer and Adorno suggest that anti-Semitism is not merely a matter of psychological prejudice but also the collective hate for the negative principle which resists the totalizing social force of objectifying categorization. The negative principle is unbearable within what has become a totalized social order reproducing itself above the heads of individuals. Individual actors need not (and perhaps cannot) be aware of the workings of the social totality as they participate in it. The negative principle is projected onto the Jews who represent, for the anti-Semite, malignant disruptors of total social cohesion and order. As such, the Jew becomes the unassimilable and uncategorizable representative of otherness, akin to the uncanny (Freud, 1919/2001c) or the return of the repressed (Freud, 1915/2001b), haunting the seemingly unified psyche and society as a symptom that challenges the wholeness the individual comes to identify with. Resistance to anti-Semitism, Horkheimer and Adorno insist, must address these social issues.

Horkheimer and Adorno's (1947/2004) approach construes anti-Semitism as the limit of enlightenment rationality and exposes the contradictions and conflicts that define the psychological domain of thought itself. While their reference to "enlightenment" rationality could lead some readers to believe that this formulation of anti-Semitism only refers to modern forms like Nazi anti-Semitism, Horkheimer and Adorno argue throughout the *Dialectic of Enlightenment* that the seeds of enlightenment thinking are present before the seventeenth- and eighteenth-century European Enlightenment in the ways that humans, even then, made equivalences for the sake of prediction and control (e.g., sacrifices to the gods or the telling of myths). The Enlightenment, which started as a project of liberation and progress, led to the totalization of these processes, and thus became regressive and oppressive to the elements of difference and negativity challenging its harmonious logic. Philosophy and science—remaining faithful to the progress of reason initiated by the Enlightenment—are unable to contend with the contradiction of a "wholly enlightened earth [...] radiant with triumphant calamity" (Horkheimer & Adorno, 1947/2004, p. 1).

In this chapter, I explore how Horkheimer and Adorno (1947/2004) renew the critical aims of philosophy in response to that calamity and the contradictory logic of anti-Semitism. They offer a dialectic of, by, and through reason with the help of what I understand to be the negative moment emphasized in psychoanalysis. Psychoanalytic theory seems to offer the authors a way to think about (and potentially resist) anti-Semitism without recourse to positive formulations of progress that might demand the elimination of conflict, contradiction, or ambivalence. As I proposed in the previous chapter, this negative dialectical project remains an ethical way of thinking about anti-Semitism and proteophobia. I conclude the chapter with a brief analysis of the continued relevance (and misuses) of this critical psychoanalytic approach—born from the study of anti-Semitism—for politics, education, and clinical work.

The Difficulty in Thinking About Anti-Semitism

As I have shown, the inherent difficulty in thinking about anti-Semitism clearly presents a major obstacle to uprooting it and its violent manifestations. Here are several questions that demonstrate this difficulty: Are Jews "White"? Is anti-Zionism anti-Semitic? Is Zionism racist? Why has it been so difficult for Jews to assimilate? Is anti-Semitism a social-structural phenomenon (like systemic racism) or merely one more instance of a petty religious or ethnic prejudice? Would anti-Semitic violence really subside if Jews and Palestinians were given a secure homeland and religious freedom? The complexity of the problem is evident in Horkheimer and Adorno's (1947/2004) assessment of anti-Semitism as the historically contingent result of collective hatred for an ineradicable negative (and constituting) principle within society. The negative, as a principle, is an important aspect *of* thinking because, to put it crudely, it allows us to distinguish between what something is and what it is not. Anti-Semitism marks the very limits of rational and categorical thinking itself. For example, Horkheimer and Adorno (1947/2004) suggest that there are two primary doctrines for categorizing Jews, one as a race or "antirace" and the other with pure religious belief (p. 137). They suggest that both of these doctrines are simultaneously true and false. In order to fight anti-Semitism, it is important to start by acknowledging the complexity of the problem, rather than trying to simplify it to make the problem go away, which will only result in an eventual return of the repressed. Psychoanalysis has provided critical theory with a model for thinking about such problems, where the problems are bound up with the difficulty in thinking; and "think we must."

Anti-Semitism and Psychoanalytic Thinking

The exodus of German-Jewish intellectuals from Germany after the rise of Nazism in 1933 marked a turning point in the academic study of anti-Semitism (Burston, 2014). Many of these scholars looked to psychoanalytic theory for their investigations, following in Freud's footsteps. In some ways, Erich Fromm (1900–1980) also paved the way for these studies with his early work on authoritarianism among blue-collar workers in the Weimar Republic (Fromm, 1984). However, theorists after Fromm suggested that looking to psychology for answers to social questions is a mistake (e.g., Fenichel, 1940), but concede that a psychology of anti-Semitism can at least illuminate one side of the problem. For example, many of the scholars in Ernst Simmel's 1946 edited volume on psychology and anti-Semitism, affirmed that anti-Semitism is rooted in the unconscious (e.g., Allport, 1946). Simmel's (1946) volume included essays from Adorno, Horkheimer, and Fenichel as well as Frenkel-Brunswik and Sanford, with whom Adorno would co-author *The Authoritarian Personality* (Adorno et al., 1950/2019).

As I pointed out in my excursus on negative psychology, Adorno came to the paradoxical conclusion that psychology is an important domain for the investigation of anti-Semitism even though he rejected the notion of a "psychology of anti-Semitism" (Adorno, 1948/2019, p. lxii). In fact, I showed how *The Authoritarian Personality* and Adorno's groundwork with Horkheimer on anti-Semitism can be read as a critique of psychology (formulated as the study of the individual subject) that emphasizes the way the psychological investigation of anti-Semitism undermines the logic of its own subject (an immanent critique). Again, Adorno (1948/2019) suggests that the failure of individuation found in the psychoanalytically informed authoritarian study is the disintegration of the concept of a psychological subject. Here, in this passage from the end of the *Dialectic of Enlightenment* (1947/2004), is another way of formulating this immanent critique:

> In the autonomy and uniqueness of the individual, the resistance to the blind, repressive power of the irrational whole was crystallized. But that resistance was made historically possible only by the blindness and irrationality of the autonomous and unique individual. (p. 200)

I called this theory "negative psychology" to characterize the investigation of how psychology dialectically becomes its opposite, namely that psychoanalysis shows the contradictory nature of the psychological subject who is not self-identical and who is constituted by the failed aims of wholeness and integration. Rensmann (2017) points out that for Adorno, this dialectical work was implicitly operating within psychoanalysis without detection by Freud, the steadfast enlightenment thinker (p. 48).[2] Psychoanalysis provides critical theory with the concepts to think contradictions such as "judgment without judging" and "perceiving without a perceiver" in thinking without criticality (i.e., instrumental rationality). Emphasizing these aspects of the psychological subject, "[Horkheimer and Adorno] attempt to show how reason, having regressed to instrumental rationality, has combined in the present era with the domination of nature and social control to form a quasi-mythical compulsion" (Noerr, 2004, p. 232). This compulsion is embodied in anti-Semitism.

Other critics of Adorno et al.'s *The Authoritarian Personality* (1950/2019) and Adorno's theory of anti-Semitism more broadly, suggest that its authors focused on right-wing anti-Semitism without

---

[2] There has been much debate on the topic of whether Freud's work aligns more with the ideals of the Enlightenment or with those of the Counter-Enlightenment. However, I believe that the challenge in categorizing Freud's work in such a binary manner highlights the productive tensions that he opened up in his theories. On the one hand, Freud's emphasis on reason and his belief in the power of scientific inquiry align with Enlightenment ideals. He sought to uncover hidden motivations and unconscious desires in human behavior, and his approach was grounded in a systematic study of the human psyche. On the other hand, Freud's work also challenges certain Enlightenment assumptions, such as the notion that human beings are inherently rational and capable of achieving self-awareness. Instead, Freud's theories suggest that much of our behavior is driven by unconscious forces that are beyond the control of the classical subject of liberal democracy.

addressing the persistence of left-wing anti-Semitism, possibly for political reasons (Burston, 2014). It is worth noting that contemporary anti-Semitism is far more prevalent on the right than on the left, especially in overt forms (Hersh & Royden, 2023). Regardless, this critique misses an important aspect of the study and its theoretical underpinnings. In the study, conservatism and religiosity are found to be highly correlated with authoritarianism by way of anti-Semitism. These characteristics are easily mapped onto right-wing politics owing to the conservatism of right-wing parties. And yet, the left *as a ticket* can be just as conservative. There is evidence for this interpretation in the groundwork laid out in the *Dialectic of Enlightenment* (1947/2004). There, anti-Semitism is conceptualized as a structural issue in human reasoning that crisscrosses political allegiances. Anti-Semitism is found in the issue of "ticket mentality itself" on both the left and right (Horkheimer & Adorno, 1947/2004, p. 172). *Ticket mentality*, here, refers to the endorsement of a political party or social platform which always requires overly broad generalizations and approximations. For instance, people vote for the democratic *ticket*, the republican *ticket*, the progressive *ticket*, a centrist *ticket*, the fascist *ticket*. "To vote for a ticket," Horkheimer and Adorno (1947/2004) argue, "means to practice adaptation to illusion petrified as reality" (p. 170). And importantly, they are not just referring to electoral voting procedures but also, rather, suggesting that thinking about social issues has, itself, become a process of adopting an ideology, ticket, or identity instead of thinking. Ticket thinking, or identity thinking as such, is always a form of petrification or rigidity that conserves something of the status quo. So-called progressives are no less an enemy of thinking-otherwise when pre-established categories if their thinking becomes fixed and conservative as a progressive *ticket*.[3]

---

[3] There is an interesting dialectical tension here in the idea of ticket mentality. As Leswin Laubscher (personal correspondence, 2023) has pointed out to me, voting for a ticket can be a form of voting against mere self-interest and in service of others and for the common good—a process tied to political responsibility and even ethics in general. I agree. And yet, I think what Horkheimer and Adorno (2004) are getting at, here, is that even though voting is an ethical act against oneself and for others and a necessary component of freedom and democracy, even so, it is also a vote for what includes more than what we have bargained for or can reasonably think through. For instance, say I believe in workers' rights, so I vote for the American Democratic Party. With that vote comes a whole lot of other stuff—a whole platform of stuff that will certainly morph later on—including,

Dialectic of Enlightenment Thinking

In the *Dialectic of Enlightenment* (1947/2004), the authors purport to trace the genealogy of the psychological subject ending in the psychoanalysis of anti-Semitism. According to Horkheimer and Adorno's (1947/2004) genealogical reflections, the human subject fighting for survival seems to have transitioned from animism to the enlightened subject of science and philosophy, intermediated by mimetic ritual practices and early mythical thinking. They insist that the thinking subject is in a crisis of its own making:

The human being's mastery of itself, on which the self is founded, practically always involves the annihilation of the subject in whose service that mastery is maintained, because the substance which is mastered, suppressed, and disintegrated by self-preservation is nothing other than the living entity, of which the achievements of self-preservation can only be defined as functions—in other words, self-preservation destroys the very thing which is to be preserved. (Horkheimer & Adorno, 1947/2004, p. 43)

Modern forms of science and technology, which are designed to control and master nature's forces, mimic the drive toward self-preservation. However, this growing mastery and control of nature's forces has also brought about the growing objectification of humanity and the dominance of instrumental reason over critical reason. This is due to the totalizing processes of exchangeability, categorizability, and synthesis on which science and philosophy have been premised. But this is not just a function of science or philosophy as institutions; the drive toward categorization is found to be the very process defining the psychological subject.

---

today, support for an oppressive Israeli government, (to name just one example). This is what was the case with some anti-Semitic parties in the 1930s and sadly with some candidates today. Some voters weren't "anti-Semitic" but voted for a party with an anti-Semitic plank in its platform. Moreover, even a party with every plank checked for the termite damage of hate and self-centeredness will not protect from the inevitable contradiction of representative governance and hiring another to do the thinking. Ticket mentality, then, is a form of instrumental reasoning that mimics this model of adopting a platform or ideology or having others think for us. We can then ask, if ticket mentality is inevitable in a democracy, perhaps even a precondition, what then?

Science and philosophy are rooted in the domination of nature. Nature, here, consists in particular differences that resist conceptual generalization *and* that force of sameness which drives humans toward processes of identification. The particularities that are stripped away in order to make things identifiable for the human subject (objectifiable and universally exchangeable) in their *genera* return as the unconscious remainder of (and in) each concept. The generalization, approximation, and abstraction utilized by enlightenment science and philosophy perform the role that myth once played for civilization in the explanation and prediction of nature. The general concepts of human thought objectify nature through a mediating distance between the concepts used to think with and the "things of nature" intuited by the senses and identified by the concepts. Myth was already a way to understand nature in order to predict and control its cycles at a distance. Accordingly, Horkheimer and Adorno (1947/2004) claim that "[t]he myths which fell victim to the Enlightenment were themselves its products" (p. 5). Myths were already scientific (as attempts to master nature), and science, which seeks to eradicate myth, is also mythical (in its totalization, telling of origins, projecting human properties onto nature). However, where science becomes mythical, the elements of particularity found in the early mimetic forms of human thinking are missing.

What are the particularities found in early forms of mimetic mythical thinking that Horkheimer and Adorno (1947/2004) suggest are missing from mythical modern science? First of all, mimesis can be defined as *direct* representation without the distance provided by general concepts and linguistic signification. Words and concepts refer *to* something at a distance beyond the word or concept itself so as to identify the nonidentical. The directness of mimesis, on the other hand, is related to the particularity of each representation, much like how a proper name refers to a particular person. To preserve themselves, humans learned to mimic their surroundings through direct representation. This was a form of control that was not yet cognitively centralized, though magical ritual was the attempt to harness that power of the mimetic directness between the human and the thing in the natural environment. In other words, the human adapted to the danger of the environment through a form of directness or camouflage such as dressing as an animal, invoking (or not invoking) the name of an animal to make it present or absent, or even ritual sacrifice. This is not an embodiment of a generalized exemplar of *an* animal but a re-presentation of *the* animal. An example of this process, referred to as taboo deformation, is the word "bear," which is commonly understood to be a euphemism for the original name for *the* bear, and etymologically comes from the word "brown." Such deformations are adopted out of fear of the mimetic directness between the name and the thing.

Yet, in the move from myth as science to science as myth, the sacrificed laboratory animal becomes the scientific exemplar stripped of its unique qualities and any contact between the animal and what it represents (Horkheimer & Adorno, 1947/2004, p. 7). The particularity of mimetic practices (magic or cultic ritual) once allowed for the direct representation of *this* sacrificial animal, *this* process. The universal generalizations and approximations of science lead to exactitude but repress particularity. Horkheimer and Adorno (1947/2004) propose that the critical analysis of this historical process might expose the logic of domination which is *in* science (as the totalizing process of ordering and classification) but also hidden *from* science. Such exposure, it is wagered, could counteract the effects of that repression, or at least keep from redoubling repression.[4]

The *Dialectic of Enlightenment* explores, performatively, the way that concepts change historically (and ambiguously) into their opposites. The new dialectical project established by the authors is a kind of psychoanalytic philosophy emphasizing the unconscious dimensions of concepts as they are employed. Through false equivalences like that of

---

[4] According to some observers, the style and form through which knowledge and verification are expressed in the *Dialectic of Enlightenment* (1947/2004) transform its content. For example, D'Arcy (2020) suggests that Horkheimer and Adorno's generalizations about myth, mimesis, and science can be understood as the performance of the same processes that are under investigation. According to D'Arcy the form of presentation in the *Dialectic of Enlightenment* is a performance of mythic narrative akin to the epic of Homer; it tells of myths and their transformations, but is, itself, an epic. Horkheimer and Adorno (1947/2004) retell the mythical origin story of the subject (as Odysseus and as the scientist) but in the form of an epic intimately linked to the particularity of their social moment (i.e., the subject as anti-Semite, fascist subject, concentration camp commandant). How is the presentation of science as myth different from the way science presents itself? D'Arcy (2020) answers that it is "just what distinguishes epic from myth, a dimension of parody or stylization in the modus operandi of the text" which requires "the ability to recognize and think through the ambiguity of language" (p. 55).

economic exchange, reason becomes unreason, psychology as the study of the individual thinking subject becomes the study of the failure of individuation, and the drive toward self-preservation becomes indistinguishable from self-destruction. Perhaps the chapter on anti-Semitism in the *Dialectic of Enlightenment*, as the limits of enlightenment, needs to be read as just such a performance, and not merely a systematic philosophical explanation for anti-Semitism. As I mentioned above, those who read it in the latter sense may be disappointed to find more contradictions and questions than answers. And perhaps this is what is so acute about its contents.

It is the purpose of this rereading of the *Dialectic of Enlightenment* (1947/2004) to demonstrate how the dialectic of enlightenment thinking, which I understand to be a kind of psychoanalytic thinking in this context of anti-Semitism explored in the next section, remains relevant for critical thinking beyond the status quo in both critical theory and psychoanalysis.

Anti-Semitism and the Limits of Enlightenment

In this section, I explore Horkheimer and Adorno's (1947/2004) psychoanalytically informed perspective on anti-Semitism as the limit of enlightenment rationality characterized by the drive toward sameness through the domination of nature and instrumental thinking. This drive toward sameness, categorization, and exchangeability produces the modern psychological subject while secretly promoting its downfall. Manifestations of anti-Semitism stem from the compulsion to destroy the ambivalence and otherness which persists in defiance of the totalizing force of the drive toward sameness. This compulsion is proteophobic. Anti-Semitism, as we have seen, has become rooted in the unconscious and marked by the projection of what is ambivalently both desired and feared onto the social other (a role historically played by the diasporic Jew). Science and philosophy (complicit in the drive toward sameness) become incapable of correcting for the violence perpetrated against ambivalence and otherness—hence the subtitle of Horkheimer and Adorno's (1947/2004) chapter "limits of enlightenment." Simultaneously, the loss of that otherness would be the loss of subjectivity, which is established through social conflict with that other. Psychoanalysis, with its emphasis on the negative principle (Freud, 1925/2001e), offers conceptual tools (e.g., the unconscious, the uncanny, projection, phobia) for analyzing the contradictory drives and for mounting a defense against anti-Semitism formulated as hate for that same negative principle and fear of the uncategorizable.

Jewishness as the Negative Principle

The historically Christian and liberal answer to the question of Jewish particularity proposes assimilation into an already existing unity through conversion or secularization; policies aimed at smoothing over differences. But assimilation, as the stripping of particularity, always fails to be completed since assimilation is always a historical process which bestows a new particularity (the Jewish convert or the secular Jew). Think here of the double bind experienced by European Jewry around the eighteenth century: Jews were persecuted if they did not assimilate, and assimilated Jews were (and continue to be) accused of undermining core modern principles of nationalism and universalism.

Horkheimer and Adorno (1947/2004) assert that "for the fascists the Jews are not a minority but the antirace, the negative principle as such; on their extermination the world's happiness depends" (p. 137). Heidegger, for instance, considered Jewish rootlessness as a dangerous and total "deracialization," evoking an earlier pre-biological and spiritual form of racial thinking (Wolin, 2023). In this form of anti-Semitism, Jews play the role of the negative principle necessary for the positivity of self-identification. The Jewish negative principle is the negative within the positive itself, exposing the imposture of the positive. In other words, the Jews come to stand (as the unassimilable and uncategorizable) for the failure of social cohesion of the national collective while at the same time defining the boundary of that collective. The destruction of the Jews, as the destruction of the negative principle, would therefore spell the death of the identity of the ingroup. For the Nazis (and their contemporary counterparts) the negative principle cannot be synthesized by way of assimilation, pushed to the outside through nationhood, nor destroyed; hence the fantasy of total erasure manifested in the Final Solution.

In the anti-Semitic imaginary, the Jew is a malevolent agent, an outsider who ruins the purity of the universal, who refuses to be "absorbed into utility by passing through the cleansing channels of conceptual order" (Horkheimer & Adorno, 1947/2004, p. 147). The particularity that escapes the universalizing force of categorization—the unassimilable aspect of Jewish particularity and difference, belonging as much to the anti-Semite who bestows it—returns like the repressed as "compulsive aversion" (Horkheimer & Adorno, 1947/2004, p. 148). In the failure to assimilate fully, owing to the historical process of assimilation itself, the Jew is positioned as the symptom of social disharmony that returns again and again.

Though shaped by historical processes, these positions are also structural; from this point of view, the ingroup and outgroup could be replaced by other groups or whatever group takes "the line of least resistance" (Adorno, 1948/2019, p. lii). This formulation is tellingly reminiscent of the function of displacement in the phobic response through the path of least resistance. And as uncomfortable as it may be to think about, for Horkheimer and Adorno (1947/2004), even the Jewish person can displace the anti-Semite in the logic of domination "as soon as he feels the power of representing the norm" (p. 140).[5] Horkheimer and Adorno are

---

[5] Here, I want to point out Badiou's assertion that the Jew has, indeed, replaced the anti-Semite. I believe that there is an unbridgeable gap that divides Badiou's assertion from Horkheimer and Adorno's (1947/2004). For Badiou, the Jew becomes the anti-Semite when the Jew insists on maintaining Jewish identity as a particular identity (rooted in what he refers to as "SIT," standing for Shoah, Israel, Talmud) which troubles a universal humanism. In a way, Horkheimer and Adorno are asserting the opposite, the Jew becomes the anti-Semite when they represent the norm and strive to erase particularity in service of the supposedly (but actually exclusive) universal. Badiou seems to recognize this potential. Therefore, he seems to be striving for a utopian universalization *of particularity* such that there is no communal identity beyond the universal, and an end to the chimerical delusion of racial identification. [How might this be different than Cèsaire's (1950/2001) universal stuffed with particulars?] I read this as a positive dialectical project. I am not convinced that this project does not amount to another erasure of otherness and institutionalization of sameness at a different scale. Synchronically, this universalism is not necessarily racist, but as Moten (2018) shows us, racism is "another mode of propagation of the very idea (of universality)" (p. 24). The diachronic propagation of the ideal of the universal cannot be other than racist. This is not unlike an attempt to return to some primordial purity of Being, a return to use-value, or sexuality without repression. And while this seems similar to Horkheimer and Adorno's (1947/2004) idea that exchangeability is the erasure of particularity, a life without it also may be the erasure of particularity. It is certainly an erasure of Jewish forms of life. More fine-grained analysis of Badiou's

not suggesting that the Jews are an arbitrary target, or that anti-Semitism has nothing to do with Jews. The Jews are, indeed, linked via similarity, proximity, and other contingencies to a kind of negativity, ambivalence, and otherness that offer the grounds for the anti-Semite's metonymic (or is it metaphoric?) substitutions.

Anti-Semitism as the Drive Toward Sameness

The image of the Jewish people harbored by many anti-Semites is that of the (sometimes) invisible strangers conspiring against society and ruining the possibility of social harmony with their inherent differences. Anti-Semitism is driven by the proteophobic wish to impose uniformity and make everyone the same so as to gain social control. Importantly, this control also happens to be the failed striving of the psychological subject. The ego which is tasked with integrating and unifying the psychological subject is also responsible for synthesizing the libidinal drives and mental content to cope with the demands of external reality. The drive toward sameness is found in the logic of identity which defines the ego. The ego unifies experience but is perpetually subverted by an uncanny remainder of disunity coming from its own "eccentric function" being "only what the objective world is for it" (Horkheimer & Adorno, 1947/2004, p. 155; See also Laplanche, 1991). In other words, the ego is constituted by recognition and processes of identification with the other. The separate wholeness defining the boundaries of the ego happens to be given by what the ego is not. (Note how this conception of the *ec*-centric function and otherness cleaves the early critical theorists remarkably close to later scholarship in psychoanalysis.)

Horkheimer and Adorno (1947/2004) show that this process of making everything and everyone the same is not just the project of anti-Semitism or the work of the ego but also the logic of commodification (following Marx) where things (and human beings on the labor market) are stripped of their qualities in order to be exchanged for a universal equivalent. Stripped of their particular qualities, everything serves a social

---

complex and theoretically rigorous philosophy is needed but is well beyond the scope of this book. He is closer to Nietzsche, here, in being anti-Judaic rather than anti-Semitic.

utility within the social totality; this goes for enlightenment science which quantifies qualities, the exchange economy which relies on equivalences, and the ego which uses concepts and categories to make the world predictable and masterable. The stripping of particular qualities and the drive toward the same is "the primeval-historical entrapment" (Horkheimer & Adorno, 1947/2004, p. 139). Paradoxically, anti-Semitism is the attempt to escape through more of the (enlightenment) logic of sameness that laid the trap to begin with. These processes amount to the exchange of meaningful qualities of life for the preservation of that life. In other words, anti-Semitism is a self-defeating response to the trappings of the totalized socio-economic and historical order which both produces psychological interiority and empties it of meaning.

The destructive consequences of socio-economic and psychological drive toward sameness are externalized in anti-Semitism. Horkheimer and Adorno explain that "[i]n the image of the Jew which the racial nationalists hold up before the world they express their own essence" (1947/2004, p. 137). The image of the Jew, simultaneously strange and familiar, operates as the uncanny, as formulated by Freud (1913/2001a). The uncanny refers to the process by which the individual subject experiences a repressed aspect of themselves as external to them, or a part of themselves that is eccentric.[6] The projection by anti-Semites may align with characteristics of Jews and Jewishness, doubling down on the uncanny anxiety, however, the Jew is not the *cause* of anti-Semitism. Traditional causal explanations seem to be inadequate in this multidirectional psychoanalytic model.

Rationality alone cannot combat anti-Semitism because, in its link to power and mastery, rationality is inculpated in the logic that brought about anti-Semitism in its current form. But this does not lead (as it might if one stopped here) to an irrationalist solution. The solution is found not merely in combating the already existing irrationalities with more rationality but also in resisting irrationality in the very process of

---

[6] In my understanding, the uncanny represents the unsettling return of the repressed, which is recalled in the act of attempting to rid oneself of it. This is not unlike the way that assimilation and destruction of what is other redoubles and inscribes the negativity to be eliminated; a fact that seems tied to the attempt made by the Nazis in their Final Solution to eliminate Jews and any trace of that elimination.

rationally formulating and justifying solutions. Any proposed solution to anti-Semitism must grapple with these contradictions to be justifiable. Any irrationality in the rational solution is unjustifiable. Think, again, of the lives overlooked in economic arguments against quarantine during the Covid-19 pandemic, or the Israeli lives lost in the fight for Palestinian self-determination and the suffering of Palestinians in Israel's fight for self-preservation, or support for the war in Ukraine. The difficulty in knowing how to respond to these human tragedies means that more critical thinking is needed, not that we need to stop thinking to start acting irrationally. To do so is to be complicit in the prevailing evil (see Adorno, 2001a).

Thinking Anti-Semitism in Terms of Mimesis and Projection

Mimesis, rooted in the work of imitation and mimicry, is a long-standing philosophical concept and constellating figure in the *Dialectic of Enlightenment* (1947/2004). Plato rejected mimesis; Aristotle defended it. It is implicitly present in Freud's theory of identification and explicitly so in Lacan's mirror stage through the influence of Roger Caillois' (1935/1984) theory of mimesis and legendary psychasthenia,[7] who was also an influence on Walter Benjamin and Adorno. Erich Auerbach published a masterful and influential work in literary criticism, entitled *Mimesis: The Representation of Reality in Western Literature* (1946/2003). Mimesis continued to be an influential concept through the twentieth century from Luce Irigaray and Jacques Derrida to Michael Taussig and Homi Bhabha.

In the *Dialectic of Enlightenment* (1947/2004), the concept of mimesis helps articulate what is repressed for the subject of science and commodity exchange, and the way that Jews represent the uncanny terror of

---

[7] Developing the idea of legendary psychasthenia, Caillois (1935/1984) explores how animals and insects can adapt their appearance to their surroundings through mimesis or mimicry sometimes in excess of their needs (e.g., chameleon, moth, praying mantis), and its connection to psychological experiences where the individual changes in response to their environment and self-preservation can become excessive and, at times, self-destructive.

facing the repressed which returns in the other (for the anti-Semite.) The anti-Semite mimics *and* attacks what they fear in themselves (difference, death, otherness, negativity, disorder), swept up in unconscious ambivalent identification. For instance, Jews have been accused of ritual crimes for centuries, but it is Hitler who becomes a magician acting out the mimetic and deadly ritual with his followers: "All the gesticulations devised by the Fuhrer and his followers are pretexts for giving way to the mimetic temptation without openly violating the reality principle" (Horkheimer & Adorno, 1947/2004, p. 151). In other words, and along the lines of what Freud (1921/2001d) had formulated, the mimetic identification with the destructive leader permits the expression of libidinal and destructive impulses, which had been repressed or projected onto the Jews, without arousing the guilt that would normally accompany them. The temptation of this mimetic process is the promise of social cohesion without sacrificing libidinal gratification. But the promise goes unkept since, in giving way, "[t]he soul, as the possibility of guilt aware of itself, decays" (Horkheimer & Adorno, 1947/2004, p. 164).

Mimesis, formulated above as direct representation, is also another way of understanding Freud's death drive (Horkheimer & Adorno, 1947/2004, p. 189; see also Matthew Potolsky, 2006, p. 143), as the drive toward losing oneself in the environment or returning to the directness of natural totality.[8] This is made especially apparent in the link between mimesis and anti-Semitism where the fear of death is answered by death. "The despoiling of graveyards is not an excess of anti-Semitism," Horkheimer and Adorno (1947/2004) assert, "it is anti-Semitism itself" (p. 150). Similar to the distinction between the death drive and the self-preserving drives in Freud, the sameness of mimesis is distinct from the sameness of synthesis, though both aim, in one way or another, for sameness (e.g., as mastery or as union). Mimesis (like Freud's uncanny) is characterized by a magical proximity to the thing and the potent force of words and thoughts. Synthesis, on the other hand, is indirect and mediated by the uniquely human symbolic system of signification. And yet the drive toward sameness is present in both mimesis and synthesis. The drive

---

[8] This is merely one possible reading of the death drive. I also find compelling Laplanche's (1991) theory of the sexual death drive as an unbinding force.

toward sameness need not lead inevitably to anti-Semitism, but it does seem to be a proto-anti-Semitic compulsion that selects its object through a path of least resistance.

The psychological subject is formed in the gap of indirectness accompanying synthetic operations of the understanding which displaces mimesis. "Bodily adaptation to nature is replaced by 'recognition in a concept,' the subsuming of difference under sameness" (Horkheimer & Adorno, 1947/2004, p. 148). The subject is formed through this displacement and transformation "from reflecting mimesis to controlled reflection" (Horkheimer & Adorno, 1947/2004, p. 148). Reflection is controlled by way of conceptual identification or bringing the object under the categorizing force of the subject's concepts by stripping it of its differences. But the mastery of nature afforded by the controlled reflection of the synthetic faculties does not fully root out the uncanny persistence of mimetic directness. Displacement of mimetic reflection preserves the feared thing displaced in the form of a repressed which returns. The symbols (words and images) used to think with have a directness which must continue to be repressed in order to avoid the uncanny terror occurring when, as Freud (1919/2001c) suggests in his formulation of the uncanny, "a symbol takes over the full functions of the thing it symbolizes, and so on" (p. 244). Think, again, of taboo deformations and euphemisms; each instance is a substitution which points to the very real directness of words or images and a proximity to something feared which must be kept at bay. The psychic interiority of the psychological subject is opened up through the distance used to defend against over-proximity. In other words, the displacement of mimetic directness—or in psychoanalytic terms repression and projection—opens a space for internality and abstract reasoning. These defenses are so central to the psychological subject that the end of someone's repression would be, according to Adorno (1982), "tantamount to the abolition of his 'psychology'" (p. 136). So, the anti-Semite's persecution of the Jews, the longing to fill the gap of indirectness, otherness, and ambivalence, is the undoing of the psychological subject who, as a subject, is constituted by the very failure to reach its own totalizing and unifying aims.

A critical project cannot aim merely to succeed positively nor to master nature definitively; it must reflect on the mediating projection, the way the perceptions of the surroundings are co-constructed through the concepts projected onto intuitions. Following Kant, human perception is the result of an unconscious synthesis of concepts (understanding) and intuitions (sensibility). In these synthesizing processes of the imagination, the unified subject comes into being as a projection which enables perception. "If mimesis makes itself resemble its surroundings, false projection makes its surroundings resemble itself" (Horkheimer & Adorno, 1947/2004, p. 154). Granted, for Horkheimer and Adorno, there is no escaping the element of projection that is inherent in all acts of perception; what characterizes false projection is the lack of reflection involved. False projection is the default mode of perception and thus critical reason must actively resist it. For Horkheimer and Adorno (1947/2004), "Every percept unconsciously contains conceptual elements, just as every judgment contains unclarified phenomenalistic ones" (pp. 159–160). The illusion of immediacy and presence hides the mediating concepts the subject uses to think with and projects into the surroundings, while at the same time judgment is evacuated of its phenomenalistic content. Critical reason involves the reflection on the one in the other. Without critical reflection on mediation and the historical aspect of concepts and categories used to think with, they can be manipulated without detection, and thus perception made up in part of these concepts can be controlled heteronomously (by an external authority). Both conceptual certainty and intuitive immediacy must be challenged by the negative and mediated moment of thought in order to resist heteronomy—a heteronomy which fosters anti-Semitism. For our thinkers, projection is not merely an intra-psychic process, and anti-Semitism by way of repression or projection is not merely a psychological phenomenon.

Anti-Semitism is a false projection because anti-Semites make the world reflect themselves instead of seeing how they are themselves a product of otherness owing to the dialectical nature of perception and projection. The theory of false projection helps to trouble any neat categories of interiority and exteriority, so-called subjective and objective realities. To argue that Horkheimer and Adorno (1947/2004) are suggesting that the anti-Semite is projecting onto the Jews and so therefore what they find in the world is not real, would be a misunderstanding (see Lapidot, 2021, for one such misunderstanding).

Horkheimer and Adorno (1947/2004) are trying to salvage enlighten-ment autonomy while acknowledging its impurity. "What is at stake," they say, "is not conservation of the past but the fulfillment of past hopes" (Horkheimer & Adorno, 1947/2004, p. xvii). They recognize that for all the paranoid delusions of projection and false immediacy, which Marxists might render as false consciousness, "such blindness is [...] a constitutive element of all judgment, a necessary illusion" (Horkheimer & Adorno, 1947/2004, p. 160). For Horkheimer and Adorno, thinking is an infinite project, and the judicious use of critical reasoning should guide that process. It will perpetually miss its mark, and the ego is even born of this failure. In other words, paranoid projection which can lead to persecution (like anti-Semitism) also gives humanity the power of judgment to fight such persecution and the autonomy and democracy worth fighting for.[9] The ego, despite its illusory properties and destructive inevitabilities must be salvaged so that reason can persist dialectically beyond its own crisis, especially since the ability to formulate the limits of reason is the work of human morality. Put differently, Adorno and Horkheimer (1947/2004) write, "Neither the certainty untroubled by thought, nor the preconceptual unity of perception and object, but only their self-reflective antithesis contains the possibility of reconciliation" (Horkheimer & Adorno, 1947/2004. p. 156). Or, as Adorno (1967/2004) will put it years later in the preface to *Negative Dialectics*, this task has always been "To use the strength of the subject to break through the fallacy of consti-tutive subjectivity" (p. xx). And only the negative and mediated moment in critical thought—reason called to account, by the suffering of the other, for the remainder which insists in its concepts and categories—can reconcile the difficulties in thinking about something as complex as anti-Semitism. It does so by reconciling not in higher synthesis or primordial mimesis but in the critical moment of thought itself which emphasizes the unconscious and ambivalent side of language as it is used. What could be more psychoanalytic?

---

[9] Horkheimer and Adorno's (2004) adoption of a kind of neo-Kantian epistemology challenges or extends the traditional Marxist notion of "false consciousness," since the intelligibility of the world, mediated through the ego's (mostly unconscious) operations always entails elements of projection, oversimplification, and hence some distortion. Similar to their (arguably) heterodox reading of Freud, where getting rid of repression would not leave an unrepressed ego but no ego at all, to get rid of false consciousness would not leave true consciousness but no consciousness at all, hence the negative work of critical theory as a form of resistance to untruth.

Bauman's Dialectic of Enlightenment

Horkheimer and Adorno (1947/2004) propose a theory of anti-Semitism that is driven by a fear of the negative principle threatening social totality, order, and categorization. The Jew is positioned as unassimilable into Christianity and modernity's universal enlightenment principles, representing that which disrupts the established order. Horkheimer and Adorno's (1947/2004) theories of anti-Semitism are grounded in psychoanalysis and formulated as a negative psychology. They situate anti-Semitism in relation to enlightenment knowledge, theories of fetishistic exchangeability, the dialectic of mimesis, and false projection. Bauman (1995) rethinks this critical project in terms of proteophobia, tracing what is left out of thinking and the rules of thought, and what is erased in the rigid drive toward sameness that manifests in rejecting, labeling, eradicating, or branding the uncategorizable. His project involves understanding the limits of categorization, examining how rigid categories exclude that which cannot be easily assimilated, and tracing the historical and contingent contexts in which these exclusions are manifest tangibly in the world.

Historian and critical theorist Johnathan Catlin (2022) provides an analysis of Adorno's impact on Bauman, who received the Theodor W. Adorno Prize in 1998. In his acceptance speech, Bauman proposes that thinking about anti-Semitism can and should aid in our understanding of modernity, rather than solely relying on modernity to comprehend anti-Semitism.

[…] Bauman cites a passage from *Negative Dialectics*: "if thinking is to be true—if it is to be true today, in any case—it must also be a thinking against itself" […]. Bauman pairs this conception of critical theory with Adorno's famous maxim that "A new categorical imperative has been imposed by Hitler upon unfree mankind: to arrange their thoughts and actions so that Auschwitz will not repeat itself, so that nothing similar will happen" […]. Taking these ideas together, Bauman reflects, helped him recognise that "the ethical imperative to make the world impervious to the madness of Auschwitz' is 'at the same time to make the mind susceptible to the reason of self-criticism.'" (Bauman, 1998, p. 6, cited in Catlin, 2022, p. 203)

Catlin (2022) reminds us that Adorno's reference to Auschwitz, cited by Bauman, should be understood to mean, according to Adorno in his 1965 lectures on Metaphysics, "not only Auschwitz but the world of torture which has continued to exist after Auschwitz and of which we are receiving the most horrifying reports from Vietnam" (p. 201, citing Adorno, 2001b, p. 101). Adorno's philosophical project, as carried forward by Bauman, offers a valuable insight into intersectionality and multidirectional thinking where events are discovered to be part of history and where struggles are interrelated. The categorical imperative, mentioned above, is renewed and changed by Jewish suffering. It is not that suffering started in Auschwitz, but it is a fact that it did not stop with Auschwitz. That is the point.

Zygmunt Bauman was critical of Adorno et al.'s *The Authoritarian Personality*, but his (Bauman's) work on anti-Semitism and proteophobia are inspired by Horkheimer and Adorno's *Dialectic of Enlightenment* (1947/2004) and Adorno's *Negative Dialectics* (1967/2004). Catlin (2022) argues that Bauman could have gained much from thinking more seriously about Adorno's psychoanalytic theory. Bauman's (1991) work on modernity and ambivalence was an attempt "to wrap historical and sociological flesh around the 'dialectics of enlightenment' skeleton" (Bauman, 1991, cited in Catlin, 2022). The backbone of this skeleton—perhaps the skeleton in the closet of contemporary thinkers of anti-Semitism—is Horkheimer and Adorno's (1947/2004) psychoanalytic thinking.

Implications of Anti-Semitism as the Limits of Enlightenment

According to the theory described above, resistance to anti-Semitism in the form of critical reason could lead to "the turning-point of history" (Horkheimer & Adorno, 1947/2004, p. 165). It is a turning point for the whole of history because anti-Semitism is not merely about anti-Jewish prejudice but also about a wide-reaching social crisis at the limits of enlightenment rationality and categorization. The processes of thought capable of countering anti-Semitism, rooted in fear of the uncategoriz-able, are also equipped to confront other forms of oppression. Critical reason is tasked paradoxically with preventing the violence operative in the marriage of thought and power or reason and force without reverting to unreason. In this formulation, and as I've already noted, Horkheimer and Adorno (and Adorno, more specifically) have been accused of quiet-ism and conformity stemming from a supposed pessimism and inopera-bility of such a position (e.g., Whitebook, 2004, p. 79; see also Hullot-Kentor, 2006).[10] Adorno (2001a) acknowledges the paradox but insists upon its importance *as* a paradox:

The situation may well demand [...] that we resist the call of practical-ity with all our might in order ruthlessly to follow through an idea and its logical implications so as to see where it may lead. I would even say that this ruthlessness, the power of resistance that is inherent in the idea itself and that prevents it from letting itself be directly manipulated for any instrumental purposes whatsoever, this theoretical ruthlessness con-tains—if you will allow me the paradox—a practical element within itself. (p. 4)

---

[10] Habermas considered Horkheimer and Adorno's analysis, and Adorno's more specifically, as an attack on the legitimacy of reason and the emancipation that reason sought to enable. "Adorno, [Habermas] insists, became entangled in a radical denunciation of reason that could not ground itself. Realizing this, the best Adorno could do was to ignore the contradiction. This was possible in Adorno's case because he could distract himself with art [...]" (Hullot-Kentor, 2006, p. 31). Habermas seems to fundamentally misunderstand Adorno's project, and fails to provide an imma-nent critique, thus leaving the fibers of the project untouched. That Habermas became the face of Frankfurt School critical theory, Hullot-Kentor (2006) suggests, is a "terrifically unlucky historical mismatch" (p. 24).

Hope for a better world lies in the refusal to justify oppression since such desperate measures obligate us to give up thinking in mid-thought. (Perhaps it is helpful to think of this refusal as a form of non-violent resistance.) I read this as the negative principle shared by strands of both psychoanalysis and critical theory, with implications for the practice of Freud's three impossible professions, each of which requires an impossible choice between social utility and thinking: *politics, education,* and *psychoanalysis.*

Implications for Politics

Stephan Grigat (2019) uses Horkheimer and Adorno's theory of anti-Semitism to propose political policy and military intervention in the turbulent Middle East. Grigat's work should be applauded for stressing the persistence and social consequences of anti-Semitism and the continued relevance of Horkheimer and Adorno's critical theory of anti-Semitism for our current historical milieu. Nevertheless, I believe that Grigat falls short of his own moral aspirations. I will spend the next few pages addressing his political theory to show that without careful critical reflection, even the most compelling ethical justification for political action against anti-Semitism can be complicit in the logic of oppression. I believe that this has become the case in many contemporary theories of anti-anti-Semitism, and I propose that careful attention to Adorno's critical thinking can help to counter this betrayal of thought.

Grigat (2019) grounds his political project on Adorno's (updated) categorical imperative: To think and act "so that Auschwitz will not repeat itself, so that nothing similar will happen" (Adorno, 1967/2004, p. 365). Adorno's imperative is a moral response to mimetic bodily agony when confronted with the other's suffering for which our categorical and conceptual understanding is forever inadequate. Grigat (2019) also appeals to a speech given by Adorno on anti-Semitism in the 1960s where Adorno seems to suggest that in the short-term "the 'available means of coercion' should be used 'without sentimentality'" (Adorno, 1964, cited in Grigat, 2019, p. 444). Grigat reads this as a justification (invoking Adorno as the moral authority) for military intervention. Grigat combines this somewhat misleading citation, Horkheimer and Adorno's theory of anti-Semitism, and Adorno's categorical imperative to justify practical and short-term military action against nations led by governments complicit in anti-Semitism. Grigat asserts that the European Union must cut off political relations with all anti-Semitic governments and give unilateral military support to Israel. Grigat is quite correct in his political demand to fight anti-Semitism and anti-Semitic forms of anti-Zionism but undermines the logic on which that demand is based, stopping short of the universal anti-Fascism (which he proposes) by reducing contemporary anti-Semitism to anti-Zionism.

Despite Grigat's consideration of Horkheimer and Adorno's theory of anti-Semitism as more than anti-Jewish prejudice, he claims "[t]he analysis of geopolitical reproduction of antisemitism in the form of *anti-Zionism* is today a central task for a critical theory of antisemitism" (Grigat, 2019, p. 445). With this, Grigat begins to reduce anti-Semitism from hate for the negative principle into something petrified in the territorialized and nationalist struggles in the Middle East:

Taking Adorno's categorical imperative seriously today means: Giving all possible support to Israel and its armed forces in their defensive struggle against antisemitism in all its forms, while focusing criticism, in both the academic and political spheres, on the anti-Israeli resentment that is encountered. (Grigat, 2019, p. 457)

In not condemning all hate for the negative principle or what is uncategorizable (be it the image of the Jew or the image of the Palestinian) he recapitulates what he wishes to critique and inadvertently undermines Adorno's categorical imperative.

Grigat (2019) systematically presents the very real anti-Semitic threat from governments and well-established institutions on the world stage. And he is rightly pointing to the problem (on the right and the left) of being unable or unwilling to challenge anti-Semitism in all its forms (implicit and explicit). Resisting anti-Semitism and condemning terror, however, should not be conflated with the support for a particular government. Grigat is not wrong: Anti-Zionism can be a form of anti-Semitism. But he is also not right. The central task for the critical theory of anti-Semitism is still the development of critical faculties, the resistance to ticket mentality in toto or proteophobia, and the opposition to suffering.

A categorical imperative must be followed in all cases to resist oppression wherever it rears its head—Iran, Israel, India, China, the United States. More in line with Adorno's critical theory, state nationalism itself (Israeli, American, Palestinian) just like ticket thinking (right and left) must be challenged. Critical theory cannot turn away from the suffering of any human beings, whether they are identified as Israeli or Palestinian. This does not lead to quietism (as is supposed) but to new and non-violent forms of action (See Butler, 2020). Those who may suggest that this is inoperable in the real world are expressing the abandonment of thought and the abandonment of those who will inevitably be excluded. Grigat can claim that his policy proposal is pragmatic, possible, and even necessary, but he is wrong to claim that it withstands the radical force of Adorno's moral imperative and the *Dialectic of Enlightenment* (1947/2004).

Reason becomes unreason when critical theory is used to endorse and justify violence. This does not mean that people should not defend themselves, but it does lead to more questions about what is meant by "people," "self," and "defense" (see Butler, 2020). Adorno's discussion of a "short-term program," promoted by Grigat (2019), refers to the recourse to authority for the sake of the de-Nazification of Germany. But this authority, Adorno (1964) goes on to explain, is the shock of moral strength. According to Adorno (1964), shock and moral strength go hand in hand (p. 102). Taking Adorno seriously, today, is to stand in solidarity with oppressed people and to recognize the way violence (of thought and action) is unjustly justified. Adorno (2001a) wrote that "[f]orce only really becomes evil the moment it misunderstands itself as [...] the sword of God" (p. 174). The immorality of violence is in its rationalization as good. Later in his speech on anti-Semitism, Adorno (1964) claims, quite rightly in my estimation, that "[a]n effective defense against anti-Semitism is inseparable from an effective defense against nationalism in any form. One can't be on the one hand against anti-Semitism, and on the other hand be a militant nationalist" (p. 103).[11] Of

---

[11] Is there communal identity without the logic of exclusion and proteophobia? Boyarin (2023) argues for a rehabilitation of a non-political national identity with a national community. It is

course, in the preliminary remarks prefacing his speech, Adorno implores the readers not to take it as authoritative; they should, rather, think critically for themselves.

Implications for Education

Much of Horkheimer and Adorno's Critical Theory points to the position of education, as the development of critical thinking, in the struggle against anti-Semitism, authoritarianism, and other forms of heteronomy. Adorno gave lectures and wrote extensively on the central role of this critical education (e.g., Adorno, 1998, 1964). I imagine that the importance of a critical education (stated as such) will not come across to informed readers as particularly extraordinary. A terminological clarification is needed, here: Where I have just written "education," Adorno refers primarily to the German *Bildung* which is a concept that contains a cultural specificity missing when translated into English directly as education or even culture, as it is often done. In German, education as pedagogy is referred to as *Erziehung*. Morelock (2017) defines *Bildung*, on the other hand, as "[…] a model state to be achieved by learners through cultivating their own wise intellectual capacities" (p. 67). He goes on to suggest that an adequate definition of *Bildung* must also convey the link between the autonomy of the individual and sociality: The autonomy achieved by *Bildung* is constituted by the ability to contribute socially. So, while education is a component of *Bildung*, when reduced to an individualistic or institutional form of education, or as a means to an end, the unique cultural characteristics of *Bildung* are missing.

---

unclear if Boyarin's concept of "nation" stands up to critiques of political nationalism (e.g., Dahbour, 2012), since it does not seem to be a demand for sovereignty. For Homi Bhabha (1994), community seems to be opposed to nation. Community, for Bhabha (1994), is a disruption of the imagined community of the nation. Community is incommensurable with national identity. "Binary divisions of social space" Bhabha (1994) goes on to explain, "neglect the profound temporal disjunction—the translational time and space—through which minority communities negotiate their collective identifications. For what is at issue in the discourse of minorities is the creation of agency through incommensurable (not simply multiple) positions" (p. 230). The Jew is a figure of disruptive incommensurability who finds their community identity in "the border problem of diaspora" (Bhabha, 1994, p. 230).

This is precisely what Adorno is concerned with: *Bildung* has been reduced to an instrumental education. Barbarism as the failure of culture is also, first and foremost, the failure of an educational system complicit in the predominance of instrumentalized reasoning and the reproduction of technicians. *Bildung* is a condition of possibility of humanity and the dialectical autonomy necessary for political participation as citizens. Without *Bildung* there is barbarism. Still, Adorno cautions not to mistake his emphasis on *Bildung* for a positive solution in itself. Echoing the dialectical processes developed above from the *Dialectic of Enlightenment* (1947/2004), Adorno recognizes that *Bildung* is also complicit in "the elimination of the subject in the interest of its own self-preservation" (Adorno, 1959, p. 18). *Bildung* has always also been a way of controlling human drives as a means of achieving social cohesion, and education has become a commodity in the totalized social order instituted by capitalism. Adorno looks to *Bildung* not as a positive utopian image but as an image for dialectical reflection.

The predominance of instrumental reasoning is not so much a consequence of a total lack of education, culture, or *Bildung* but what Horkheimer and Adorno (1947/2004) refer to as a *"Halbbildung"* (i.e., half-education or pseudo-culture). The concept is best articulated in Adorno's essay *"Theorie der Halbbildung"* (1972) originally published in 1959 and translated into English under the title "Theory of pseudo-culture" (1959/1993). *Halbbildung* leads to the application of formulas and methods without fostering the self-reflexivity and critical thinking needed to root out unreason and proteophobia in one's own reason. Perhaps *Halbbildung* is the establishment of categories motivated by proteophobia without reflection on the inevitable failure of those same categories. Currently, *Halbbildung* can be witnessed in some critiques of anti-Semitism and in many facets of contemporary institutional learning and is aggressively present in the growing movement to defund liberal arts programs in the United States (Morelock, 2017). Yet, it should be noted that the resuscitation of the liberal arts (like a return to *Bildung* itself) would not constitute a solution. *Bildung* is opposed to *Halbbildung*, but a return to traditional *Bildung* is not the answer. "The measure of the bad new," Adorno (1959/1993) reminds his readers, "is only the bad old" (p. 23). *Bildung* is struck through with contradictions and requires an immanent critique. For instance, the cultural facet of *Bildung* presupposes autonomy but is given heteronomously. The individual can only become autonomous by taking in knowledge from an outside authority. "Thus," Adorno (1959/1993) writes, "the moment [*Bildung*] exists, it already ceases to exist" (p. 24). The solution, then, is not a return to the older form of *Bildung*, nor is it an embrace of a *Halbbildung*, but a critical reflection on the failure of *Bildung and Halbbildung*.

In not being able to be corrected directly through pedagogy (i.e., reality testing, transfer of information, teaching methods, etc.) *Halbbildung* functions much like the unconscious. Accordingly, Adorno (1959/1993) offers a somewhat unexpected assertion: "Only a deep psychological approach could counteract this tendency in such a way as to prevent its ossification in the early developmental stages and to strengthen critical reflection" (p. 36). This assertion should be qualified with reference to Adorno's reading of psychology: The psychological approach must be a negative psychology—psychoanalysis.

Implications for Psychoanalysis

Much of Adorno's reading of psychoanalytic theory corresponds to negativity, otherness, and ambivalence, and emphasizes the constitutive tensions and contradictions between—and, crucially, within—the individual and society.[12] "The greatness of Freud," Adorno (1952/2014) writes, "[…] consists in that he leaves such contradictions unresolved, and he scorns the pretended systematic harmony where things in themselves are torn asunder" (p. 337). Although Adorno insisted on the pivotal role of psychoanalysis in critical thinking and education, he was reproving of what he saw as the inevitably normalizing aims of (psychiatric) clinical practice from which those theories originated and toward which those theories seem to return unchallenged, as if harmonious with that practice. Nevertheless, I believe that Adorno's work, informed as it is by psychoanalytic theory, can (in a neat reciprocity) offer clinicians—especially clinicians hesitant to endorse the social status quo—a model of ethical

---

[12] Adorno (1952/2014) was critical of social psychoanalysis that reduced society to interpersonal relationships with other egoic subjects.

and dialectical thinking attuned to what is left out of many normative practices: the non-identical, nonconceptual, uncategorizable, unconscious. This is relevant to the current study on anti-Semitism because Adorno's perspective on anti-Semitism is deeply grounded in psychoanalytic theory and has much to offer psychoanalytic thinkers and practitioners. Exploring and expanding on Adorno's critical approach to psychoanalysis may assist us in contemplating strategies to address proto-anti-Semitic tendencies within the realm of clinical psychology.

In Adorno's essay "Education after Auschwitz" (1966/1998), he proposes that the dissemination of psychoanalytic theory is an integral feature of his vision of critical education capable of countering anti-Semitism in the wake of Nazism (p. 191).[13] Adorno recognized that, in conjunction with psychoanalysis, education as pedagogy (*Erziehung*) is still crucial to developing the capacity for critical reflection rather than being limited to mere *Halbbildung* and instrumental reasoning. Critical education converges with the field of psychoanalysis in a number of ways, including the position of authority, identity, and contradiction and the processes involved in learning to learn. Psychoanalytic theory can help establish critical practices in education, but can psychoanalysis uproot anti-Semitism in the clinic? No, not directly and not without a change in social and material conditions—*so, maybe?*

Psychologists and psychiatrists noted, early on, that anti-Semitism may not be something that can be clinically cured person by person (Simmel, 1946). This seems understandable in that those with explicit prejudices or implicit ideological commitments do not generally come to therapy to be cured of them. What would a psychotherapy that addresses a patient's anti-Semitism be, then? Is this an instance of a more general therapeutic issue, namely, can I treat the patient for something for which they do not seek treatment or don't even know they have? On the one hand, in a psychotherapeutic culture in which the patient is regarded as a customer or client (i.e., someone who pays for a service or an experience), where the treatment is understood as the delivery of pre-established treatment protocols, and where effectiveness is measured by pre-established

---

[13] "Education after Auschwitz" (1966/1998) was first published in German as "*Erziehung nach Auschwitz*" (1966/2012). I note this because of his use of *Erziehung* and not *Bildung*.

objectives and agreed-upon goals, the idea of offering a treatment beyond what is sought, other than what is asked for, as it were, may be considered controversial. The presumption to intervene therapeutically in a manner that is not consistent with the client's/customer's explicit requests appears contrary to the principles of consumerist exchange, where the customer is always right; more seriously, it appears to be contrary to the principle of informed consent, where the patient is entitled to information about the treatment on offer. However, if the patient's presenting problem stems from ambivalence or from unconscious desires, it appears contrary to the principles of psychoanalysis to exclusively address concerns that the person recognizes at the outset of treatment.[14] This is not to suggest that a patient who comes to therapy complaining about work-related distress will leave being treated for anti-Semitism. No. But it may mean that a patient that comes to therapy complaining about work-related distress will leave having been treated for proteophobia, intolerance of ambivalences, or underlying structural patterns of social relation implicated in proto-anti-Semitic potentials.

All that being said, can any social issue (like anti-Semitism) be addressed through an individual approach? Is there any evidence that this makes a difference for anti-Semitism or racism? Would it not necessitate economic, political, and educational reforms? Psychoanalysis does not usually claim to cure social issues like anti-Semitism; that is, even if there is a social otherness at the core of individuals. Instead, psychoanalysis plays a part within and against larger social networks such as academia, literature, scientific research, health care, social work, and social media, producing and challenging norms of authority and identity. Indeed, perhaps introducing dialectical and less conventional methods of treatment, which avoid normalizing or pacification, could be considered a social intervention aligned with broader social transformations. This parallels how education appears to focus on individual students and individual achievement despite the historical introduction of public education and the ongoing societal implications of educational reforms. Such potential psychoanalytic   interventions   may   involve   improving   treatment

---

[14] In Lacanian analysis, the patient's demand (initial complaint or presenting concern) is never the same as their desire (or what they don't know they desire).

accessibility and prioritizing alternative measures of goal-setting and effi-cacy (see Laplanche, 2015). They may also emphasize sitting with, toler-ating, or working through ambivalence and otherness, rather than focusing solely on curing perceived disorders or restoring the patient to normalcy. Additionally, practicing psychoanalysts continuously develop psychoanalytic theory based on their engagement with individuals, and that theory has the potential to influence social practices and discourse.

The works of French psychoanalysts Jacques Lacan and Jean Laplanche provide valuable insights into clinical theory that align with what I am envisioning as an Adorno-inspired critical psychoanalysis.[15] For these psychoanalysts, psychotherapeutic goals and treatment is always radically particular to the individual patient, but the particular coordinates of that patient's symptoms are always in relation to the other's desires, rules, and enigmatic messages.[16] An important practice of these psychoanalytic treatments takes the form of "no"-ing and not knowing. This is exem-plary of a negative dialectical approach in the clinic. Do I really know what my patient means by what they say? This could look like repeating a patient's statement with an added negation, so that the patient's state-ment, "The dream was not about my mother," gets returned as, "The dream was not *not* about my mother." Or the "no" can be a refusal on the therapist's part to say "yes" to a certain pattern of relating set out in the patient's original demand and repeated in the therapeutic dyad. Sometimes this is as simple as saying "no" to an unfinished sentence: "You said, 'The dream was…,' what were you about to say?" Often, the form of the patient's address to the therapist exposes the unconscious issue (or desire), whereas the content (or demand) seems to obscure it. Since their desire lies elsewhere, a patient who comes to therapy and demands a solution to their problem may get upset either way, when the therapist offers a solu-tion or refuses to give one. The non-oppositional "no" to the demand, on

---

[15] Lacan's thinking may have been influenced by the *Dialectic of Enlightenment* (Roudinesco, 1997, p. 312). There is an uncanny similarity between Lacan's (1966/2006) essay on Kant and Sade, origi-nally published in 1963, and the chapter on Kant and Sade published much earlier in *Dialectic of Enlightenment* (1947/2004).

[16] Verhaeghe (2008) defines the Other, for simplicity's sake, as that which,

indicates the totality of typically human elements present in the concept of nurture (education, culture, teaching, media, etc.). These elements exert themselves in every individual through lan-guage and, hence, through the Other, particularly during development. (p. 12; footnote)

the other hand, may offer an alternative, a different relation to desire. There are countless variations of this "no"-ing and not knowing.

The suspension of knowing on the part of the therapist, who is supposed to know, leads to curiosity on the part of the patient about enigmas and unconscious processes. "What is it that my therapist is so curious about?" And, "What is happening to me?" In the best cases (with many but not all patients), the subject who is supposed to know (Dr. So and so), and yet who doesn't seem to know and so (and so) continues to show curiosity beyond the patient's demand, ends up lending that curiosity to the patient. The establishment of boundaries and limits (i.e., the therapeutic frame), the injunction to "say whatever comes to your mind, as it comes to your mind with as little censorship as possible," combined with the "no" to the fixity of pre-established schemas, ends, and plans for therapeutic action may lead to a "hollowed-out transference" (as Laplanche [1991] refers to it). This form of transference provides a hospitable hollow for free-associations and dis-associations that permits—or rather, refrains from prohibiting—new and unexpected meanings and patterns to emerge.[17] Shoshana Felman (2003) calls this (or something like this), "radical negativity," which is neither the negative nor the positive but the "no" as a scandalous nonopposition (p. 104); a "no" in service of an openness to the future. This openness is dangerous, I will admit, since any openness to the unknown, as is always the case in an ethics that prioritizes otherness, could be replaced with something potentially worse than what is already known (See Rose, 1993, for such a perspective). And yet, within this openness lies the hope for transformation that neither therapist nor patient can see coming ahead of time.[18] Psychoanalyst and translator

---

[17] We could say that this is a negation of a negation (perhaps also *Verneinung* or denegation), a "no to the no," or a determinate negation without a positive moment of affirmation (Horkheimer & Adorno, 2004, pp. 17–18; Adorno, 2001b).

[18] This is in the temporal register of what Freud called, *Nachträglichkeit* (*après-coup*, afterwardness, retroactivity, or deferred action) and a grammatical tense of the future anterior; an unconscious, a repression, and end of analysis that will have been (see Laplanche, 2017 for an extended study of *Nachträglichkeit* and *après-coup*). The therapeutic project within this temporal register works with the subject of language:

I identify myself in language, but only by losing myself in it as an object. What is realized in my history is neither the past definite as what was, since it is no more, nor even the perfect as what has been in what I am, but the future anterior as what I will have been, given what I am in the process of becoming. (Lacan, 1966/2006, p. 247)

Bruce Fink (1997) addresses this openness in clinical work: "Although the therapist can promise neither happiness nor cure, he or she can, if need be, hold out for the analysand the promise of a new approach to things, a new way of dealing with people, a new way of operating in the world" (p. 10). It is not newness or change for its own sake; far from it. Instead, it is a resistance to the recurrent relational patterns that seem to be perpetuating the patient's suffering. As a therapist I do not know and cannot know what needs to happen, but I can take an educated guess about what needs to *not happen*. Clinical work offers the hope and hap for such not-happenings.

As I noted at the outset, combating anti-Semitism seems to require a prior definition, hence the centrality of the definition question in anti-Semitism studies. In the previous chapters we witnessed the failure of these definitions owing to a difficulty in thinking about anti-Semitism and categorizing its multi-form Jewish target. I offered Adorno's theory of constellations as his alternative to the problem of definition in research, which Hullot-Kentor (2006) observes is inspired by psychoanalytic free-association. Psychoanalytic treatment is also stifled by pre-established categorizations. Psychodiagnostics that rely on symptom checklists, for instance, have been notoriously unreliable (Vanheule, 2014; Verhaege, 2008). Adorno's negative dialectics also helps to reorient and disorient psychoanalysis away from such normalizing schemas. As Mariotti (2009) notes, "Adorno's practice of negative dialectics works to unsettle and disrupt the kind of thinking most starkly represented in the DSM [American Psychiatric Association's *Diagnostic Statistical Manual*]" (p. 175) Unlike the medical diagnostics, psychodiagnostics are not reducible to the individual but must take the other into account. In a reversal of the medical model of diagnosis, psychodiagnostics (at least *a la* Lacan, see Verhaeghe, 2008) seems to require that the more I learn about a patient, the more particular their cases become and the less general their diagnosis can be. The less general the case, the weaker the ready-made categories and manualized answers to action become, and the more difficult it is to determine how I, as a therapist, should respond. The difficulty in knowing how to respond shows me that more thinking is needed. As Verhaeghe (2008) notes, psychodiagnosis can never be made at the outset of a treatment; analytic treatment doesn't stem from the diagnosis like it does for medical professionals. Instead, the process of diagnosis—the process of gathering information and thinking carefully about the particularities of a patient's speech—coincides with the treatment.

Still, I witness in the literature and in those around me an impatience with this conflict between social utility (e.g., affordable treatments, clear answers, determined truths, terminable therapies) and thinking (e.g., not knowing, seeking to know). This conflict has led to anti-intellectualism in clinical settings and perhaps even proteophobia.[19] A psychoanalytic practice informed by Adorno's version of psychoanalysis therefore needs to wrestle with the tension within and between social utility (normalization) and critical thought (the persistence of not-knowing), without insisting on a solution. This kind of psychotherapy traffics in difficult questions and impossible contradictions, and may arouse therapists' anxiety. Indeed, thinking on the part of the therapist seems to break off in mid-thought in moments of discomfort and ambivalence when, for pragmatic reasons we therapists say, "okay, enough thinking; just take action" (i.e., enough history-taking, make a treatment plan; enough theory, we need technique), perhaps for insurance companies, perhaps to alleviate the anxiety of the therapist, or perhaps in response to a desperate demand from the patient or their families. This breaking off of thought for the sake of action will always be somewhat irrational.[20] *And yet...*there is nothing more irrational—in the sense of rationality offering a justification—than being faced with the immanent suffering of the other and asking them to pause...at the precipice of a refuge (the consulting room door, say) while I 'take my thinking to its necessary conclusion' (as the philosopher might say) before inviting them in. On the other hand, beyond the structural requirement to invite the patient to keep talking, sometimes the best intervention is stopping myself from assuming I know what needs to happen (a "no" to the know) and to keep my mouth closed. This contradiction between theory and practice—or between the

---

[19] This is not to advocate for intellectualization in the clinic in the sense of making interpretations, but in the sense of thinking carefully about what it is that we are doing or trying to do in the clinic.

[20] A strange idea "somewhat irrational." It's a little like Adorno's (1951/2005) "Minima Moralia" or minimum morality.

requirements of clinical thinking and the demands of suffering—is an opportunity to think critically (in that critical thinking is an active challenge to thought). Maybe we should read Adorno's (1967/2004) statement, "the need to lend voice to suffering is the condition of all truth," (p. 17) in reverse such that it reads, "the condition of lending voice to suffering is the need for all truth."[21] This idea—at the confluence of psychoanalysis and critical theory, theory and practice—gives ethical imperative to analyses of oppression, like the present study of anti-Semitism, which seeks truth instead of pragmatic solutions (a sometimes ridiculous vigilance at the expense of brevity and elegance) with the hope that this obligation to truth will lend voice to those Jews and non-Jews suffering from the violence of anti-Semitism.

Indispensable to psychoanalytic talk therapy are questions about what it is to be human, to have psychic interiority (or not), to participate in language, and to make meaning—but also meaninglessness and the unintelligibility of trauma, as that which overwhelms speakability, and which at some level brings each patient to the clinic. The clinic can still be one of enigmatic signifiers, of the other's desire, of retroactivity, of unresolved contradiction—what Adorno (1952/2014) recognized as important in Freud's work—between and within the psychological and the social, speech and the unspeakable, meaning and trauma, categorizing and the uncategorizable. How do we do justice to the question of suffering, the truth of it, without erasing it with our fears and anxieties, without tearing it asunder? "The most terrible thing is not suffering" James Wood (2019) writes, evoking the memory of Primo Levi, "it is to have the reality of one's suffering erased" (np).

---

[21] I find the clinic to be a scene of knowledge production much like philosophy, but it is also a place where knowledge production runs aground on the rocky shores of the uncategorizable unconscious and the kernel of the real that haunts that unconscious. Theory not just does inform how the therapist should intervene but also is challenged in the room.

Negative Psychology of Anti-Semitism in Terms of Proteophobia

Let me gather together some of the themes from this chapter: Horkheimer and Adorno (1947/2004) develop critical theory as a resistance to untruth through a psychoanalytic inquiry into anti-Semitism as the limits of enlightenment reason. They emphasize the negative moment of thought so as to oppose what they call a "false clarity" reinforcing the status quo (Horkheimer & Adorno, 1947/2004, xvii). Clarity can be reasonable and false at the same time, since clarity can be grounded in the facts of perception that may be controlled heteronomously by authoritarians, fascists, or social totalities. Without the emphasis on the negative moment of thought and dialectics, the resistance to anti-Semitism can and has been used by lucid thinkers to justify oppression and militant nationalism which perpetuate cycles of violence. The drive toward sameness which manifests as anti-Semitism is found in the development of the psychological subject that comes into being through the illusion of false equivalences and in the processes of language formation. Critical reason in the form of immanent critique as developed in the *Dialectic of Enlightenment* (1947/2004) can counteract the rational processes usurped by the automatism of the drive toward sameness motivated by proteophobia which manifests in anti-Semitism.

Many contemporary scholars of anti-Semitism acknowledge the relevance of Adorno's various projects in their work, and still, his thinking often remains on the sidelines (and in psychology even further beyond the periphery). This sidelining can be attributed to various limitations and difficulties in Adorno's work, which pose challenges to employing it instrumentally. However, I believe that embracing these challenges as an opportunity to engage in critical thinking *with* Adorno, rather than merely utilizing his ideas, shows the continued relevance and enduring pertinence of his work, enabling us to foster a more discerning examination of anti-Semitism and other manifestations of proteophobia.

Adorno recognized that the nature of anti-Semitism lies beyond psychology, but he found a backdoor by which to resist anti-Semitism through the study of the way the psychological subject undermines itself.

Thought of as negative psychology, psychoanalysis presents itself as an ally of critical reason, constantly calling the ego's syntheses into question and tracing the perpetual self-undermining of conscious conceptions, words, and narratives. Ideally, like the processes of critical education and *Bildung*, psychoanalysis is not merely about the content taught by an outside authority but also about the discovery and fostering of the critical faculties in each individual to resist untruth and *Halbbildung*. This entails the ability of each individual to see and carve out a hollow for the non-identical in identity, the nonconceptual in concepts, the unconscious in consciousness, and indeed, the uncategorizable in categorization.

Although Horkheimer and Adorno (1947/2004) borrow and extend a number of psychoanalytic concepts, Adorno was explicitly skeptical of the prospects of a clinical work that could function clinically (toward health or normality, say) without simultaneously reinforcing the status quo. I disagree with Adorno's rejection of the clinical project, though he is right to be concerned with its potential normalizing force. I believe that psychoanalysis can and should learn from and extend critical theory in clinical thinking. Psychoanalysis as a clinical project can learn from critical theory to develop treatments that move away from the reliance on narratives of progress and the individualism inherent in the disease model of mental illness and toward change which is unforeseeable and perhaps even beyond the individual.[22] This may help psychoanalysis maintain a critical edge in the face of overwhelming pressure to adapt to the status quo of randomized controlled trials and manualized treatments. There are a number of clinical projects which are already pushing against the false clarity and positivism found in contemporary mainstream psychology (e.g., Ashter, 2021; Fink, 1997; Fischer et al., 2016; Hook, 2017; Lacan, 1966/2006; Laplanche, 1991, 2015; McWilliams, 2020; Nobus & Quinn, 2005; Rogers, 2016; Sass, 2019; Vanheule, 2017; Verhaeghe, 2008). Resistance to normative conceptions of health and well-being could lead to the development of new ways of relating to identity and authority, breaking with those most susceptible to anti-Semitism and other forms of oppression.

---

[22] As Laplanche (2015) would put it: a psychoanalysis beyond subjective or psychological reality to include psychical reality and the reality of the message.

Recently, scholars have been revisiting the intersection of critical theory and psychoanalysis (e.g., Allen, 2020; Allen & Ruti, 2019; Burston, 2020; Butler, 2020; Dews, 1987; Fong, 2016; Honneth, 1995; Whitebook, 1996), with Allen (2020) suggesting the indispensability of psychoanalysis for critical theory, and I will add: of psychoanalysis for the critical theory of anti-Semitism. I would further argue that psychoanalysis also greatly benefits from critical theory. Adorno's negative dialectics, in particular, offers valuable insights into grappling with the seemingly impossible in clinical practice and the significance of confronting the impossible, whether it involves the transformation of psychical symptoms or the fight against anti-Semitism.

References

Adorno, T. W. (1964). Zur Bekämpfung des Antisemitismus heute (Fighting anti-Semitism today). In *Das Argument, 29*. My translation. (Transcript of a speech given November 3, 1962).

Adorno, T. W. (1972). Theorie der Halbbildung. In G. Schriften, (Ed.), *Band 8: Soziologische Schriften 1* (pp. 93–121). Suhrkamp Verlag. (Original work published 1959)

Adorno, T. W. (1982). Freudian theory and the pattern of fascist propaganda. In A. Arato & E. Gephardt (Eds.), *The essential Frankfurt School reader* (pp. 118–137). Continuum. (Original work published 1951)

Adorno, T. W. (1993). Theory of pseudo-culture (1959). *Telos, 95,* 15–38. https://doi.org/10.3817/0393095015

Adorno, T. W. (1998). Education after Auschwitz. In *Critical models: Interventions and catchwords* (pp. 191–204, H. W. Pickford, Trans.). Columbia University Press.

Adorno, T. W. (2001a). *Problem of moral philosophy* (T. Schröder, Ed. & T. Livingstone, Trans.). Stanford.

Adorno, T. W. (2001b) *Metaphysics: Concepts and problems* (R. Tiedemann, Ed. & E. Jephcott, Trans.). Stanford University Press.

Adorno, T.W. (2004). *Negative dialectic* (E. B. Ashton, Trans.). Routledge. (Original work published 1967)

Adorno, T. W. (2012). Erziehung nach Auschwitz. In U. Bauer, U. H. Bittlingmayer, & A. Scherr (Eds.), *Handbuch Bildungs- und*

Erziehungssoziologie. Bildung und Gesellschaft. VS Verlag für Sozialwissenschaften, Wiesbaden. https://doi.org/10.1007/978-3-531-18944-4_7 (Original work published in 1966)

Adorno, T. W. (2014). Revisionist psychoanalysis (N. -N. Lee, Trans.). *Philosophy and Social Criticism, 40*(3), 326–338. (Original work published 1952)

Adorno, T. W. (2019). Remarks on the authoritarian personality. In T. W. Adorno, E. Frenkel-Brunswik, D. J. Levinson, & R. N. Sanford (Authors), *The authoritarian personality* (pp. xli–lxvi). Verso. (Original work drafted 1948)

Adorno, T. W., Frenkel-Brunswik, E., Levinson, D. J., & Sanford, R. N. (2019). *The authoritarian personality.* Verso. (Original work published 1950)

Allen, A. (2020). *Critique on the couch: Why critical theory needs psychoanalysis.* Columbia University Press.

Allen, A., & Ruti, M. (2019). *Critical theory between Klein and Lacan: A dialogue.* Bloomsbury.

Allport, G. W. (1946). Preface. In E. Simmel (Ed.), *Anti-Semitism, a social disease.* International Universities Press.

Ashter, G. (2021). *Exigent psychoanalysis: The interventions of Jean Laplanche.* Routledge.

Auerbach, E. (2003). *Mimesis: The representation of reality in Western literature.* Princeton University Press. (Original work published 1946)

Bahbah, H. (1994). *The location of culture.* Routledge.

Bauman, Z. (1991). *Modernity and ambivalence.* Polity.

Bauman, Z. (1995). *Life in fragments. Essays in postmodern morality.* Basil Blackwell.

Bauman, Z. (1998). Allosemitism: Premodern, modern, postmodern. In B. Cheyette & L. Marcus (Eds.), *Modernity, culture, and "the Jew".* Polity Press.

Boyarin, D. (2023). *The no-state solution: A Jewish manifesto.* Yale University Press.

Burston, D. (2014). Anti-Semitism. In T. Teo (Ed.), *Encyclopedia of critical psychology.* Springer.

Burston, D. (2020). *Critical theory and the problem of authority: Psychoanalysis, politics and the postmodern university.* Palgrave.

Butler, J. (2020). *The force of nonviolence.* Verso.

Caillois, R. (1984). Mimicry and legendary psychasthenia (J. Shepley, Trans.). *October, 31,* 17–32. https://doi.org/10.2307/778354 (Original work published 1935)

Catlin, J. (2022). Bauman, the Frankfurt School, and the tradition of enlightened catastrophism. In J. Palmer & D. Brzeziński (Eds.), *Revisiting modernity and the Holocaust.* Routledge. https://doi.org/10.4324/9781003120551

Cèsaire, A. (2001). *Discourse on colonialism*. Monthly Review Press. (Original work published 1950)

D'Arcy, M. (2020). Dialectic of enlightenment: Origin stories of Western Marxism. In K. Freeman & J. Munro (Eds.), *Reading the postwar future: Textual turning points from 1944* (pp. 43–59). Bloomsbury Academic.

Dahbour, O. (2012). *Self-determination without nationalism: A theory of postnational sovereignty*. Temple University Press.

Dews, P. (1987). *Logics of disintegration: Post-structuralist thought and the claims of critical theory*. Verso.

Felman, S. (2003). *The scandal of the speaking body: Don Juan with J.L. Austin, or seduction in two languages*. Stanford University Press.

Fenichel, O. (1940). Psychoanalysis of anti-Semitism. *American Imago, 1B*(2), 24–39.

Fink, B. (1997). *A clinical introduction to Lacanian psychoanalysis: Theory and technique*. Harvard University Press.

Fischer, C. T., Laubscher, L., & Brooke, R. (2016). *The qualitative vision for psychology: An invitation to a human science approach*. Duquesne University Press.

Fong, B. (2016). *Death and mastery: Psychoanalytic drive theory and the subject of late capitalism*. Columbia University Press.

Freud, S. (2001a). Totem and taboo. In J. Strachey (Ed. & Trans.), *The standard edition of the complete psychological works of Sigmund Freud, volume XIII (1912–1913)*. Vintage Books. (Original work published 1913)

Freud, S. (2001b). Repression. In J. Strachey (Ed. & Trans.), *The standard edition of the complete psychological works of Sigmund Freud, volume XVI (1914–1916): On the history of the psychoanalytic movement, papers on metapsychology and other works*. Vintage Books. (Original work published 1915)

Freud, S. (2001c). The 'uncanny'. In J. Strachey (Ed. & Trans.), *The standard edition of the complete psychological works of Sigmund Freud, volume XVII (1917–1919): An infantile neurosis and other works* (pp. 217–256). Vintage Books. (Original work published 1919)

Freud, S. (2001d). Group psychology and the analysis of the ego. In J. Strachey (Ed. & Trans.), *The standard edition of the complete psychological works of Sigmund Freud, volume XVIII (1920–1922)* (pp. 65–143). Vintage. (Original work published 1921)

Freud, S. (2001e). Negation. In J. Strachey (Ed. & Trans.). *The standard edition of the complete psychological works of Sigmund Freud, volume XIX (1923–1925): The ego and the id and other works*. Vintage Books. (Original work published 1925)

Fromm, E. (1984). *Working class in Weimar Germany: A psychological and sociological study*. Berg Publishers.

Grigat, S. (2019). The fight against antisemitism and the Iranian regime: Challenges and contradictions in the light of Adorno's categorical imperative. In A. Lange, K. Mayerhofer, D. Porat, & L. Schiffman (Eds.), *Volume 1 comprehending and confronting antisemitism* (pp. 441–462). De Gruyter. https://doi.org/10.1515/9783110618594-034

Hersh, E., & Royden, L. (2023). Antisemitic attitudes across the ideological spectrum. *Political Research Quarterly, 76*(2), 697–711. https://doi.org/10.1177/10659129221111081

Honneth, A. (1995). *The struggle for recognition: The moral grammar of social conflicts*. Polity.

Hook, D. (2017). *Six moments in Lacan: Communication and identification*. Routledge.

Horkheimer, M., & Adorno, T. W. (2004). *Dialectic of enlightenment: Philosophical fragments* (G. S. Noerr, Ed. & E. Jephcott, Trans.). Stanford. (Original work published 1947)

Hullot-Kentor, R. (2006). *Things beyond resemblance: Collected essays on Theodor W. Adorno*. Columbia University Press.

Lacan, J. (2006). *Écrits: The first complete edition in English* (J. A. Miller, Ed. & B. Fink, Trans.). W.W. Norton & Co. (Original work published 1966)

Laplanche, J. (1991). *New foundations for psychoanalysis*. Basil Blackwell.

Laplanche, J. (2015). *Between seduction and inspiration: Man* (J. Mehlman, Trans.). The Unconscious in Translation.

Laplanche, J. (2017). *Après-coup* (J. House, Trans.). The Unconscious in Translation.

Mariotti, S. (2009). Damaged life as exuberant vitality in America: Adorno, alienation, and the psychic economy. *Telos, 149*, 169–190. https://doi.org/10.3817/1209149169

McWilliams, N. (2020). *Psychoanalytic diagnosis: Understanding personality and structure in clinical process* (2nd ed.). Guilford Press.

Moten, F. (2018). *Stolen Life*. Duke University Press.

Morelock, J. (2017). Authoritarian populism contra "Bildung": Anti-intellectualism and the neoliberal assault on the Liberal Arts. *Cadernos CIMEAC, 7*(2), 63–81. https://doi.org/10.18554/cimeac.v7i2.2429

Nobus, D., & Quinn, M. (2005). *Knowing nothing, staying stupid: Elements for a psychoanalytic epistemology*. Routledge.

Noerr, G. S. (2004). Editor's afterward. In T. W. Adorno & M. Horkheimer *Dialectic of enlightenment: Philosophical fragments* (G. S. Noerr, Ed. & E. Jephcott, Trans.). Stanford University Press.

Potolsky, M. (2006). *Mimesis. Routledge.* https://doi.org/10.4324/978020 3401002

Rensmann, L. (2017). *Politics of unreason: The Frankfurt School and the origins of modern antisemitism.* SUNY.

Rogers, A. (2016). *Incandescent alphabets: Psychosis and the enigma of language.* Routledge.

Rose, G. (1993). *Judaism and modernity: Philosophical essays.* Verso.

Roudinesco, E. (1997). *Jacques Lacan* (B. Bray, Trans.). Columbia University Press.

Sass, L. (2019). Three dangers: Phenomenological reflections on the psychotherapy of psychosis. *Psychopathology, 52*(2), 126–134. https://doi.org/10.1159/000500012

Simmel, E. (Ed.). (1946). *Anti-Semitism, a social disease.* International Universities Press.

Vanheule, S. (2014). *Diagnosis and the DSM: A critical review.* Palgrave.

Vanheule, S. (2017). Conceptualizing and treating psychosis. *British Journal of Psychotherapy, 33*(3), 388–398. Wiley.

Verhaeghe, P. (2008). *On being normal and other disorders: A manual for clinical psychodiagnostics* (S. Jottkandt, Trans.). Karnac.

Whitebook, J. (1996). *Perversion and utopia: A study psychoanalysis and critical theory.* MIT Press.

Whitebook, J. (2004). The marriage of Marx and Freud: Critical theory and psychoanalysis. In F. Rush (Ed.), *The Cambridge companion to critical theory* (pp. 74–102). Cambridge University Press. https://doi.org/10.1017/CCOL0521816602

Wolin, R. (2023). *Heidegger in ruins: Between philosophy and ideology.* Yale University Press.

Wood, J. (2019). *Serious noticing: Selected essays 1997–2019.* Farrar, Straus, and Giroux. eBook.

7

Conclusion, or Not *Not* Anti-Semitism

"Tell Me If Anything Was Ever Done"

In the preceding pages, I made the case that anti-Semitism is hard to categorize, stemming, at least in part, from the difficulty in categorizing what it is to be Jewish, which seems to be multi-form (a figure of thought, a race, an ethnicity, a religion, a nation, none of the above). In thinking about the difficulty in categorization I constellated various instances of anti-Jewish practices across historical epochs where the Jew stands in the changing and ambivalent position of the troubling outside(r)-within—for others and, as it turns out, for Jews as well. Moreover, I found that the difficulty in thinking categorically is mimicked in the very scholarly study of anti-Semitism, my own included. As I showed, this difficulty in the research processes need not keep us from working toward a deeper understanding which could offer the tools to counter contemporary anti-Semitism. Instead, I employed a critical methodology and psychoanalytic attitude examining "culturally pre-formed objects" and psychological principles while continually questioning assumptions wherever they appeared. While this critical vigilance may have made for difficult thinking, I found that the complex subject matter itself—anti-Semitism (and

Jewishness)—called for such thinking, and I offered several instances (in education, psychotherapy, and politics) where this vigilance is found to have a concrete impact, if only a humble one. There are many studies of anti-Semitism which aim toward pragmatic solutions; I have chosen instead to aim at theoretical vigilance hoping that it will lead to ever-more-just practices.

To account for that double difficulty (in the matter and its study), I turned to Zygmunt Bauman's theory of proteophobia, or the anxious fear of the multi-form, form-changing, and what doesn't fit into clear-cut categories. Bauman was inspired by psychoanalysis and Frankfurt School Critical Theory (Catlin, 2022), and I offered a methodology for studying anti-Semitism and proteophobia through the return to the Frankfurt School's psychoanalytic critical theory, specifically Adorno's formulation of a negative dialectics and negative psychology. I proposed that thinking about the historical specificity of anti-Semitism in relation to proteophobia can help scholars think about anti-Semitism (and Jewishness) without lapsing into essentialism, exceptionalism, or eternalism. This question regarding tension between analyzing the principles underlying anti-Semitism, which give it conceptual cohesion, and analyzing the specificity of historical moments of anti-Semitism—especially in contradistinction to other forms of racism, oppression, and proteophobia—remains unanswered, but formulated in what I believe is a unique and uniquely productive manner, in the above chapters. Looking to the future, the concept of proteophobia could help to inform and perhaps even constellate projects adjacent to this one in the fields of psychoanalysis and critical theory.[1]

To reiterate, I found that anti-Semitism can be understood through the constellation of difficulties in thinking about anti-Semitism and Jewishness and the unique historical circumstances of Jews, Jewishness, and Judaism—*the concept of proteophobia is worth developing in response to this constellation.* Adorno's theoretical work provided something of a model for doing so. Yet, not so simply, this line of investigation led me to

---

[1] At this very moment, I have in mind projects such as Derek Hook's (2017, 2018) Lacanian theory of jouissance in racism, Eric Santner's (2001) Freudian/Rosenzweigian theory of "Egyptomania" (p. 7), and Gila Ashter's (2021) Laplanchian theory of "erotophobia." Expanding upon these connections could easily fill several volumes.

some seemingly impossible but no less necessary interventions at the level of politics, education, and psychoanalysis, each of which demands a kind of "staying with the trouble" (Haraway, 2016) in (dis)order to "lend a voice to suffering" (Adorno, 1967/2004, p. 17) and to remain open to unimaginable but no less necessary futures. This made for some admittedly heady thinking—"very, very heady," psychologist Leswin Laubscher (Personal communication, 2023) tells me—but also heavy thinking.

Is anti-Semitism still a problem? How could one say, no? White supremacists increasingly perpetrate violent attacks and terrorize Jewish people regardless of whether Jews consider themselves to be White or not. And, in recent years, conspiracy theories revolving around the Jews have gained new currency, especially in right-wing and online (mis) information-sharing circles. Anti-Semitism also persists, though perhaps in a distinct form, among progressive and on the left wing of the political spectrum. This can take the form of exclusionary practices or reducing Jewish identity to religious faith in (much needed) "diversity, equity, and inclusion" initiatives on college campuses and elsewhere. Additionally, among social justice minded folks, there can be an association between Jews and money, capitalism, power, Whiteness, and Israel, and where anti-Semitism can accompany legitimate struggles against violence. Anti-Semitism is still a troubling issue for Jewish people, and should be troubling for all those who wish to better comprehend the assumptions, myths, and ideologies that shape contemporary societies.

Not *Not* Anti-Semitism

In what follows, a conclusion but also an epilogue of sorts, I will share some reflections on the work above; but I will also make one last call to "stay with the trouble" in the sense that Donna Haraway (2016) gives the phrase, something like staying with the complexities *as complexities*, or questions *as questions* (what I consider a critical and psychoanalytic attitude) and as a force of resistance to destructive solutions. Haraway (2016) writes:

Staying with the trouble requires making oddkin; that is, we require each other in unexpected collaborations and combinations, in hot compost piles. We become-with each other or not at all. (p. 4)

We must stay with the trouble of Jewish questions as Jewish questions for and about Jews and Jewishness, but also for others. In May 2023, as I was editing the first complete draft of my manuscript and reflecting on what I uncovered in my investigation, the US White House announced a "First-Ever U.S. National Strategy to Counter Antisemitism." And in May of the next year (2024), as I was putting the final touches on the book, the US House of Representatives passed the Antisemitism Awareness Act, controversial on both the left and right wings of the political spectrum. Such initiatives are promising in taking the issue seriously. Still, I'm afraid that without critical research and scholarship, such initiatives could make things worse by misunderstanding the nature of the anti-Semitism. It is not enough to acknowledge that anti-Semitism is still a question for our time that must be answered by urgent action. True as it may be—no *Dayenu*—it is not enough. Sometimes, in our efforts to *achieve* social justice, we can unwittingly perpetuate the very thing we are striving to dismantle. Working for self-preservation or self-determination, for example, we easily miss what that "self" has meant and could mean. What then is this self? Or perhaps more apropos, "what is the Jews?" as Boyarin (2023) asks. If critical theory is still necessary—and I think it is—it is to ask such questions to prevent that kind of injustice committed in the name of justice, the injustice that looks so convincingly like justice.[2] Therefore, my aim has been to find ways of addressing anti-Semitism without neglecting other marginalized groups, or reinforcing anti-Semitism by collapsing Jewish forms of life into the broader domains of race and religion, or of the whitewashed categories of the European, the Judeo-Christian, and the Western.[3]

---

[2] Drucilla Cornell called this form of critical theory—namely, deconstruction, psychoanalysis, negative dialectics—philosophy of the limit. What could also be considered, following Sergey Dolgopolski (2009), a philosophy of disagreement.

[3] In 7th grade Social Studies, I failed the test on Judaism by offering wrong answers to questions like, "What is the name of the Jewish God?" The correct answer, apparently, was "Yahweh." I put down several other answers: Hashem, Adonai, Elohim, Hamelech. I had never once, in my five years of Jewish education at Hillel Academy, heard or seen the word, "Yahweh," the English and

Jewish people continue to debate, discuss, agree, and disagree on what it means to be Jewish and what it means to say "anti-Semitism." I am one of those Jews. Yet, I find that fighting anti-Semitism often involves solutions (e.g., definitions, bias training, "return" to Israel, assimilation, isolation, attacks on anti-Zionism) that seem to make Jewishness—which is so intertwined with those questions—disappear. Perhaps the Jewish answer to the Jewish Question really is another question, as Vivian Liska (2021a) so wittily suggests. After all—debate, conversation, discussion, questioning, indeed the Talmud and *machloykes*[4]—if there is something that constitutes Jewish thinking, as stereotypical as it might seem, is this not it?

The difficulty in categorizing Jewishness and anti-Semitism and the subsequent proteophobic responses correlate with a set of contentions: questions of Israel, Palestine, and Diaspora; questions of competitive memory (Holocaust, colonialism, and slavery); questions of anti-Semitism across the political spectrum; questions of race, religion, and nation; questions of visibility and invisibility of Jewishness; questions of Jewish ways of thinking and being. I argued, in the study of these questions in the preceding chapters, that the unique historical position of Jewish people and Jewish thought breaks the binary logic through which contemporary society solves social problems and organizes itself: oppressor/oppressed, colonialized/colonizer, White/nonwhite, traumatizer/traumatized, right/left, minority/majority, other/same, race/religion, nation/religion, philosophy/religion, progress/regress, civic/private, heredity/faith, Jewish/Greek, among others. It is evident that attempting to fit Jewishness into these preconceived categories or reconciling them into a

---

Christian transliterated verbalization for the four Hebrew letters (Tetragrammaton) that refer to the name of G-d, that is, in itself, as far as I was taught, unknowable and unsayable.

[4] *Machloykes* is a Yiddish word for disagreement, controversy, or debate, and characteristic of the kind of discourse found in the Talmud between Rabbis.

positive dialectical synthesis erases something of that Jewishness.[5,6] It is a loss I am not willing to accept.

Now, in reflecting on my efforts, I find myself asking questions about this Jewishness. What is it that I am seeking to protect? While staying with the trouble of these difficult questions, I noticed that I was changing as I proceeded. How could I not change, unless I already knew what I was going to say beforehand? And if I already knew, could I truly consider that as research? Throughout this process, I discovered a self that was in a constant state of transformation—blurry, messy, and quite possibly not entirely my own. I found that my ethics were intertwined with my Jewishness which was intertwined with the struggles of others through otherness and ambivalence. Perhaps it was unavoidable, given that in some way, and as I stated at the outset, the method must match the matter-at-hand. To borrow words from poet Ocean Vuong (2022), "How you say what you mean changes what you say" (p. 50). There may be some justified disagreement about how well I succeeded in saying it, stumbling over my lines, as I did, at times. Now, in good Jewish (and psychoanalytic) fashion, I will answer a question with another question, and another, and another, and another, as I endeavor to explore a little further the forms of thinking and doing of the Jewish collective and its potentials, this Jewishness that Daniel Boyarin (2023) calls *Yiddishkeit, Judaïtè, Judezm*e.[7]

---

[5] As a therapist on Psychology Today, Jewish is only a religious affiliation. Not even that, the site uses the word "Faith" in asking, "What is your identified faith?" which in no uncertain terms refers to faith in the Christian sense.

[6] As Boyarin (2023) points out,

Both Zionists and anti-Zionists seem to agree that it is only by defining the Jews as a religion," and not a "nation," that the inexorability of a "Jewish state"—with all that implies for all of the inhabitants of Palestine—can be avoided. Both of these choices, however, seem both inapt and inept [...] (pp. 1–2).

Categorizing the Jews as a nation requiring a state seems to undermine what it is to be Jewish and categorizing the Jews as a religion transforms Jewishness into Christianity. And Christianity, as we have seen, defines itself as what is not Jewish. These reductions come at the unjust cost of Jewish forms of life and values worth protecting, and must be considered an anti-Jewish practice, if not a form of anti-Semitism.

[7] In *No-State Solution* (2023), Boyarin develops a "diasporist vision for the future of the Jews doubly situated at home and abroad in their *doikayt*, their here and now," which is essentially a "commitment to the welfare of the people and their culture among whom one lives" (p. 90). This ambivalence between *Yiddishkayt* (Jewishness) and *doikayt* (Bundist hereness or Diasporism) may also be

Four Questions: מה נשתנה

The Question out of the Jews

I faced several (more or less) subterranean challenges in writing the previous chapters, one of which is particularly disconcerting: the stubborn feeling that my work would leave something out or make things worse. After I had already completed the first draft of my manuscript, I received Daniel Boyarin's *No-State Solution* (2023) in the mail, a slim volume that I had excitedly pre-ordered and immediately read three times over. It was there that I was introduced to Elad Lapidot's *Jews out of the Question: A Critique of Anti-Anti-Semitism* (2021), a book that posed inescapable questions for my work relating to that stubborn feeling. At first, I considered rewriting the whole book in light of these questions, but my friends and colleagues dissuaded me from such a foolhardy endeavor and encouraged me to explore these questions here. So, that's what I am doing. I will try to keep using this more personal voice, but please excuse me if I slip back into a slightly more heady style, it is not for lack of trying; there just seems to be no direct path to the end. (I will try to keep the "very, very heady" discussion in the footnotes, for the more adventurous among you.)

Lapidot's (2021) main gripe is the lack of attention to Jewishness and Jewish practices in the scholarly discourse surrounding anti-Semitism. The Jewish target of anti-Semitism is said to have little or nothing to do with "real" Jews. Where it is given attention, Jewishness seems to be formulated as something empty (as a kind of negativity defined completely by what is not Jewish or by anti-Semites) or not really Jewish. Lapidot (2021) is critical of the discourse of those who claim to be combating anti-Semitism—what he refers to as anti-anti-Semitism[8]—and seems to

---

the founding principle of Jewish identity, as such. Boyarin's (2023) Jewish manifesto describes an intrinsic ambivalence between the here and now of living with others in the Diaspora and the then and there of Jewishness always tied to historical materiality, resistant to present injustices, and seeking a more just, though unimaginable, world in the future. Boyarin (2023) argues that the most pressing question is not what the Jews have been (and they have been so many things) but rather, it is a question of values: "What kind of social identity do we want for the Jews?" (p. 9).

[8] What would happen if we read this anti-antisemitism in relation to Muñoz anti-antirelationalism and Fredric Jameson's anti-antiutopianism (Muñoz, 2019, p. 14)?

find in it only a complicity in the erasure of Jewish forms of life and thinking. Lapidot (2021) calls it a Jewish "epistemicide," the killing or silencing of a Jewish knowledge system. It's a powerful message. Perhaps even more startlingly, though, the focus of his criticism is on scholars such as Max Horkheimer and Theodor W. Adorno, David Nirenberg, and others. In my participation in working to combat anti-Semitism and my agreement with so much of Adorno's thinking and Nirenberg's scholarship, am I, too, inadvertently erasing something of this Jewishness?[9]

For the most part, I follow Lapidot's (2021) logic and take his warning to heart. But I also get the sense that his aim is slightly off, and he misses his target. Let me offer the first example that comes to mind, possibly the lowest-hanging fruit. David Nirenberg (2013) is one of those anti-anti-Semites that Lapidot (2021) takes issue with. Lapidot (2021) claims that for Nirenberg, anti-Judaism "has nothing to do with real Jews" (Lapidot, 2021, p. 66). This is not quite accurate. Nirenberg (2013) sought to set aside the material causes and consequences of anti-Judaism for Jews in order to show how Judaism and anti-Judaism are produced in part by non-Jews and function as antithetical concepts for many non-Jews in the

---

[9] One of the main points here is that the use of the figure of the Jew remains a tool for understanding the world. "There are no more Semites today than there are Aryans," Gil Anidjar (2007) points out (p. 18), and yet, "Semites and the condition that have produced, divided, and effaced them, still have a hold on us" (p. 9). This hold, for Anidjar (2007), is established through the production of a series of differential binaries, the differential condition that produced the concept of Semites as opposed to Aryans, or put another way, the Orient opposed to the Christian Occident, or yet another way, the Christian division of life into religious and secular—these discursive moments still have a hold on us. We are still conditioned by the terms "Jewish" and "anti-Semitism" just as we cannot help but still think in terms of religion and race, even or especially in suggesting that we are secular and post-racial. This discursive force is what Anidjar (2007) calls, following Derrida, the theological priority of one term, in a differential dialectic, over the other. It is theological because the one term is prioritized by way of revelation and not reason (and by this privileging, the one term becomes valued more/differentially; and then, in the next step, becoming naturalized, as the timeless and natural order of things and the true). This theological prioritization is inevitable and necessary but too often, or even always, veiled.

There are a series of dialectical productions that erase one side but really produce both sides. I understand negative dialectics, deconstruction, and perhaps even semiology as parallel processes through which the prioritization is exposed as a theological one. The theological is not false or irrational, but conditions truth and rationality. To follow the truth is merely to show that something is being naturalized and something is being erased in the process of history. The theory of proteophobia helps us think about how it may be that Jewishness is not the representation of the other, as the representation of the Occident, the Religious, the Racial, the Counter-national. It is that which challenges the smooth operation of the theological prioritization of functional binaries.

West and continue to constrain thought today. I find the idea to be quite compelling. In bracketing the relationship between Jews and anti-Judaism, Nirenberg (2013) is not making that relation disappear but bracketing and bringing it before our eyes for analysis. Nirenberg (2013) directly contradicts Lapidot's (2021) claim, and poses a set of guiding questions to introduce his project:

> Why did so many diverse cultures—even many cultures with no Jews living among them—think so much about Judaism? What work did thinking about Judaism do for them in their efforts to make sense of their world? Did that work in turn affect the ways in which future societies could or would think with Judaism? And how did this history of thinking about Judaism affect the future possibilities of existence for living Jews? (Nirenberg, 2013, p. 2)

In not emphasizing the Judaism of the Jewish collective, Nirenberg (2013) is not erasing or ignoring Jewishness or even Judaism for Jews, as Lapidot (2021) might suggest.[10] Instead, as I see it, Nirenberg (2013) offers his readers the opportunity to explore how these ideas affect Jewish and non-Jewish lives in societies grounded in a previously underexplored anti-Judaism. So, conceivably in Nirenberg's (2013) case, it makes some sense to omit what it is to be Jewish for Jews for the sake of answering other important (though, undoubtedly interconnected) research questions.

Still, according to Lapidot (2021), anti-anti-Semites continue to erase Jewishness by characterizing anti-Semites as nonrational or pathological and the Jewish target "as *mere* perception, construction, projection, imagination, fantasy, and myth" (p. 9; emphasis original). Have I not done just that? Lapidot (2021) distinguishes his own methods from these anti-anti-Semites, by including what he calls epistemic phenomenon or, in other words, Jewish forms of thinking, knowing, and making sense of the world. "It is only and strictly in this sense" Lapidot (2021) writes, "of rendering visible historical Jewish being, that anti-Semitism may be said

---

[10] Daniel Boyarin is explicit in his work *Judaism* (2019) that he is formulating a way of thinking Jewishness back into David Nirenberg's framework in *Anti-Judaism* (2013).

to hold some 'truth'" (Lapidot, 2021, p. 194).[11] According to Lapidot (2021) anti-Semitic rhetoric reveals something of the truth of what it is to be Jewish for the mere fact that they are talking about Jewish people, that Jewish people are something to think about and talk about. What an unsettling claim!

Are anti-Semites projecting something of their own ambivalent fears and desires out into the world onto the figure of the Jew, or are they capturing something true about Jews? Perhaps Lapidot is merely saying that to know which is the case, we need to think about Jewishness; I can follow him in that line of thinking. And couldn't some anti-Semites be doing one thing, and some the other, and some both at the same time? Still, when the anti-Semite says that they hate Jewish greed, social work, bad hygiene, good hygiene, femininity, macho-ness, control of global financial institutions, dual loyalties, isolationism, rigid rule following, promotion of communism, ritual murder—are they really talking about what Jewish people are or do as Jews? Boyarin (1993, 2023), for one, famously discusses the carnality or femininity of the Jews as concrete examples of some knowledge that some anti-Semites know about some Jews.

A social group, like the Jewish people, can be considered to exist and endure through performative reiterations. These reiterations encompass collective practices, traditions, and actions. These shared forms of knowing and doing play a crucial role in the group's continuity and identity over time. Indeed, Jewish people may do things that anti-Semites hate. Perhaps anti-Semites have an aesthetic distaste for small hats? I'm joking. But in all seriousness, it is possible (and productive, even) to consider that along with hating things that Jews do not do, many anti-Semites hate what Jews do do. Here is a general account of the components and choreography of the performative reiterations of Jews pulled together by Daniel Boyarin (2023). I quote it at length because it shows something of the knowledge about the Jews that Lapidot (2021) suggests is a missing component in most studies of anti-Semitism. I find it to be a remarkably compelling and relatable articulation of Jewishness:

---

[11] To riff on the phenomenological axiom, consciousness of "Jews" is consciousness of something.

The practices that constitute Jewish identity—and perhaps more broadly ethnic or national identities in general, *mutatis mutandis*—consist of the speaking of Jewish languages or the use of markedly Jewish forms of language (Throw Mama from the train—a kiss), modes of walking, body language, telling stories, singing songs, as well as the study of Talmud, practicing the rituals of the holidays, eating this food and not that. The sharing of these repetitious performances is what produces kinship bonds. Here I must again refer to Patricia Williams's perfect description [...], that it is not biology that produces ancestral bonds but "the inheritance of linguistically and rhetorically embedded traditions passed on in habits of speech. I am composed of the voices of those who bred me. We are talked into the world by our forebears: by how they parsed words or not."

None of these performances apply to all Jews, nor need they. At the very beating heart of such narratives, practices, representations, scripts, doings, all the performances that produce *Judaïtè*, are Torah, primarily, but not necessarily or only the study of the Talmud (with all of its ramifications for forms of Jewish speech and speech practices), and the performance of the Jewish doings, whether or not they are conceived of as divine commandments. As that Torah itself reminds us: "Forever let a person study the Torah even not for its own sake, for from such study, they will come to study for its own sake." (Boyarin, 2023, pp. 57–58)

I see myself in these words and acknowledge that there is something that can be known and said about the Jews in this precise sense; Jews speak a set of languages, eat certain foods, perform a constellation of rituals.[12] Nevertheless, the idea that *anti-Semitism may be said to hold some "truth"* does not seem to hold up in all or even most cases of the anti-Semite's supposed knowledge about the Jews. Do the Jews really drink the blood of Christian babies? Are Jews plotting to replace White Christian American citizens with illegal Muslim immigrants of color? The answer is, no. These claims reflect the projective and phobic

---

[12] Yiddishist musician, Daniel Kahn (2020) sings "Learn to be a Jew," in a remarkable performance of this Jewish being.

processes of the anti-Semite, not a quality of Jews.[13,14] Am I missing something here?

In some instances, though certainly not all or even most instances, anti-Semites are talking about and targeting this Talmudic Jewishness directly (seemingly without projection or displacements). And on those rare occasions, mainly restricted to intellectual anti-Judaism, the anti-Semite knows what they are talking about, but Boyarin (2023) says, "they just get their values upside down" (p. 125). To my mind, this softens

---

[13] That is, even if the anti-Semitic assertions are psychic condensations and displacements using, for such assertions, the raw material of what Jews do or have done, like circumcision, social justice, and immigrant rights. This raw material functions as does the memory traces from the day's residue in the manifest content of the dreamwork.

[14] We can imagine a fantasy world where some Jews do drink the blood of Christian babies, or we can imagine that such a claim is a condensation of Christian obsession with blood and Talmudic circumcision rituals. In either case, as Langmuir (1996) points out, this still wouldn't logically allow for the statement "the Jews X" to be true in the sense that Lapidot (2021) refers to as "rendering historical Jewish being." Langmuir (1996) reminds us of the logical distinction between potentially rational knowledge and less justifiable assertions. Specifically (the reader may recall this from Chap. 3), he discusses the distinction between the assertion that "some Jews X" and the categorical assertion that "the Jews X." While the former assertion may be rational insofar as they are based on observations, the latter is used in the context of xenophobia and anti-Semitism and is often irrational or even nonrational. As Žižek (1992/2009) points out, to function as anti-Semitism and not merely prejudice; the Jew must be hated for what is "in Jew more than Jew" (p. 107), something always in excess of any accurate positive Jewish characteristics. To be anti-Semitism, there must be something in excess or surplus of Jewish characteristics, no matter the positive content. Žižek (1992/2009) helps to unpack this insight:

[…] at first, 'Jew' appears as a signifier connoting a cluster of supposedly 'effective' properties (intriguing spirit, greedy [sic] for gain, and so on), but this is not yet anti-Semitism proper. To achieve that, we must invert the relation and say: they are like that (greedy, intriguing …) because they are Jews. This inversion seems at first sight purely tautological—we could retort: of course it is so, because 'Jewish' means precisely greedy, intriguing, dirty … But this appearance of tautology is false: 'Jew' in 'because they are Jews' does not connote a series of effective properties, it refers again to that unattainable X, to what is 'in Jew more than Jew' and what Nazism tried so desperately to seize, measure, change into a positive property enabling us to identify Jews in an objective-scientific way. (pp. 106–107)

For Žižek (1992/2009), this "unattainable X" is not in the Jew but the signifying operation of language. This only seems to contradict the claim that anti-Semites hold some knowledge about the Jews. For Žižek (1992/2009), this is beside the point when trying to understand anti-Semitism which is always in surplus of that Jewishness, since "the ideological figure of a Jew is a way to stitch up the inconsistency of our own ideological system" (p. 49). Lapidot's counterpoint might be that instead of exposing the surplus as surplus (and what is displaced in the symbolic via projection, etc.), anti-anti-Semites reject the claims made by anti-Semitism entirely, and end up rejecting the Jewishness that is not surplus, too. The baby with the bathwater. Both points seem to be correct.

Lapidot's attack and makes room for the multi-form ways of doing and talking Jewishness, but also fighting anti-Semitism.

On the one hand, the idea that there could be some truth to the anti-Semite's assertions may hold up in terms of some anti-Judaism and some philosophical anti-Semitism (e.g., Kant, 1793/2008 and Nietzsche, 1895/2005), but it does not seem to hold up in terms of conspiracy theories or racial and biological anti-Semitism which have little to do with Jewish performative reiterations. On the other hand, though the content and form of racial discourse is clearly irrational (Fields & Fields, 2012), the projection involved in it is not random and may even come to socially construct what it means to be Jewish for Jews in certain historical moments. The Jews as race—we are forced by this false attribution (once-upon-a-time accepted by many Jews) to ask, if not race, what? Religion? No. Nation? Not in the traditional sense. The false attribution does reveal a truth in the form of a question—what Boyarin (2023) calls the New Jewish Question: "What is the Jews?"

So, are the Jews wealthy, white, capitalists, globalists, socialists? Do they have dual loyalties? Do they conspire? Certainly, some Jews are wealthy, some are socialists, and some are doctors, lawyers, merchants, and actors. Heck, I'm a psychotherapist. Some of us do come together to talk about changing the world—especially on Saturdays.[15] While wealth is not an essential aspect of being Jewish, social engagement and changing the world may very well be. It is not that the Jews are essentially powerful, even though some Jews have power. Some of these Jews may take power in the name of Jewishness (as in the case of Israel), but cannot (or at least should not, in my opinion) be said to be powerful because they are Jewish. Jews may be doctors and actors but the statement, "The Jews control the medical industry and the media," is still an anti-Semitic

---

[15] I say this rhetorically, of course. Actually, Shabbat is not always the time for changing the world or even planning to change it, even if the conversations at Shul do seem to focus on the work of making the world a better place. In its most ideal, Shabbos is positioned as a time for rest, fostering relationships, and deep contemplation—a moment for being rather than doing. The focus shifts from actively creating to enjoying the existing creations. This day of rest not only provides an opportunity but also dictates the importance of reflecting on the toil and labor, as well as on the complexities and contradictions inherent in observing such a commandment. Paradoxically, Shabbat remains profoundly linked to the world-changing endeavors of the other six days of the week, as it offers a moment to question one's most fundamental assumptions about life and work.

assertion. If anything, Jews use might and harness power in spite of their Jewishness. "Not by might, nor by power, but by my Spirit, says the Lord of hosts" (Zachariah, 4:6). I agree with Lapidot (2021) and Boyarin (2023) that we should think about Jewishness—both are doing the important work of reintroducing something of Jewish thought and activity into the discourse of combating anti-Semitism—but we need to take more care in our criticism of, at least, those who take care with that anti-anti-Semitism.

The Question of Jewish Non-Identity

Liska (2021b) summarizes Lapidot's (2021) argument as follows:

> Lapidot defines antisemitism as the "de-semanticization of the Jew," an emptying out of the Jew's "epistemic content." More simply stated, the antisemitic discourses do not grant the existence of Jewish thought. He then shows that anti-anti-Semitism—far from its pretense to fight anti-Semitism—in fact collaborates in this emptying out, presumably because anything said of the Jew is considered stereotypical, a generalization, a negation. Anti-anti-Semitism accords no affirmation of a positive episteme to what Lapidot calls "the Jewish." At first glance, as a negation of a negation anti-anti-Semitism should rescue a "positive" content of the Jewish. But Lapidot shows that it instead merges with this negation. (Liska, 2021b, np)

I find this to be a fairly accurate encapsulation of Lapidot's argument in *Jews Out of the Question* (2021). I want to highlight the scare quotes surrounding the word "positive." On the one hand, Lapidot (2021) argues that Horkheimer and Adorno (1947/2004) and Nirenberg (2013) are problematic in focusing on the anti-Semite, since they seem to neglect the positive content of Jewishness; an erasure by omission. On the other hand, Lapidot (2021) contends that Horkheimer and Adorno (1947/2004) embody a "positive" Jewish epistemology when their arguments take the form of negation of reification and the false (such as false projection, false immediacy, false clarity, untruth). He finds this at the very heart of their work (Lapidot, 2021, p. 86). (And so do I.) "Thus,"

Lapidot (2021) writes, "not only do [Horkheimer and Adorno] recognize a Jewish episteme, Jewish epistemology looms as the historical paradigm of critical theory itself" (p. 69). I find this to be a confusing but no less intriguing contradiction, best expressed in terms of Adorno's concept of non-identity.

The question in the previous section was prompted by my reading of Lapidot (2021), which I found by way of Boyarin (2023). This next section's question is posed by Liska (2021b) by way of Lapidot (2021) by way of Boyarin (2023). Liska (2021b) suggests that the problem articulated by Lapidot (2021), regarding the erasure of Jewishness in the battle against anti-Semitism, occurs "when the Jew is taken to epitomize non-identity, non-place, and no-time" (np). Is this not the case?[16] The non-identity and non-place *of* the Jews seem to refer to what Jews *are*—Liska (2021b) is right to caution against this epitomization, as she does above—but might this also or more primarily refer to what Jews do?[17] Rather than abandoning the concepts of non-place and non-identity, I offer that these concepts refer to a signature Jewish ethical relations and the very "positive" practice of doing Jewishness. In this sense, the non-place of Jews is effectively ethical. In addition to non-place (noun) of Diaspora and the Talmud—the traveling homeland (Boyarin, 2015)—we can think of non-place as ethically refusing to place (verb) the other; a refusal to construe the other or to impose finite limits upon the other in a way that leads to injustice.[18] This is Jewishness at its very best, as moral consciousness. So a non-place refers to the refusal to impose one's own place, my place—certainly a positive and embodied, indeed carnal and Diasporic, place—onto the other. This refusal, I do believe, creates a hollow for the

---

[16] To my mind, Jews do epitomize negativity for some non-Jews, especially as non-placeable and non-identifiable.

[17] When I italicize the preposition "of" in "non-X *of* the Jews" in the sentence above, I am invoking the polyvalence of the preposition "of" as in Kant's Critique *of* Pure Reason (where it could refer to a critique carried out by pure reason and a critique carried out on pure reason).

[18] For instance, there exists a kind of non-place "grounded" in Diaspora and a moving non-placeable place within books, historically the Torah and Talmud, which Boyarin (2015) refers to as a traveling homeland (see also Boyarin & Boyarin, 2002). Jews most certainly have a positive place from which they positively identify—I am a Diaspora Jew living in California; I am a Jew who lives in Israel; I am a Jew who finds community in synagogue. I am not saying that the non-place of Jews is the non-place of the positive Jewish identity. Instead, I see it as the non-place of Jewish ethics and Jewish thinking.

other in me, and remains open to the multiplicity of ways—each an ethical relation to the Other, the Neighbor, the Stranger—of doing Jewishness today.[19]

Similarly, to speak of the non-identity of the Jews is not to say that the Jew *is* non-identity or has no identity. I, for instance, identify as Jewish. (You may have noticed.) The non-identity *of* the Jews is about a positive practice of making a place in the world for non-identity (not being or non-being, but otherwise-than-being [Levinas, 1974/2006]). Could we not say, however, that each Jew is, indeed, non-identical, not because they are Jewish, but because everyone carries something of the non-fungible and uncategorizable? (Is this not what Levinas [1961/1969] might call the face of the other? Or more radically still, the diachronic other which hollows out the self in substitution [Levinas, 1974/2006]?) If this is potentially true for all human subjects, what of it is particularly true for Jews? Being Jewish, then, may be about making a place or hollow for the non-identity beyond my grasp and by recognizing that the identity of the non-identical is not the truth.[20] Moreover, it is about being called by Jewish practices, literature, laws, communally performative reiterations, other people, the voice of suffering, etc., to make such a hollow for the other. (This is what I understand by Jewish "chosenness.")

As I noted above, Lapidot (2021) seems to point to this form of non-identity as a properly Jewish form of knowledge, and he finds it in the early chapters of Horkheimer and Adorno's *Dialectic of Enlightenment* (1947/2004). Here is one such section quoted at length, where Horkheimer and Adorno (1947/2004) discuss this directly in terms of *Bilderverbot* (the Jewish ban on the idolatrous image of G-d, the infinite, truth, utopia, the future, etc.):

> The disenchanted world of Judaism propitiates magic by negating it in the idea of God. The Jewish religion brooks no word which might bring solace

---

[19] This is not just there in Jewish thinking but also potentially the very structure of human psychical reality (see Laplanche, 1991).

[20] Eric Oberle (2018) develops Adorno's theory of non-identity into a persuasive theory of negative identity and as a new social and liberatory phenomenology. According to Oberle (2018), this theory of negative identity was forged in Adorno's theory of anti-Semitism.

to the despair of all mortality. It places all hope in the prohibition on invoking falsity as God, the finite as the infinite, the lie as truth. The pledge of salvation lies in the rejection of any faith which claims to depict it, knowledge in the denunciation of illusion. Negation, however, is not abstract. The indiscriminate denial of anything positive. [...] The self-satisfaction of knowing in advance, and the transfiguration of negativity as redemption, are untrue forms of the resistance to deception. The right of the image is rescued in the faithful observance of its prohibition. Such observance, "determinate negation," is not exempted from the enticements of intuition by the sovereignty of the abstract concept, as is skepticism, for which falsehood and truth are equally void. Unlike rigorism, determinate negation does not simply reject imperfect representations of the absolute, idols, by confronting them with the idea they are unable to match. Rather, dialectic discloses each image as script. It teaches us to read from its features the admission of falseness which cancels its power and hands it over to truth. Language thereby becomes more than a mere system of signs. With the concept of determinate negation Hegel gave prominence to an element which distinguishes enlightenment from the positivist decay to which he consigned it. However, by finally postulating the known result of the whole process of negation, totality in the system and in history, as the absolute, he violated the prohibition and himself succumbed to mythology. (Horkheimer & Adorno, 1947/2004, pp. 17–18)

Here, Horkheimer and Adorno (1947/2004) are offering a form of Jewishness,[21] but it is not a positive identity (or re-semanticization, if you will) of Jewish people which could so easily violate the *Bilderverbot* being described.[22]

---

[21] See Martin Jay (2020) for more on the relationship between the Frankfurt School, Jewishness, and *Bilderverbot*.

[22] Is the negativity formulated by the early Frankfurt School theorists distinct from the negative conception of Jewishness found in Sartre (1965) and Memmi (1962)? Sartre famously formulated Judaism as a kind of pure cultureless negativity emerging through the entrails of the anti-Semite. Memmi countered this view by demonstrating that Jewish culture encompasses both negative and positive aspects. He pointed to the cultural advancements in Israel as evidence of this positive dimension. Sartre, after visiting Israel, acknowledged the presence of a positive Jewish culture. While Horkheimer and Adorno's (1947/2004) critical formulation of negativity differs from Sartre and Memmi's phenomenological approaches, there appears to be an oversight in philosophical discourse regarding the emphasis on the prohibition against idolatry and the Jewish ban on images, neglecting or downplaying the fact that 248 of the 613 *mitzvot* are considered positive commandments.

Liska (2021b), too, refuses to offer an image of positive Jewish life, despite her repudiation of non-identity. "I myself hesitate to spell this out," Liska (2021b) tells us, "mainly out of fear of essentializing, fixing, pinning down and narrowing our understanding of what is Jewish" (np). She insists upon a positive Jewish identity, but stops just short of defining it. "A similar hesitation is," Liska (2021b) believes," shared by some (though not all) the anti-anti-Semites Lapidot addresses" (np). Is this not the refusal of idolatry that might keep Horkheimer and Adorno (1947/2004) from including an image of "real" Jewish people into their critique of anti-Semitism? *Bilderverbot* is not a resistance to the image as such, to the idea that people have faces, or the idea that Jews are people with identities. No, it is a resistance to the re-presentation of those faces and identities as idols and as the truth. This, I do believe, is the non-identity of the Jews.[23]

Boyarin (2023) seems less concerned with *Bilderverbot* when describing a positive Jewish identity. He shows that Jewish forms of life can be identified in the very doings and the goings-on of the various Jewish collectives—the stories, literature, languages, humor, food, values, culture, rituals, tonality, gestures, music, and controversies of Jewish people constellated by the Talmud—without, seemingly, limiting the possible

---

[23] The non-identity of Jews does not occlude thinking or promote a kind of faith (in the non-identical). Jewishness can be thought about, for some Jewish thinkers quite rationally. For Levinas (1963/1997), reason and language are a spiritual order that has nothing to do with supernatural miracles, irrationalism, or mysticism (p. 7). He suggests that mystical and irrational forms of Jewishness can lapse into an idolatry of faith. The Sacred in Levinas' Judaism is "one's relation to man" (p. 16). Elsewhere, he writes:

[…] saying that the meaning [sens] of reality is understood in terms of ethics is tantamount to saying that the universe is sacred. But it is in an ethical sense [sens] that it is sacred. Ethics is an optics of the Divine. Henceforth, no relation with God is direct or immediate. The Divine can be manifested only through my neighbour. For a Jew, Incarnation is neither possible nor necessary. (Levinas, 1963/1997, p. 159)

Such a non-mystical divinity that Levinas (1963/1997) finds in Judaism "entails the risk of atheism" (p. 15). Indeed, despite the refusal of divine incarnation, Levinas (1963/1997) says that "[a]dhering to the Sacred is infinitely more materialist than proclaiming the incontestable value of bread and meat in the lives of ordinary people" (p. 7). If I understand correctly, Levinas (1963/1997) is suggesting with this "an inversion of the apparent order" (p. xiv). The meat and potatoes of materialism can sometimes hide its own metaphysical foundations (for us) by ignoring the workings of language. Even the sacred in Jewish life is a matter of material doings. But only the other's hunger is sacred, as Levinas writes: "There is no bad materialism other than our own. This first inequality perhaps defines Judaism" (p. xiv).

futures open to those collectives. As Boyarin (2023) succinctly puts it, "The Talmud was considered not only or even primarily as a text, as a book, but as a set of practices, and these practices are quintessentially diasporic, even foundational for the Jewish Diaspora as a positive form of life, as opposed to a negative space of deprivation" (p. 100); I imagine Liska (2021b) would agree. The tension between this identity and non-identity of Jews is important to think through, debate, discuss, and not one to make disappear, conclude, define. I will leave this as an open question.

In *Difficult Freedom: Essays on Judaism*, Levinas (1963/1997) illustrates this ambivalence of Jewish non-identity through the Talmud. Levinas invokes the sages in the Talmud's "Tractate Tannith" who say that a day of rain is greater than the resurrection of the dead (redemption), greater than the day when the Torah was given (revelation), and even greater— yes, even greater—than the day when the earth was created (creation), since the day of rain is universally given to just and unjust people, alike. Levinas (1963/1997) interprets this to mean, "There is a subordination of every possible relationship between God and man—redemption, revelation, creation—to the instruction of a society in which justice, instead of remaining an aspiration of individual piety, is strong enough to extend to all and be realized" (p. 21). Those very Jewish forms of knowledge, content, and identity that Levinas is so justifiably hesitant to relinquish (redemption, revelation, creation), are subordinate to the rain; and this is Jewish and what Levinas calls Jewish messianism. The Jewish both is and is not the exemplar of itself. One can picture, with some straining of the eyes and mind, in the words of Levinas (1963/1997), "loving the Torah even more than God" (p. 145) or even a Jewish atheism, but a day of rain that is more Jewish than the Torah? It is impossible to picture. This seems to erase the very sources of Jewish epistemology and identity, that is, unless this is exactly that.

This Jewish messianism—illustrated in the Tractate, above—requires a self that is not itself or merely for itself. Here, Levinas' formulation evokes Rabbi Hillel's foundational Jewish ethical problematic: "If I am not for myself, who will be for me? But, if I am only for myself, what am I? And if not now, when?" If I am not a self that is for myself, who will stand in for me in the name of justice? And if I am only for myself and my own, *what* am I? Can I truly call myself a Jew? This is my reading. Hospitality, Derrida (1998) says, requires a simultaneous attachment and letting go of my own. Perhaps Levinas betrays this Jewishness—as, for example, his critics have noted, when he fails to extend to Palestinians this hospitality or even the status of ethical subjects. If so, might this betrayal arise from a fear that if he is not for his own, to purposefully mis-paraphrase Hillel, for Jewish people above others, there will be no Jews in the future? It is certainly a risk to "let ourselves go" as Moten (2018, p. xi; See Kleinberg, 2021) might put it, but without taking that risk, annihilation is certain, since this is the heart of being-Jewish. Is this what Levinas (1963/1997) *calls* "difficult freedom" (p. 272)? And it is a calling, this difficult freedom—one that Levinas did not always live up to—but a no less imperative one.[24]

The Question of Anti-Anti-Anti-Semitism

Now, I will return from Liska (and the strange concept of non-identity) back to Lapidot (2021), for a very brief moment, to consider his

---

[24] "[…T]o 'be' a Jew," Butler (2013) writes, "is to be departing from oneself, cast out into a world of the non-Jew, bound to make one's way ethically and politically precisely there within a world of irreversible heterogeneity" (p. 15). Clearly, not all Jews identify with the form of Jewishness, *Yiddishkeit*, or *Judaïtè* that is being described in relation to non-identity, diaspora, heterogeneity, the Talmud, otherness, negativity, ambivalence. In reading Muñoz (2019), I noticed that perhaps this is not unlike the way that not all gay and lesbian individuals resonate with the Queerness of Queer Theory. Muñoz (2019) refers to mainstream gay identities as the "pragmatic gay politics" of the "broken-down present" (p. 30). In his masterful *Cruising Utopias*, Muñoz (2019) highlights the work of (thinkers associated with being Jewish such as) Adorno, Marcuse, Derrida, and Bloch, thereby indirectly bringing Jewishness and Queerness into proximity. Although Queer struggles and Jewish struggles are not the same or equivalent, I hope you can pardon my use of a few local analogies. Mendelsohn (2022) suggests that Jews are to Europe what gay people are to patriarchy—unassimilable. Muñoz (2019) shows that Queerness is always in the future, impossible but hoped for. And, if I understand him correctly, glimpses of the as-of-yet-unknown future are recognized in the present in the precarious happiness of radically particular moments. Queerness is between the two—the disappointing moment of fleeting happiness and the utopian future—and not in either of them. It could be thought of as a performance that troubles pre-existing categories and not an identity one occupies. Likewise, *Judaïtè* à la Boyarin (2023) and Levinas (1963/1997) is less an assertion about what Jews are or have been, than performative reiterations and practices related to what could be and a set of identities and texts open to a future and not worshiped as a golden calf. Perhaps this is what Liska (2021b) means by the moment "when the Jew is taken to epitomize…no-time" (np).

provocative (and a little scandalizing) solution to the problem he finds in anti-anti-Semitism. Lapidot (2021) champions the cause of anti-anti-anti-Semitism (and of Heideggerian phenomenology),[25] which he insists is a promotion of neither anti-Semitism nor anti-anti-Semitism. According to Lapidot, Jewish thought is denied existence ("dis-figuration") when, in fighting anti-Semitism, any engagement with the figure of Jews, Jewishness, or Semites is dismissed as merely chimerical, illusory, or anti-Semitic. One such instance occurs when people promoting anti-anti-Semitism erase the hyphen in anti-Semitism and use the term "antisemitism," as in the IHRA Working Definition of Antisemitism. This rhetorical use of the term "antisemitism," at times (and I want to emphasize this "at times"), enact a refusal to consider the Semitic or anti-Semitism or even Jewishness as worthy of consideration in any critical way.[26]

In engaging with the theory of "anti-anti-anti-Semitism," I am rising to a new theoretical register which may come across as over-intellectual and absurd, to say the least. It is worth touching on, nonetheless, for a few reasons. First of all, Lapidot uses it to critique Horkheimer and Adorno's anti-anti-Semitism. Second, to take up anti-anti-anti-Semitism, for Lapidot (2021), is not merely to be against those against those against the Jews or more plainly to be against Jews. Anti-anti-anti-Semitism is, instead, against a particular body of discourse referred to as "anti-anti-Semitism." It is the acknowledgment, one that seems too often ignored, that one can be *against* (anti-) a particular discourse of anti-anti-Semitism without being *for* anti-Semitism. Lastly, Lapidot (2021) claims that the vigilance of thought leading to this seemingly absurd "anti-anti-anti-" points to the very positive thing that he finds in Jewish forms of knowing.

---

[25] Lapidot (2021) is ambiguous here, as he also calls for a non-anti-anti-Semitism approach to the Jewish Question.

[26] Readers may have noticed that I have used anti-Semitism instead of antisemitism throughout the project. Still, it does not seem accurate to say that all such cases of using the term "antisemitism" involve the dis-figuration of the Jewish, especially in academic writing. Langmuir's *Towards a Definition of Antisemitism* (1996) may be one such exception, as is Frosh's *Antisemitism and Racism* (2023).

Lapidot (2021) argues that although certain aspects of Jewishness targeted by anti-Semites may indeed be Jewish in nature (e.g., carnality, but perhaps also negativity, otherness, ambivalence, and non-identity), the refusal to acknowledge the potential accuracy of their knowledge, based on the assumption that anti-Semitism is always delusional, forces those combating anti-Semitism to reject any Jewish epistemic significance, *regardless of its validity.* Lapidot's (2021) methodology shares significant similarities with Nirenberg's (2013) perspective. Nirenberg (2013) states that anti-Judaism is not necessarily pathological. But that lack of reflection on the place of anti-Judaism in Western civilization, *that* is pathological. Nirenberg (2013) quotes Horkheimer and Adorno (1947/2004) who write that "what is pathological about anti-Semitism is not projective behavior as such, but the absence of reflection in it" (Nirenberg, 2013, p. 299).[27] It is crucial to clarify that this does not imply, or at least I hope it does not, that the anti-Semites are correct—clearly, they are not. And I can't imagine that Lapidot is suggesting we go around seriously considering whether Jews are subhuman, rats, or parasites. To my mind, there seems to be room to explore anti-Semitic projections *and* the figures (e.g., otherness) labeled Jewish by both Jews and anti-Semites.[28]

At its most modest, Lapidot's project is a call to think about Jewishness and a warning that sometimes in the discourse of those trying to protect Jews from anti-Semitism (what he is calling anti-anti-Semitism), any talk about the Jewishness of those Jews is considered anti-Semitic.[29] It is not. Notably, Horkheimer and Adorno (1947/2004) contend that they are not talking about Jews but about anti-Semitism.

Lapidot (2021) takes his anti-anti-anti-Semitism a step further (perhaps for some, a step off the cliff) claiming that "anti-anti-anti-Semitism is accordingly an introduction to Jewish thought, to thinking as it has

---

[27] Nirenberg (2013) goes so far as to suggest that,

The goal of my project, like Horkheimer and Adorno's, is to encourage reflection about our "projective behavior," that is, about the ways in which our deployment of concepts into and onto the world might generate "pathological" fantasies of Judaism. (p. 468)

[28] Langmuir's (1996) analysis does just that with his schema of rational, irrational, and nonrational assertions (see Chap. 3).

[29] This, much like how any talk about Blacks, as a cohesive group, can be considered part of racialized, that is racist, discourse (see Fields & Fields, 2012).

historically been deployed in and as Jewish being, to thinking as *machloykes*" (p. 18). "Anti-anti-anti-Semitism" he continues, "is introduction to Talmud" (Lapidot, 2021, p. 18).[30] What a claim! In other words, anti-anti-anti-Semitism is somehow quintessentially Jewish. (A provocation, if there ever was one.) If I follow Lapidot in this, and I'm not so sure that I do, it begs the seemingly absurd question of anti-anti-anti-anti-Semitism as an even better introduction to the Talmud, and so on. This moment of absurdly adding the "anti-," I would suggest, is what may be most helpful in Lapidot's (2021) thinking. My own critique of anti-anti-Semitism—and this book is one—is also a critique of anti-Semitism without, I hope, erasing and thereby hiding any culturally preformed "anti-." Jewish forms of thinking and knowing may take the form of the continual addition of the "anti-" and the continued debate that this entails. Still, do any of these discourses help us think about anti-Semitism and the Jewish people who face oppressive forms of that anti-Semitism? I don't think it is enough to critique anti-anti-Semitism or to promote anti-anti-anti-Semitism. The work of justice demands more deliberation, more time.

The Question of Hope and Pessimism in Jewish Thinking

I was surprised (and you may be surprised at my surprise) to find that my investigation into anti-Semitism seemed to inevitably lead me to so many questions about Jewishness. I found that the Jews represent negativity, ambivalence, otherness, non-identity, and the uncategorizable for anti-Semites in a variety of historical contexts, and that these concepts may be figural to the Jewish experience as well. How do I reconcile this with positive forms of my own Jewish identity and those of other *Menorah* lighting and *Mezuzah* tapping Jews around the world? Is there a fullness to the Jewish relationship *with* negativity, ambivalence, otherness, etc.? And if there is such a fullness, what are the relationships between these concepts and the performative reiterations of Jewish doings? Allow me to offer

---

[30] Anti-anti-anti-Semitism is here considered to be an introduction to the Talmud, but so, Lapidot (2021) apparently thinks, is the philosophy of Martin Heidegger.

some last thoughts for consideration—some more heady, some more hearty, and some more poetic or spleen. None conclusive.

Jewish literature and, arguably, Jewish life, starts with the Torah and G-d as alterity. It is hardly controversial to state that Jewishness has *something* to do with G-d, and that the Jewish G-d is historically and perennially formulated as unique and singular.[31] Erich Auerbach (1946/2003), German-Jewish philologist and progenitor of literary criticism, observes that "the concept of God held by the Jews[32] is less a cause than a symptom of their manner of comprehending and representing things" (p. 8). Inspired by Auerbach's (1946/2003) analysis, Daniel Mendelsohn (2020)—famed author of the extraordinary book, *The Lost: The Search for Six in Six Million* (2006)—explores this Jewish way of thinking as reflected in the Jewish doings of literature. I find that Mendelsohn's writing style is itself a manifestation of this Jewish manner.

Mendelsohn (2020), following Auerbach (1946/2003), finds an alternative manner in the Greek literature of Homer, where the protagonist Odysseus, one might remember, becomes homeless and finds his way home, where digressions come back around to contribute ever more detail to the main narrative, and where all digressions and dilatory wanderings contribute to an unbroken complete story. As Auerbach (1946/2003) notes, "[…] the present lying open to the depths of the past, is entirely foreign to the Homeric style; the Homeric style knows only a foreground, only a uniformly illuminated, uniformly objective present" (p. 7). Homer produces a world where we have total mastery over the past. The uniform world—the whole of what is—is open to radiating circles of ever greater understanding where moments of ambivalence are reconciled.

The Jewish manner, on the other hand, could be characterized by what Auerbach (1946/2003) calls "multilayeredness," which relates to a kind of ambivalence or openness:

---

[31] To think of G-d as One in the sense of uniqueness (Cohen, 1964) is not to understand G-d as the Other (another Being) or the Negative (non-being), but to recognize radical alterity beyond being positive or negative.

[32] It is worth noting that the bible speaks of Hebrews and Israelites but not necessarily "Jews."

[…] the most important thing is the "multilayeredness" of the individual character; this is hardly to be met with in Homer, or at most in the form of a conscious hesitation between two possible courses of action; otherwise, in Homer, the complexity of the psychological life is shown only in the succession and alternation of emotions; whereas the Jewish writers are able to express the simultaneous existence of various layers of consciousness and the conflict between them. (p. 13)

This multilayeredness is enabled by ambivalence as well as the gaps and cracks in the narrative. What happens to Abraham and his caravan on the three-day trip to Moriah? How does Isaac react to his binding? The text doesn't tell us. The reader of the text is confronted with an incomplete story. Naturally, the incompleteness invites readers to provide their own interpretive insights, in pursuit of meaning and understanding. Paradigmatically, the Talmud is both a record of this ongoing process and a reminder of its inevitable unfinished makeup. Moreover, Auerbach (1946/2003) is saying something beyond this; the gaps and cracks and ambivalences are not just a failure of historical or literary accounting but also an accurate depiction of the ambivalences and cracks in the world of the story, its author(s), and its readers. The Jewish manner "derives its uncanny power and devastating realism," Mendelsohn (2020) writes, "precisely from that which cannot be represented" (p. x). I find this to be an endlessly inspiring idea.[33]

Jewish literature—to my mind, from the Talmud to Daniel Mendelsohn's *Three Rings* (2020)—is filled with these ambivalences and incompleteness; indeed, so is Adorno's "Essay as Form" (1958/2019) and the whole of Freud's oeuvre, for that matter. But where does that literature lead us? Perhaps to what Mendelsohn (2020), taken slightly out of context, refers to as "a series of locked doors to which there is no key" (p. 99).[34] A series of locked doors with no key—Mendelsohn (2020) calls

---

[33] See also Frosh (2013) for more on this idea.

[34] Laplanche (2015) suggests we ditch the search for keys and use a screwdriver to dismantle the lock:

For the key that is used to open is also, and above all, used to close. Psychoanalytic method, in its origins, makes use not of keys but of a screwdriver. It dismantles locks and does not open them. It is only in that manner, like a burglar breaking and entering, that it attempts to approach the terrible and ludicrous treasure of unconscious signifiers. (p. 216)

this the pessimistic model. I would add a measure of messianic hope to this so-called pessimism. Adorno is often considered a pessimistic thinker, but his so-called pessimism, and what I might call a Jewish pessimism, is anything but pessimistic. As Hullot-Kentor (2006) insists:

> The charge of pessimism is more pessimistic than the pessimism it claims to perceive. Even pessimism is dialectical, and especially in Adorno's case the relentlessness of his life's work can hardly be attributed to a lack of hope for change, but only to the most naive optimism, which was continually transformed—by the refusal to compromise—into an instrument of cognition. (p. 29)

As Adorno (1951/2005) writes, in one of his most widely cited (and misunderstood; see Hullot-Kentor, 2006) passages: "Perspectives must be fashioned that displace and estrange the world, reveal it to be, with its rifts and crevices, as indigent and distorted as it will appear one day in the messianic light" (p. 247).

When pressed on the question of whether there is hope, "pessimistic" writer Franz Kafka said to his friend Max Brod, "Oh, plenty of hope, an infinite amount of hope—but not for us" (Kafka, cited in Benjamin, 1969/1999, p. 116). Or, to invoke Walter Benjamin's (1991) famous aphorism, *"Nur um der Hoffnungslosen willen ist uns die Hoffnung gegeben"* (p. 201), translated into something like, "Only for the sake of the hopeless ones have we been given hope." My hope will be disappointed, as Muñoz (2019) reminds me, but must be hoped nonetheless. What is hoped for is not necessarily a key to the door or access to what is beyond it. In Kafka (1925/2009), it is a series of unenterable doors, each guarded by a doorkeeper. "No one else could be granted entry here," Kafka's (2009) doorkeeper says, "because this entrance was intended for you" (p. 155). For me? The unenterable gate is just for me. Yet hope may not be for me but hoped for another. Chambers-Letson et al. (2019) write in the forward to Muñoz' *Cruising Utopias,*

I really like this passage. It reminds me of another one of my favorites; the Deleuzian aphorism: *A concept is a brick, it can be used to build a courthouse of reason, or thrown through the window;* and in a similar vein, Adorno's aphorism: *art is an uncommitted crime.*

Hope is work; we are disappointed; what's more, we repeatedly disappoint each other. But the crossing out of "this hoping" is neither the cancellation of grounds for hope, nor a discharge of the responsibility to work to change present reality. It is rather a call to describe the obstacle without being undone by that very effort. (p. x)

The locked door is not the end but the beginning of a disappointing description. Perhaps we are facing backward toward the door, like Benjamin's (1969/1999) angel of history standing before the pile of historical rubble and blown backward by the winds of paradise. Everywhere we turn, though, there seems to be rifts, crevices, gaps, hollows, cracks. Once a lyric, now a slogan on a coffee mug: "There is a crack in everything/That's how the light gets in" Leonard Cohen (1992) sang. And, I'll add, especially coming from underneath the door. Or maybe the door is non-identical. Maybe the door is not a door. Maybe it's ajar. A jar Wallace Stevens placed in Tennessee. Heidegger's jug. The broken vessel. Maybe the door *is* the crack. "By the facade," Levinas (1961/1969) says (the face, the mug, the door, the jar) "the thing which keeps its secret is exposed enclosed in its monumental essence and in its myth, in which it gleams like a splendor but does not deliver itself" (p. 193). Exposed enclosed, *Dayenu*, I digress, associate, return.

In *Three Rings: A Tale of Exile, Narrative, and Fate* (2020), Mendelsohn presents a masterfully crafted and personal treatise on method, criticism, history, and diaspora. There, he performs the tension I've been describing between Jewish and Greek models. He brings these two models together, explains how they seem to be reconciled, but doesn't reconcile them. If anything, we readers try to bind them together to make sense of Mendelsohn's (2020) own knotted and multilayered narrative. Sense is made, but it is a sense that seems open, ambivalent; *it does not deliver itself*. In particular, Mendelsohn (2020) explores the "ring composition" found in Homer's *Odyssey* and studied by the mysterious scholar, W. A. A. Van Otterlo. Ring composition is an optimistic and European style where there is a circle or ring of understanding that goes out into a digression—about a scar on Odysseus' leg or the adventures of Telemachus, for instance—and comes back, wanders and returns, giving an ever more complete account of the story. Mendelsohn (2020) compares this circular and optimistic Greek form to the perforated and pessimistic Jewish form.[35] The Greek optimistic form—the hermeneutic or even philosophical form, one could say—seems to be a reconciliation of the pessimistic and optimistic as if two parts of another, higher, circular whole; thus it functions dialectically like a reconciliation of identity and non-identity in a higher identity, agreement and disagreement in a higher agreement, the Jewish and Greek into the Christian, or dare I say Diaspora and *Shlilat Ha'golah* (negation of exile) in the State of Israel.[36]

Mendelsohn (2020) finds in Proust's magnum opus, *In Search of Lost Time* (1992), "two ways" which map onto these Jewish and Greek ways. They are like two half circles that form a ring of sorts. He compares Proust's ring composition to what I might call W. G. Sebald's ring constellations.[37] The rings gleam like splendor but do not deliver.

> Like Proust's digressions and "ways," Sebald's meanderings ultimately form a giant ring that ties together many disparate tales and experiences; but if Proust's ring appears to us as a container, filled with all of human experience, Sebald's way embraces a void: a destination to which, as in some narrative version of Zeno's paradox, no amount of writing can deliver us. (Mendelson, 2020, p. 99)

Mendelsohn ends *Three Rings* (2020) with this reflection on W. G. Sebald. A German author born to a Nazi sergeant in 1944, Sebald left Germany to teach in England and in a way, spent his life undermining his father's ideology. Sebald implements this pessimistic and (one could say) Jewish style in taking up the question of Jewish suffering and German barbarism. Sebald, the *luftmensch*, the Jewish non-Jew—a figure that breaks, once again, any sense of categorical clarity.

---

[35] It is curious to note that Mary Douglas looks to the "Old Testament" as well for a ring composition.

[36] Hegel's dialectics is often imagined to be ring-shaped. Circles within circles that lead to an absolute science.

[37] My first associations are with Lacan's three rings (the imaginary, symbolic, and real), the toroid, and the Klein bottle.

As many have noted, the word "Holocaust" is missing from Sebald's work like the hole in the middle of a ring. It is a ring of tales and experiences that constellate to form a figure of human suffering without a center. It is the absence absent from the book. There is a refusal of closure but an insistence in writing. There is an expansive opening up and outward beyond the text, as if to say, this book in your hands is a question and not an answer. Hope is found in this moment of unanswered questioning when thought recognizes that it cannot dominate its material, and instead follows footprints in the sand. It is in reference to Sebald's style that Mendelsohn invokes the locked door metaphor. An apt metaphor, seeing, now, that Sebald's hope, his writing, really was *for all those others without hope.*

Wanderers, refugees, exiled scholars and clergy, father and son, an unfinished model of the temple in Jerusalem, a Greek scholar fleeing Istanbul, a Muslim from Spain, a Huguenot from France, a Jew from Germany to Istanbul—the world that Mendelsohn (2020) describes is filled with associations and unlikely combinations of storylines across time and space. It seems neat and tidy, the way these pieces fit together. Mystical, even. And the ring seems round and smooth. Too smooth. Indeed, it is an illusion. The ring circles around a void, a hollow. Mendelsohn (2020) pulls on the threads of association, which unravel to reveal something which is not the reconciliation of the associated ideas into a higher category. Instead, it estranges and challenges what we thought we already knew. The Jewish and Greek styles do not make up a perfect whole (World, Europe, Christianity, nature, secular society) without remainder. As Adorno (1951/2005) reminds us, "the whole is the false" (p. 50).[38] There is a hole in the whole. Something circumcised.

---

[38] Hullot-Kentor (2006) offers an insightful reading of Adorno's well-worn phrase:

For if the whole is indeed the false, driven to the point that it is aware that it is not the absolute, the whole becomes the capacity of the truth. This is the central idea of Adorno's philosophy. It is worth restating. The idea that the whole is the false is by its own measure, by its own insight, the idea that the false is known only by the power of the whole. (Hullot-Kentor, p. 165)

References

Adorno, T.W. (2004). *Negative dialectic* (E. B. Ashton, Trans.). Routledge. (Original work published 1967)

Adorno, T. W. (2005). *Minima moralia: Reflections from damaged life*. Verso. (Original work published in 1951)

Adorno, T. W. (2019). *Notes on literature* (R. Tiedemann, Ed. & S. E. Nicolson, Trans.). Columbia University Press. (Original work published 1958)

Anidjar, G. (2007). *Semites*. Stanford University Press.

Ashter, G. (2021). *Homo psyche: On queer theory and erotophobia*. Fordham University Press.

Auerbach, E. (2003). *Mimesis: The representation of reality in Western literature*. Princeton University Press. (Original work published 1946)

Benjamin, W. (1991). *Gesammelte Schriften: Band 1* (R. Tiedemann & H Schweppenhauser, Eds, with participation from T. W. Adorno & G. Scholem). Suhrkamp.

Benjamin, W. (1999). *Illuminations* (H. Arendt, Ed. & H. Zohn, Trans.). Schocken. (Original work published 1969)

Boyarin, D. (1993). *Carnal Israel: Reading sex in Talmudic culture*. University of California Press.

Boyarin, D. (2015). *A traveling homeland: The Babylonian Talmud as Diaspora*. University of Pennsylvania Press.

Boyarin, D. (2019). *Judaism: The genealogy of a modern notion*. Rutgers University Press.

Boyarin, D. (2023). *The no-state solution: A Jewish manifesto*. Yale University Press.

Boyarin, J., & Boyarin, D. (2002). *Powers of diaspora: Two essays on the relevance of Jewish culture*. University of Minnesota Press.

Butler, J. (2013). *Parting ways: Jewishness and the critique of Zionism*. Columbia University Press.

Catlin, J. (2022). Bauman, the Frankfurt School, and the tradition of enlightened catastrophism. In J. Palmer & D. Brzeziński (Eds.), *Revisiting modernity and the Holocaust*. Routledge. https://doi.org/10.4324/9781003120551

Chambers-Letson, J., Nyong'o, T., & Pellegrini, A. (2019). Preface. In J. E. Muñoz (Ed.), *Cruising utopia: The then and there of Queer futurity* (2nd ed, pp. ix–xii). NYU Press.

Cohen, H. (1964). *Reason and hope: Selections from the Jewish writings of Hermann Cohen* (E. Jospe, Ed.). Schocken.

Cohen, L. (1992). Anthem [Recorded by Leonard Cohen]. On the future [CD]. Columbia Records.

Derrida, J. (1998). *Of hospitality*. Stanford University Press.

Dolgopolski, S. (2009). *What is Talmud?: The art of disagreement*. Fordham University Press.

Fields, B. J., & Fields, K. E. (2012). *Racecraft: The soul of inequality in American life*. Verso.

Frosh, S. (2013). *Hauntings: Psychoanalysis and ghostly transmissions*. Palgrave.

Frosh, S. (2023). *Antisemitism and racism: Ethical challenges for psychoanalysis*. Bloomsbury.

Haraway, D. (2016). *Staying with the trouble: Making kin in the Chthulucene*. Duke University Press.

Hook, D. (2017). What is "enjoyment as a political factor"? *Political Psychology, 38*(4), 605–620. https://www.jstor.org/stable/45094377

Hook, D. (2018). Racism and jouissance: Evaluating the 'racism as (the theft of) enjoyment' hypothesis. *Psychoanalysis, Culture and Society, 23*(3), 244–266.

Horkheimer, M., & Adorno, T. W. (2004). *Dialectic of enlightenment: Philosophical fragments* (G. S. Noerr, Ed. & E. Jephcott, Trans.). Stanford. (Original work published 1947)

Hullot-Kentor, R. (2006). *Things beyond resemblance: Collected essays on Theodor W. Adorno*. Columbia University Press.

Jay, M. (2020). *Splinters in your eye: Essays on the Frankfurt School*. Verso.

Kafka, F. (2009). *The trial* (M. Mitchell, Trans.) Oxford University Press. (Original work published 1925)

Kahn, D. (2020). The Jew in You [Song]. On *The Unternational: The Fourth Unternational* (Arranged with P. Korolenko). Auris Media.

Kant, I. (2008). *Religion within the limits of reason alone* (T. M. Greene & H. H. Hudson, Trans.). HarperOne. (Original work published 1793)

Kleinberg, E. (2021). *Emmanuel Levinas's Talmudic turn: Philosophy and Jewish thought*. Stanford University Press.

Langmuir, G. (1996). *Towards a definition of antisemitism*. University of California Press.

Lapidot, E. (2021). *Jews out of the question: A critique of anti-anti-Semitism*. SUNY Press.

Laplanche, J. (1991). *New foundations for psychoanalysis*. Basil Blackwell.

Laplanche, J. (2015). *Between seduction and inspiration: Man* (J. Mehlman, Trans.). The Unconscious in Translation.

Levinas, E. (1969). *Totality and infinity: An essay on exteriority*. Duquesne University Press. (Original work published 1961)

Levinas, E. (1997). *Difficult freedom: Essays on Judaism*. The Johns Hopkins University Press. (Original work published 1963)

Levinas, E. (2006). *Otherwise than being, or beyond essence.* Duquesne University Press. (Original work published 1974)

Liska, V. (2021a). *The Jew as a problem: Thoughts on Judaism and Identity* [Video]. YouTube. Van Leer Jerusalem Institute. https://www.youtube.com/watch?v=O4fm5c8eLdI

Liska, V. (2021b). Vivian Liska on Elad Lapidot: Is the Talmud a discourse of negation? *Marginalia.* https://themarginaliareview.com/talmud-negation/

Memmi, A. (1962). *Portrait of a Jew.* Penguin.

Mendelsohn, D. (2020). *Three rings: A tale of exile, narrative, and fate.* University of Virginia Press.

Mendelsohn, D. (2022). Interview with Daniel Mendelsohn (III): The USA, Europe and the Jews. Retrieved May 8, 2023, from https://k-larevue.com/en/interview-with-daniel-mendelsohn-iii-the-usa-europe-and-the-jews/

Moten, F. (2018). *Stolen life.* Duke University Press.

Muñoz, J. E. (2019). *Cruising utopia, 10th anniversary edition. The then and there of queer futurity.* New York University Press.

Nietzsche, F. W. (2005). The anti-Christ. In A. Ridley & J. Norman (Eds.). *Nietzsche: The anti-Christ, ecce homo, twilight of the idols: And other writings* (J. Norman, Trans.). Cambridge University Press. (Original work published 1895)

Nirenberg, D. (2013). *Anti-Judaism: A Western tradition.* Norton.

Oberle, E. (2018). *Theodor Adorno and the Century of Negative Identity.* Standford University Press.

Santner, E. L. (2001). *On the psychotheology of everyday life: Reflections on Freud and Rosenzweig.* The University of Chicago Press.

Sartre, J. P. (1965). *Anti-Semite and Jew: An exploration of the etiology of hate.* Schocken. (Original work published 1946)

Žižek, S. (2009). *Sublime object of Ideology.* Verso. (Original work published 1992)

8

Afterword

A Memory for a Blessing

"If we didn't eat, it didn't happen," Rabbi Brenner told me at my son's *Bris* and baby naming, taking a bite of gefilte fish and horseradish on a piece of dry unsalted *Matzah*. The *Bris* and baby naming took place in the month of *Nissan* in the year 5783, smack-dab in the middle of Passover. In Ashkenazi Jewish culture, children are named after those who have died. My son, Zev Y. Strosberg, is named for my father's father, Wovel, Zev in Hebrew, and later called William and Bill when he arrived in the United States from the displaced persons camp in Germany after the war. *May his memory be for a blessing* (ז״ל). Bill Strosberg lived with us when I was a teenager. I have fond memories of him before his dementia, waking me up at 5 a.m. to do a set of push-ups and sit-ups, and then going out for pancakes down the street, where we would get the senior special. There are more disturbing memories too, of course, like finding a plastic grocery bag filled with his feces in the fridge, ready to be taken to the doctor for analysis. Mainly they are good memories, though, hazy no doubt with the glow of nostalgia. Who can forget Passover with Bill Strosberg? Passover is an important holiday for Jews. That night, our door

© The Author(s), under exclusive license to Springer Nature Switzerland AG 2024
B. B. Strosberg, *Anti-Semitism at the Limit*, Studies in the Psychosocial,
https://doi.org/10.1007/978-3-031-72025-3_8

was open, and we prepared a long table with a white tablecloth that would be burgundy with spilled wine by the end of the night. We had an equally long meal that could go late into the evening or even into the morning, or so it seemed. On Passover, even the children get tipsy on wine provided by one's grandparents under the table. It is a holiday of both joy and seriousness. We are called both to recline in our seats and to remember the suffering of others as our own suffering. A cup and plate were always set on the table for a stranger, and a cup for Elijia. I remember saying this together as a family: "We shall not wrong a stranger or oppress them, for we were strangers in the land of Egypt." Not they, but we. My grandfather would recite the "Dayenu" song in monotone Hebrew without its usual thousand-year-old, upbeat melody. Something like: "If *Hashem* had given us Shabbat;" and we would all say, "*Dayenu*" (meaning, "it would have been enough"). "If *Hashem* had led us to Mount Sinai." "*Dayenu*." "If *Hashem* had given us the Torah." "*Dayenu*." And so on. He would read it so fast we could hardly get in a "*Dayenu*" before he started the next line. We were practically just yelling, "*Dayenu, Dayenu, Dayenu.*" ("Enough, Enough, Enough.") We would all begin to laugh, the wine setting in by then, but Bill Strosberg never broke his stride.

We survived the Holocaust as strangers hiding beneath the Lesniak family barn. (*Dayenu.*) They never gave us up, but it came at a cost. There was always an ambivalent sense of thanks and apprehension when talking about the Lesniaks. And then we were refugees, strangers in Utica, New York. (*Dayenu.*) In Utica, New York, my grandparents saved, raised children, opened Empire Furniture in 1957, and attended an orthodox synagogue on holidays. Yet, my grandparents never once talked about G-d or faith. I know somehow, perhaps my father told me, that after the war they didn't have faith in any traditional sense. And yet, to me, they were the epitome of Jewish. (*Dayenu.*)

One of two who survived of a family of eight children, Wovel was born on September 12, 1912, and grew up in the small village of Nowy Korczyn, son of well-respected and observant Jews, Esther and Josef Strosberg ז״ל. Even the Polish non-Jews in the village, many of whom had little sympathy for their Jewish neighbors and who were not unhappy to see the Jews carted away on November 2, 1942, shook their heads and said, "What a shame!," when they saw Josef Strosberg at the forefront of the line waiting to board the cattle cars for the Treblinka extermination camp. Or so the story goes. After *Shabbos* on Friday nights, Josef would invite poor people from the village to his home for the *Shabbos* meal. Again, so the story goes.

In September 1939, when the Germans invaded Poland, Wovel son of Josef, was sent with the Polish army to the front lines. For the weeks that Poland took its feeble stand against the Germans, Wovel was a machine gun operator. I can only imagine the anti-Semitism he had to endure in the Polish army. But if my grandfather had anything, it was endurance. When the Poles retreated, my grandfather started his journey home—to Łódź, where his brother had a knitting factory, or to Nowy Korczyn? I'm not so sure, no one is alive to tell me. But one thing is for sure, on a return journey much like his, eleven members of our family were corralled into a barn in Brzeziny, just seven miles outside of Łódź, along with many other Jews, women and children, and burned alive. German soldiers stood outside and shot anyone who managed to escape. Memory is all that remains.

Wovel must have been with a different traveling party, since he was not in the barn that night, *Baruch Hashem*. There is a legend that keeps circling in my mind these past few weeks, about my grandfather's return. When he eventually returned home to a house he shared with several other Jews his age, he found it in shambles. A real mess. A pigsty. According to the story, Wovel walked in and said, "If you want to live like animals, let's live like animals." In the middle of the living room, he dropped his trousers, took a squat, and *kakt* on the floor. My grandfather had *Chutzpah*. He survived the war in hiding with my grandmother Tema ז״ל, who was his girlfriend at the time, first in a bunker he built on the side of the riverbank and then under the floorboards of the Lesniak family barn just outside Nowy Korczyn. The stories I've heard from those years are as horrifying as they get.

Why am I telling you this, here at the end of *our* journey? One night, as I was reflecting on the manuscript, I had a dream. In the dream, my wife, Madeline, was squatting in the middle of the living room of the house where I grew up. Squatting like she did during the birth of our son two weeks earlier. She took a shit on the hardwood floor. I knew my father would be arriving soon, and so I cleaned it up as best I could to avoid the embarrassment. "Undigested material" was the only phrase that came to mind.

Psychoanalysts have, in their astute observations, remarked that the child's fascination with poop arises from its particular quality of being both a part of their corporeal self, and yet, simultaneously removed from it. The fecal matter can serve as a precious, odorous offering for the mother figure. During the arduous phase of toilet training, children learn to master themselves and impose order. Birth, too, is associated with excretion; the newborn has, for the child's mind, exited through the navel or, indeed, the rectum. Though these are my associations, as a clinical psychologist, let us not succumb to shallow cocktail-hour interpretations.

Let me continue to free-associate. The dream came after I was asked by my doctor to take a sample of my stool for an analysis. The excavation process required was very disturbing. No one knows what's wrong with my stomach. Something of my body seems to resist the scientific order of the universe. I had remembered the dream in the midst of talking with my analyst about my book. Of course, talking about the book may be a defense against the emotional weight of becoming a father; as in, "my father is coming…" or "a father is coming…" or "a father is coming…me." *Dayenu*. "Enough / Time is a mother," writes the poet Ocean Vuong (2022, p. 49). "Enough is enough / *Time is a motherfucker*, I said to the gravestones, alive, absurd" (p. 50). Life is a mess of undigested material. "Body, doorway that you are, be more than what I'll pass through" (Vuong, 2022, p. 50). Sometimes I think I made a mess of this. Then again, I wanted to write about a messy life that needs to be borne. Something carried into being like a weight. "The need to lend a voice to suffering is a condition of all truth," Adorno (1967/2004) writes, "For suffering is objectivity that weighs upon the subject […]" (pp. 17–18).

Very very heady, very very heavy. "And I was lifted, wet and bloody, out of my mother, into the world, screaming and […]" (Vuong, 2022, p. 50). *Dayenu.*

References

Adorno, T.W. (2004). *Negative dialectic* (E. B. Ashton, Trans.). Routledge. (Original work published 1967)
Vuong, O. (2022). *Time is a mother*. Penguin Press.

References

Abromeit, J. (2011). *Max Horkheimer and the foundations of the Frankfurt School.* Cambridge University Press.

Ackerman, N. W., & Jahoda, M. (1950). *Anti-Semitism and emotional disorder: A Psychoanalytic interpretation.* Harper.

Adorno, T. W. (1964). Zur Bekämpfung des Antisemitismus heute (Fighting anti-Semitism today). In *Das Argument, 29.* My translation. (Transcript of a speech given November 3, 1962).

Adorno, T. W. (1967-8). Sociology and psychology (i & ii). *New Left Review 46,* 67–80; *47,* 79–97.

Adorno, T. W. (1972). Theorie der Halbbildung. In G. Schriften, (Ed.), *Band 8: Soziologische Schriften 1* (pp. 93–121). Suhrkamp Verlag. (Original work published 1959)

Adorno, T. W. (1982). Freudian theory and the pattern of fascist propaganda. In A. Arato & E. Gephardt (Eds.), *The essential Frankfurt School reader* (pp. 118–137). Continuum. (Original work published 1951)

Adorno, T. W. (1993). Theory of pseudo-culture (1959). *Telos, 95,* 15–38. https://doi.org/10.3817/0393095015

Adorno, T. W. (1998a). *Critical models* (H. W. Pickford, Trans.). Columbia University Press.

Adorno, T. W. (1998b). Education after Auschwitz. In *Critical models: Interventions and catchwords* (pp. 191–204, H. W. Pickford, Trans.). Columbia University Press.

Adorno, T. W. (2001a). *Problem of moral philosophy* (T. Schröder, Ed. & T. Livingstone, Trans.). Stanford.

Adorno, T. W. (2001b) *Metaphysics: Concepts and problems* (R. Tiedemann, Ed. & E. Jephcott, Trans.). Stanford University Press.

Adorno, T.W. (2004). *Negative dialectic* (E. B. Ashton, Trans.). Routledge. (Original work published 1967)

Adorno, T. W. (2005). *Minima moralia: Reflections from damaged life.* Verso. (Original work published in 1951)

Adorno, T. W. (2008). *Lectures on negative dialectics: Fragments of a lecture course 1965/1966* (R. Tiedemann, Ed. & R. Livingston, Trans.). Polity.

Adorno, T. W. (2012). Erziehung nach Auschwitz. In U. Bauer, U. H. Bittlingmayer, & A. Scherr (Eds.), *Handbuch Bildungs- und Erziehungssoziologie. Bildung und Gesellschaft. VS Verlag für Sozialwissenschaften,* Wiesbaden. https://doi.org/10.1007/978-3-531-18944-4_7 (Original work published in 1966)

Adorno, T. W. (2014). Revisionist psychoanalysis (N. -N. Lee, Trans.). *Philosophy and Social Criticism, 40*(3), 326–338. (Original work published 1952)

Adorno, T. W. (2019a). *Notes on literature* (R. Tiedemann, Ed. & S. E. Nicolson, Trans.). Columbia University Press. (Original work published 1958)

Adorno, T. W. (2019b). Remarks on the authoritarian personality. In T. W. Adorno, E. Frenkel-Brunswik, D. J. Levinson, & R. N. Sanford (Authors), *The authoritarian personality* (pp. xli-lxvi). Verso. (Original work drafted 1948)

Adorno, T. W. (2019c). *Ontology and dialectics: 1960–61* (N. Walter, Trans.). Polity.

Adorno, T. W., Frenkel-Brunswik, E., Levinson, D. J., & Sanford, R. N. (2019). *The authoritarian personality.* Verso. (Original work published 1950)

Ahmed, S. (2007). A phenomenology of whiteness. *Feminist Theory, 8*(2), 149–168. https://doi.org/10.1177/1464700107078139

Allen, A. (2020). *Critique on the couch: Why critical theory needs psychoanalysis.* Columbia University Press.

Allen, A., & Ruti, M. (2019). *Critical theory between Klein and Lacan: A dialogue.* Bloomsbury.

Allington, D. (2021). Conspiracy theories, radicalisation and digital media. In *The Global Network on Extremism and Technology (GNET).* King's College London.

Allport, G. W. (1946). Preface. In E. Simmel (Ed.), *Anti-Semitism, a social disease*. International Universities Press.

Allport, G. W. (1979). *The nature of prejudice*. Addison-Wesley. (Original work published 1954)

American Jewish Committee (AJC). (2022). American Jewish committee surveys German general and Muslim populations on antisemitism. Retrieved February 10, 2023, from https://www.ajc.org/news/american-jewish-committee-surveys-german-general-and-muslim-populations-on-antisemitism

Amery, J. (1966). *At the mind's limit*. Indiana University Press.

Anderson, B. (2016). *Imagined communities: Reflections on the origin and spread of nationalism*. Verso.

Anidjar, G. (2007). *Semites*. Stanford University Press.

Anti-Defamation League (ADL). (2020). Antisemitic attitudes in the U.S.: A guide to ADL's latest poll. Retrieved March 10, 2021, from https://www.adl.org/news/press-releases/anti-semitic-stereotypes-persist-in-america-survey-shows

Arendt, H. (1951). *Origins of totalitarianism*. Schocken.

Arendt, H. (2006). *Eichmann in Jerusalem: A report on the banality of evil*. Penguin. (Original work published 1963)

Ashter, G. (2021a). *Exigent psychoanalysis: The interventions of Jean Laplanche*. Routledge.

Ashter, G. (2021b). *Homo psyche: On queer theory and erotophobia*. Fordham University Press.

Auchincloss, E. L., & Samberg, E. (Eds.). (2012). *Psychoanalytic terms and concepts*. Yale University Press. https://doi.org/10.2307/j.ctv6jm9bp

Auerbach, E. (2003). *Mimesis: The representation of reality in Western literature*. Princeton University Press. (Original work published 1946)

Pirkei Avot. (2023). Sefaria. https://www.sefaria.org/ https://www.sefaria.org/search?q=desist&tab=text&tvar=1&tsort=relevance&svar=1&ssort=relevance

Badiou, A., Hazan, E., & Segrè, I. (2013). *Reflections on anti-Semitism*. Verso.

Bahbah, H. (1994). *The location of culture*. Routledge.

Barthes, R. (1991). *Mythologies* (A. Lavers, Trans.). Noonday Press. (Original work published 1957)

Basri, C. (2002). The Jewish refugees from Arab countries: An examination of legal rights - A case study of the human rights violations of Iraqi Jews. *Fordham International Law Journal, 26*(3), 656–720. https://ir.lawnet.fordham.edu/ilj/vol26/iss3/6

Bateson, G. (1972). *Steps to an ecology of mind: Collected essays in anthropology, psychiatry, evolution, and epistemology*. University of Chicago Press.

Baudrillard, J. (1994). *Simulacra and simulation*. University of Michigan Press.

Bauman, Z. (1991). *Modernity and ambivalence*. Polity.

Bauman, Z. (1995). *Life in fragments. Essays in postmodern morality*. Basil Blackwell.

Bauman, Z. (1998). Allosemitism: Premodern, modern, postmodern. In B. Cheyette & L. Marcus (Eds.), *Modernity, culture, and "the Jew"*. Polity Press.

Bauman, Z. (2000). *Liquid modernity*. Polity Press.

BDS. (2023). *Boycott, divestment, and sanctions*. https://bdsmovement.net.

Beinart, P. (2023, June 5). Antisemitism in the US is not a Bipartisan problem. *The Beinart notebooks*. https://open.substack.com/pub/peterbeinart/p/antisemitism-in-the-us-is-not-a-bipartisan?utm_campaign=post&utm_medium=web

Benjamin, J. (1977). The end of internalization: Adorno's social psychology. *Telos, 32*, 42–64. https://doi.org/10.3817/0677032042

Benjamin, W. (1991). *Gesammelte Schriften: Band 1* (R. Tiedemann & H Schweppenhauser, Eds, with participation from T. W. Adorno & G. Scholem). Suhrkamp.

Benjamin, W. (1999a). *Illuminations* (H. Arendt, Ed. & H. Zohn, Trans.). Schocken. (Original work published 1969)

Benjamin, W. (1999b). *The arcades project*. Harvard University Press. (Original work drafted 1927-1940)

Bernasconi, R. (2021). Racism. In S. Goldberg, S. Ury, & K. Weiser (Eds.), *Key concepts in the Study of Antisemitism. Palgrave critical studies of antisemitism and racism*. Palgrave Macmillan. https://doi.org/10.1007/978-3-030-51658-1_19

English Standard Version Bible. (2001). *ESV* Online. https://esv.literalword.com/

Billig, M. (1991). *Ideology and opinions: Studies in rhetorical psychology*. Sage Publications.

Blake, A. (2022) Trump's long history of trafficking in antisemitic tropes. *The Washington Post*. Retrieved January 2023, from https://www.washingtonpost.com/politics/2022/10/17/trump-history-antisemitic-tropes/

Bloch, B. (2019). The origins of Adorno's psycho-social dialectic: Psychoanalysis and neo Kantianism in the young Adorno. *Modern Intellectual History, 16*(2), 501–529. https://doi.org/10.1017/S147924431700049X

Borges, J. L. (1998). *Collected fictions* (A. Hurley, Trans.). Viking.

Boyarin, D. (1993). *Carnal Israel: Reading sex in Talmudic culture*. University of California Press.

Boyarin, D. (2015). *A traveling homeland: The Babylonian Talmud as Diaspora.* University of Pennsylvania Press.

Boyarin, D. (2019). *Judaism: The genealogy of a modern notion.* Rutgers University Press.

Boyarin, D. (2023). *The no-state solution: A Jewish manifesto.* Yale University Press.

Boyarin, J., & Boyarin, D. (2002). *Powers of diaspora: Two essays on the relevance of Jewish culture.* University of Minnesota Press.

Brunner, J. (1994). Looking into the heart of the workers, or: How Erich Fromm turned critical theory into empirical research. *Political Psychology, 15*(4), 631–654. https://doi.org/10.2307/3791624

Burston, D. (2014). Anti-Semitism. In T. Teo (Ed.), *Encyclopedia of critical psychology.* Springer.

Burston, D. (2020). *Critical theory and the problem of authority: Psychoanalysis, politics and the postmodern university.* Palgrave.

Burston, D. (2021). *Anti-Semitism and analytical psychology.* Routledge.

Butler, J. (2013). *Parting ways: Jewishness and the critique of Zionism.* Columbia University Press.

Butler, J. (2020). *The force of nonviolence.* Verso.

Caillois, R. (1984). Mimicry and legendary psychasthenia (J. Shepley, Trans.). *October, 31,* 17–32. https://doi.org/10.2307/778354 (Original work published 1935)

Carroll, L. (1893). *Sylvie and Bruno concluded.* Macmillan and Co.

Catlin, J. (2022). Bauman, the Frankfurt School, and the tradition of enlightened catastrophism. In J. Palmer & D. Brzeziński (Eds.), *Revisiting modernity and the Holocaust.* Routledge. https://doi.org/10.4324/9781003120551

Cèsaire, A. (2001). *Discourse on colonialism.* Monthly Review Press. (Original work published 1950)

Chambers-Letson, J., Nyong'o, T., & Pellegrini, A. (2019). Preface. In J. E. Muñoz (Ed.), *Cruising utopia: The then and there of Queer futurity* (2nd ed, pp. ix–xii). NYU Press.

Cheyette, B. (1994). *Constructions of 'the Jew' in English literature and society: Racial representations, 1875–1945.* Cambridge University Press.

Cheyette, B. (2013). *Diasporas of the mind: Jewish and postcolonial writing and the nightmare of history.* Yale University Press.

Cheyette, B. (2020). *The ghetto: A very short introduction.* Oxford University Press.

Cheyette, B., Rothberg, M., & Axster, F. (2019). Relational Thinking: A Dialogue on the Theory and Politics of Research on Antisemitism and Racism. *Lernen Aus De Geshichte.* https://lernen-aus-der-geschichte.de/Lernenund-Lehren/content/14651 (accessed August 10, 2023)

Chiang, T. (2019). The truth of fact the truth of fiction. In *Exhalations: Stories*. Alfred A Knopf.

Chotiner, I. (2022). Is anti-Zionism anti-Semitism? *The New Yorker*. Retrieved April 30, 2024, from https://www.newyorker.com/news/q-and-a/is-anti-zionism-anti-semitism

Cohen, H. (1964). *Reason and hope: Selections from the Jewish writings of Hermann Cohen* (E. Jospe, Ed.). Schocken.

Cohen, L. (1992). Anthem [Recorded by Leonard Cohen]. On the future [CD]. Columbia Records.

Cohen, S. J. D. (1999). *The beginnings of Jewishness: Boundaries, varieties, uncertainties*. University of California Press.

Cohen, M. R. (2008). *Under the crescent and cross: Jews in the Middle Ages*. Princeton University Press.

Condor, S. (1997). And so say all of us?: Some thoughts on 'experiential democratization' as an aim for critical social psychologists. In T. Ibáñez & L. Íñiguez (Eds.), *Critical social psychology* (pp. 111–146). Sage. https://doi.org/10.4135/9781446279199.n8

Cornell, D. (1992). *Philosophies of the limit*. Routledge.

D'Arcy, M. (2020). Dialectic of enlightenment: Origin stories of Western Marxism. In K. Freeman & J. Munro (Eds.), *Reading the postwar future: Textual turning points from 1944* (pp. 43–59). Bloomsbury Academic.

Dahbour, O. (2012). *Self-determination without nationalism: A theory of postnational sovereignty*. Temple University Press.

Daniel, K., & Daniel, S. (2022). *Everything, everywhere, all at once*. (Movie). A24.

Demirjian, K., & Stack, L. (2023). In congress and on campuses, 'from the river to the sea' inflames debate. *The New York Times*. Retrieved April 30, 2024, from https://www.nytimes.com/2023/11/09/us/politics/river-to-the-sea-israel-gaza-palestinians.html

Derrida, J. (1992). Force of law: The "mystical foundation of authority". In D. Cornell, M. Rosenfeld, & D. G. Carlson (Eds.), *Deconstruction and the possibility of justice* (pp. 3–67). Taylor and Francis.

Derrida, J. (1998). *Of hospitality*. Stanford University Press.

Dews, P. (1987). *Logics of disintegration: Post-structuralist thought and the claims of critical theory*. Verso.

Dion, K. L., & Earn, B. M. (1975). The phenomenology of being a target of prejudice. *Journal of Personality and Social Psychology, 32*(5), 944–950. https://doi.org/10.1037/0022-3514.32.5.944

Dolgopolski, S. (2009). *What is Talmud?: The art of disagreement*. Fordham University Press.

Eco, U. (1995). On the impossibility of drawing a map of the empire on a scale of 1 to 1. In *How to travel with a salmon & other essays* (pp. 95–106). Houghton Mifflin Harcourt.

Edelman, L. (2004). *No future: Queer theory and the death drive.* Duke University Press.

Erwin, E. (Ed.). (2002). *The Freud encyclopedia: Theory, therapy, and culture.* Routledge.

Evans, D. (1996). *An introductory dictionary of Lacanian psychoanalysis.* Routledge. https://doi.org/10.4324/9780203135570

Fanon, F. (2008). *Black skin white masks* (C. L. Markmann, Trans.). Pluto Press. (Original work published 1952)

Felman, S. (2003). *The scandal of the speaking body: Don Juan with J.L. Austin, or seduction in two languages.* Stanford University Press.

Fenichel, O. (1940). Psychoanalysis of anti-Semitism. *American Imago, 1B*(2), 24–39.

Fenichel, O. (1948). Elements of a psychoanalytic theory of anti-Semitism. In E. Simmel (Ed.), *Anti-Semitism: A social disease* (pp. 11–32). International Universities Press.

Fields, B. J., & Fields, K. E. (2012). *Racecraft: The soul of inequality in American life.* Verso.

Fields, J., & Weisberg, J. (2022). *The patient* (TV series). HBO Max.

Fink, B. (1997). *A clinical introduction to Lacanian psychoanalysis: Theory and technique.* Harvard University Press.

Fischer, C. T., Laubscher, L., & Brooke, R. (2016). *The qualitative vision for psychology: An invitation to a human science approach.* Duquesne University Press.

Flasch, P. (2020). Antisemitism on college campuses: A phenomenological study of Jewish students' lived experiences. *Journal of Contemporary Antisemitism, 3*(1).

Fong, B. (2016). *Death and mastery: Psychoanalytic drive theory and the subject of late capitalism.* Columbia University Press.

Freud, S. (2001a). The interpretation of dreams. In J. Strachey (Ed. & Trans.), *The standard edition of the complete psychological works of Sigmund Freud, volumes IV–V.* Vintage Books. (Original work published 1900)

Freud, S. (2001b). Totem and taboo. In J. Strachey (Ed. & Trans.), *The standard edition of the complete psychological works of Sigmund Freud, volume XIII (1912–1913).* Vintage Books. (Original work published 1913)

Freud, S. (2001c). Repression. In J. Strachey (Ed. & Trans.), *The standard edition of the complete psychological works of Sigmund Freud, volume XVI (1914–1916): On the history of the psychoanalytic movement, papers on metapsychology and other works.* Vintage Books. (Original work published 1915)

Freud, S. (2001d). The 'uncanny'. In J. Strachey (Ed. & Trans.), *The standard edition of the complete psychological works of Sigmund Freud, volume XVII (1917–1919): An infantile neurosis and other works* (pp. 217–256). Vintage Books. (Original work published 1919)

Freud, S. (2001e). Group psychology and the analysis of the ego. In J. Strachey (Ed. & Trans.), *The standard edition of the complete psychological works of Sigmund Freud, volume XVIII (1920–1922)* (pp. 65–143). Vintage. (Original work published 1921)

Freud, S. (2001f). Negation. In J. Strachey (Ed. & Trans.). *The standard edition of the complete psychological works of Sigmund Freud, volume XIX (1923–1925): The ego and the id and other works.* Vintage Books. (Original work published 1925)

Freud, S. (2001g). Civilization and its discontents. In J. Strachey (Ed. & Trans.), *The standard edition of the complete psychological works of Sigmund Freud, volume XXI. The future of an illusion, civilization and its discontents and other works (1927–1931)* (pp. 57–145.) Vintage Books. (Original work published 1930)

Freud, S. (2001h). Analysis terminable and interminable. In Strachey, J. (Ed. & Trans.) *The standard edition of the complete psychological works of Sigmund Freud: Volume XXIII (1937–1939)* (pp. 209–253). Vintage Books. (Original work published 1937)

Freud, S. (2001i). A comment on anti-Semitism. In J. Strachey (Ed. & Trans.) *The standard edition of the complete psychological works of Sigmund Freud, volume XXIII (1937–1939): Moses and monotheism, an outline of psychoanalysis and other works* (pp. 289–293). Vintage Books. (Original work published 1938)

Freud, S. (2001j). Moses and monotheism. In J. Strachey (Ed. & Trans.), *The standard edition of the complete psychological works of Sigmund Freud, volume XXIII: Moses and monotheism, an outline of psycho-analysis and other works.* Vintage Books. (Original work published 1939)

Fromm, E. (1984). *Working class in Weimar Germany: A psychological and sociological study.* Berg Publishers.

Fromm, E. (1994). *Escape from freedom.* Holt. (Original work published 1941)

Frosh, S. (1989). *Psychoanalysis and psychology: Minding the gap.* Macmillan.

Frosh, S. (2005). *Hate and the 'Jewish Science': Anti-Semitism, Nazism and psycho-analysis*. Palgrave Macmillan.

Frosh, S. (2013). *Hauntings: Psychoanalysis and ghostly transmissions*. Palgrave.

Frosh, S. (2023). *Antisemitism and racism: Ethical challenges for psychoanalysis*. Bloomsbury.

Geisinger, G. (May 2022). Everything everywhere all at once directors are glad to talk about 'Big Nose' controversy. *Digital Spy*. Retrieved December 27, 2022, from https://www.digitalspy.com/movies/a39902848/everything-everywhere-all-at-once-big-nose-jewish-antisemitism/

George, S., & Hook, D. (2021). *Lacan and race: Racism, identity, and psychoanalytic theory*. Routledge.

Gilman, S. L. (1991). *The Jew's body*. Routledge.

Gordon, P. E. (2019). Introduction by Peter E. Gordon. In T. W. Adorno, E. Frenkel-Brunswik, D. J. Levinson, & N. Sanford (Authors), *The authoritarian personality* (pp. xiii–xl). Verso.

Gough, B. (Ed.). (2017). *The Palgrave handbook of critical social psychology*. Palgrave Macmillan. https://doi.org/10.1057/978-1-137-51018-1

Grigat, S. (2019). The fight against antisemitism and the Iranian regime: Challenges and contradictions in the light of Adorno's categorical imperative. In A. Lange, K. Mayerhofer, D. Porat, & L. Schiffman (Eds.), *Volume 1 comprehending and confronting antisemitism* (pp. 441–462). De Gruyter. https://doi.org/10.1515/9783110618594-034

Grillo, T., & Wildman, S. M. (1991). Obscuring the importance of race: The implication of making comparisons between racism and sexism (or other-isms). *Duke Law Journal, 1991*(2), 397–412. https://doi.org/10.2307/1372732

Gross, J., & Vigdor, N. (2022, February). *ABC suspends Whoopi Goldberg over Holocaust comments*. Retrieved January 2023, from https://www.nytimes.com/2022/02/01/us/whoopi-goldberg-holocaust.html

Haberman, M., & Feuer, A. (2022, November). Trump's latest dinner guest: Nick Fuentes, white supremacist. *New York Times*. Retrieved December 28, 2022, from https://www.nytimes.com/2022/11/25/us/politics/trump-nick-fuentes-dinner.html

Hacker, P. M. S. (2015). "Forms of Life," in "Wittgenstein and Forms of Life," special issue. *Nordic Wittgenstein Review, 17*, 1–20.

Haraway, D. (2016). *Staying with the trouble: Making kin in the Chthulucene*. Duke University Press.

Hegel, G. W. F. (1979). *Phenomenology of spirit* (A. V. Miller, Trans.). Oxford University Press. (Original work published 1807)

Hersh, E., & Royden, L. (2023). Antisemitic attitudes across the ideological spectrum. *Political Research Quarterly, 76*(2), 697–711. https://doi.org/10.1177/10659129221111081

Hirsh, D. (2018). *Contemporary left antisemitism*. Routledge.

Honneth, A. (1995). *The struggle for recognition: The moral grammar of social conflicts*. Polity.

Hook, D. (2004). Fanon and the psychoanalysis of racism. In D. Hook (Ed.), *Critical psychology* (pp. 114–137). Juta Academic Publishing.

Hook, D. (2017a). *Six moments in Lacan: Communication and identification*. Routledge.

Hook, D. (2017b). What is "enjoyment as a political factor"? *Political Psychology, 38*(4), 605–620. https://www.jstor.org/stable/45094377

Hook, D. (2018). Racism and jouissance: Evaluating the 'racism as (the theft of) enjoyment' hypothesis. *Psychoanalysis, Culture and Society, 23*(3), 244–266.

Hook, D. (2024). Whiteness at the abyss: Reflections on a scene of attack. Special issue. *Psychoanalytic, Culture, and Society*.

Horkheimer, M. (2004). *Eclipse of reason*. Continuum. (Original work published 1947)

Horkheimer, M., & Adorno, T. W. (2004). *Dialectic of enlightenment: Philosophical fragments* (G. S. Noerr, Ed. & E. Jephcott, Trans.). Stanford. (Original work published 1947)

Hullot-Kentor, R. (2006). *Things beyond resemblance: Collected essays on Theodor W. Adorno*. Columbia University Press.

Freedom For Humanity. (2023, July 22). In Wikipedia. https://en.wikipedia.org/wiki/Freedom_for_Humanity.

Ibáñez, T., & Íñguez, L. (Eds.). (1997). *Critical social psychology*. Sage. https://doi.org/10.4135/9781446279199

Intactivism. (2023). https://www.circumstitions.com/

International Holocaust Remembrance Alliance. (2016). Working definition of antisemitism. https://www.holocaustremembrance.com/resources/working-definitions-charters/working-definition-antisemitism

Irigaray, L. (1985). *This sex which is not one*. Cornell University Press.

Jay, M. (1980). The Jews and the Frankfurt School: Critical theory's analysis of anti-Semitism. *New German Critique, 19*, 137–149. https://doi.org/10.2307/487976

Jay, M. (1984). *Marxism and totality: The adventures of a concept from Lukacs to Habermas*. University of California Press.

Jay, M. (1996). *The dialectical imagination: A history of the Frankfurt School and the Institute of Social Research, 1923–1950.* University of California Press. (Original work published 1976)

Jay, M. (2020). *Splinters in your eye: Essays on the Frankfurt School.* Verso.

Jay-Z. (2017). "The story of O.J." In 4:44. ROC Nation.

Judaken, J. (2013). Deconstructing anti-Semitism and eternal anti-Judaism: Jonathan Judaken on David Nirenberg's *Anti-Judaism: The Western Tradition. Marginalia.* Retrieved December 28, 2022, from https://themarginaliareview.com/deconstructing-anti-semitism-and-eternal-anti-judaism/

Judaken, J. (2018). Introduction. *The American Historical Review, 123*(4), 1122–1138. https://doi.org/10.1093/ahr/rhy024

Judaken, J. (2021). Anti-Semitism (historiography). In S. Goldberg, S. Ury, & K. Weiser (Eds.), *Key concepts in the study of antisemitism* (pp. 25–38). Springer.

Kafka, F. (2009). *The trial* (M. Mitchell, Trans.) Oxford University Press. (Original work published 1925)

Kahn, D. (2020). The Jew in You [Song]. On *The Unternational: The Fourth Unternational* (Arranged with P. Korolenko). Auris Media.

Kant, I. (2008). *Religion within the limits of reason alone* (T. M. Greene & H. H. Hudson, Trans.). HarperOne. (Original work published 1793)

Kestenbaum, S. (2016, December 21). "White nationalists create new shorthand for the 'Jewish Question'". *The forward.*

Kleinberg, E. (2021). *Emmanuel Levinas's Talmudic turn: Philosophy and Jewish thought.* Stanford University Press.

Knafo, D. (1999). Anti-Semitism in the clinical setting: Transference and countertransference dimensions. *Journal of the American Psychoanalytic Association, 47*(1), 35–63. https://doi.org/10.1177/00030651990470010801

Kovacs, A., & Fischer, G. (2021). *Antisemitic prejudices in Europe: Survey in 16 European countries.* Action and Protection League.

Lacan, J. (1997) *The seminars of Jacques Lacan book III: The psychosis* (R. Grigg, Trans.). W.W. Norton.

Lacan, J. (1998). *The seminars of Jacques Lacan book XI: The four fundamental concepts of psychoanalysis* (J. A. Miller, Ed. & A. Sheridan, Trans.). Norton.

Lacan, J. (2006). *Écrits: The first complete edition in English* (J. A. Miller, Ed. & B. Fink, Trans.). W.W. Norton & Co. (Original work published 1966)

Lacan, J. (2021). *The object relation: The seminar of Jacques Lacan, book IV* (J. A. Miller, Ed. & A. Price, Trans.). Polity.

Langmuir, G. (1990). *Towards a definition of antisemitism.* University of California Press.

Langmuir, G. (1996). *Towards a definition of antisemitism*. University of California Press.

Lapidot, E. (2021). *Jews out of the question: A critique of anti-anti-Semitism*. SUNY Press.

Laplanche, J. (1991). *New foundations for psychoanalysis*. Basil Blackwell.

Laplanche, J. (1996). Psychoanalysis as anti-hermeneutics (L. Thurston, Trans.). *Radical Philosophy, 79*(12), 7–12. https://www.radicalphilosophy.com/article/psychoanalysis-as-anti-hermeneutics

Laplanche, J. (1999). *Essays on otherness*. Routledge.

Laplanche, J. (2002). *The unfinished Copernican revolution* (L. Thurston, Trans.). The Unconscious in Translation.

Laplanche, J. (2007). Gender, sex, and the sexual (S. Fairfield, Trans.). *Studies in Gender and Sexuality, 8*(2), 201–219. https://doi.org/10.1080/15240650701225567

Laplanche, J. (2015). *Between seduction and inspiration: Man* (J. Mehlman, Trans.). The Unconscious in Translation.

Laplanche, J. (2017). *Après-coup* (J. House, Trans.). The Unconscious in Translation.

Laplanche, J., & Pontalis, J. B. (1968). Fantasy and the origins of sexuality. *The International Journal of Psychoanalysis, 49*(1), 1–18.

Laplanche, J., & Pontalis, J. B. (1988). *The language of psychoanalysis*. Karnac. (Original work published 1967)

Laubscher, L., Hook, D., & Desai, M. (Eds.). (2021). *Fanon, phenomenology and psychology*. Routledge.

Lerman, A. (2022). *Whatever happened to antisemitism?: Redefinition and the myth of the 'collective Jew'*. Pluto Press.

Levinas, E. (1969). *Totality and infinity: An essay on exteriority*. Duquesne University Press. (Original work published 1961)

Levinas, E. (1997). *Difficult freedom: Essays on Judaism*. The Johns Hopkins University Press. (Original work published 1963)

Levinas, E. (2006). *Otherwise than being, or beyond essence*. Duquesne University Press. (Original work published 1974)

Lewin-Epstein, N., & Cohen, Y. (2019). Ethnic origin and identity in the Jewish population of Israel. *Journal of Ethnic and Migration Studies, 45*(11), 2118–2137. https://doi.org/10.1080/1369183X.2018.1492370

Liska, V. (2021a). The Jew as a problem: Thoughts on Judaism and Identity [Video]. YouTube. Van Leer Jerusalem Institute. https://www.youtube.com/watch?v=O4fm5c8eLdI

Liska, V. (2021b). Vivian Liska on Elad Lapidot: Is the Talmud a discourse of negation? *Marginalia.* https://themarginaliareview.com/talmud-negation/

Loewenstein, R. (1951). *Christians and Jews: A psychoanalytic study.* International Universities Press.

Lowenthal, L. & Guterman, N. (2021). *Prophets of deceit: A study of the techniques of the American agitator.* Verso. (Originally published 1949)

Lyotard, J-F. (1990). *Heidegger and "the Jews"* (A. Michel & M. S. Roberts, Trans.). University of Minnesota Press.

Macdonald, B., & Young, K. E. (2021). Critical theory, fascism, and antifascism: Reflections from a damaged polity. *Emancipations: A Journal of Critical Social Analysis, 1*(1), 1–33. https://doi.org/10.54718/WOOW5695

Magid, S. (2006). In search of a critical voice in the Jewish diaspora: Homelessness and home in Edward Said and Shalom Noah Barzofsky's Netivot Shalom. *Jewish Social Studies: History, Culture, Society, 12*(3), 193–227.

Marcus, K. (2015). *The definition of antisemitism.* Oxford University Press.

Marcuse, H. (1955). *Eros and civilization: A philosophical inquiry into Freud.* Beacon Press.

Mariotti, S. (2009). Damaged life as exuberant vitality in America: Adorno, alienation, and the psychic economy. *Telos, 149,* 169–190. https://doi.org/10.3817/1209149169

Marks, J. D. (2010). Rousseau's use of the Jewish example. *The Review of Politics, 72*(3), 463–481. https://www.jstor.org/stable/20780332

Marx. K. (1994). Thesis on Feuerbach. In L. H. Simon (Ed.). *Marx: Selected writings.* Hackett. (Original work published 1888)

Marx, K. (2012). On 'the Jewish Question'. In J. J. O'Malley (Ed.), *Marx: Early political writing.* Cambridge University Press. (Original work published 1844)

Mbembe, A. (2015). *Necropolitics.* Duke University Press.

McWilliams, N. (2020). *Psychoanalytic diagnosis: Understanding personality and structure in clinical process* (2nd ed.). Guilford Press.

Memmi, A. (1962). *Portrait of a Jew.* Penguin.

Mendelsohn, D. (2006). *The lost: A search for six of six million.* Harper Perennial.

Mendelsohn, D. (2020). *Three rings: A tale of exile, narrative, and fate.* University of Virginia Press.

Mendelsohn, D. (2022). Interview with Daniel Mendelsohn (III): The USA, Europe and the Jews. Retrieved May 8, 2023, from https://k-larevue.com/en/interview-with-daniel-mendelsohn-iii-the-usa-europe-and-the-jews/

Merriam-Webster Dictionary. (2022). Meme. *Merriam-Webster dictionary online.* https://www.merriam-webster.com/dictionary/meme

Mielants, E., Gordon, L., & Grosfoguel, R. (2009). Global anti-Semitism in world-historical perspective: An introduction. In L. Gordon, R. Grosfoguel, & E. Mielants (special guest co-editors), *Anti-Semitism in the world system: Past, present and future*, special issue of *Human architecture: Journal of the sociology of self-knowledge, 7*(2), 1–14.

Mills, C. (2019). *The racial contract.* Cornell University Press. (Original work published 1997)

Morelock, J. (2017). Authoritarian populism contra "Bildung": Anti-intellectualism and the neoliberal assault on the Liberal Arts. *Cadernos CIMEAC, 7*(2), 63–81. https://doi.org/10.18554/cimeac.v7i2.2429

Morss, J. R. (1995). *Growing critical: Alternatives to developmental psychology.* Routledge. https://doi.org/10.4324/9780203130797

Morton, T. (2013). *Hyperobjects: Philosophy and ecology after the end of the world.* University of Minnesota Press.

Moten, F. (2018). *Stolen life.* Duke University Press. https://doi.org/10.2307/j.ctv111jj9x

Muñoz, J. E. (2019). *Cruising utopia, 10th anniversary edition. The then and there of queer futurity.* New York University Press.

Nägele, R. (1982). The scene of the other: Theodor W. Adorno's negative dialectic in the context of poststructuralism. *Boundary 2, 11*(1/2), 75. https://doi.org/10.2307/303018

Hearing Voices Network. (2022). Voices and visions. Retrieved December 28, 2022, from https://www.hearing-voices.org/voices-visions/

Neumann, F. (2009). *Behemoth: The structure and practice of National Socialism, 1933–1944.* Rowman. (Originally published 1942)

Newman, A. (1993). The death of Judaism in German protestant thought from Luther to Hegel. *Journal of the American Academy of Religion, 61*(3), 455–484. https://www.jstor.org/stable/1465125

Nietzsche, F. W. (2005). The anti-Christ. In A. Ridley & J. Norman (Eds.). *Nietzsche: The anti-Christ, ecce homo, twilight of the idols: And other writings* (J. Norman, Trans.). Cambridge University Press. (Original work published 1895)

Nirenberg, D. (2013). *Anti-Judaism: A Western tradition.* Norton.

Nobus, D., & Quinn, M. (2005). *Knowing nothing, staying stupid: Elements for a psychoanalytic epistemology.* Routledge.

Nock, A. J. (1941). *The Jewish problem in America.* The Atlantic. Retrieved February 10, 2023, from https://www.theatlantic.com/magazine/archive/1941/06/the-jewish-problem-in-america/306268/

Noerr, G. S. (2004). Editor's afterward. In T. W. Adorno & M. Horkheimer *Dialectic of enlightenment: Philosophical fragments* (G. S. Noerr, Ed. & E. Jephcott, Trans.). Stanford University Press.

Oberle, E. (2018). *Theodor Adorno and the Century of Negative Identity*. Standford University Press.

Ogden, T. (1989). *The primitive edge of experience*. Jason Aronson.

Osserman, J. (2022). *Circumcision on the couch: The cultural, psychological, and gendered dimensions of the world's oldest surgery*. Bloomsbury.

Ostow, M. (1995). *Myth and madness: The psychodynamics of anti-Semitism*. Transaction Publishers.

Parker, I. (Ed.). (2015). *Handbook of critical psychology*. Routledge.

Pateman, C. (1988). *The sexual contract*. Polity Press.

Paybarah, A. (2022, December). *Kanye West draws fresh denunciation for Hitler praise in Alex Jones interview*. Washington Post. Retrieved December 28, 2022, from https://www.washingtonpost.com/politics/2022/12/01/kanye-west-alex-jones-hilter-interview/

Pew Research Center. (2011). Global Christianity—A report on the size and distribution of the world's Christian population. Retrieved December 28, 2022, from https://www.pewresearch.org/religion/2011/12/19/global-christianity-exec/

Pew Research Center. (2021). 9. Race, ethnicity, heritage and immigration among U.S. Jews. *Jewish Americans in 2020*. Retrieved December 28, 2022, from https://www.pewresearch.org/religion/2021/05/11/race-ethnicity-heritage-and-immigration-among-u-s-jews/

Po-Chia Hsia, R. (2018). Judaism and Protestantism. In J. Karp & A. Sutcliffe (Eds.), *The Cambridge history of Judaism, volume 7: The early modern world 1500–1815*. Cambridge University Press.

Poliakov, L. (2003) *The history of Anti-Semitism: Vol 1–4* (G. Klin, Trans.). University of Pennsylvania Press.

Potolsky, M. (2006). *Mimesis*. Routledge. https://doi.org/10.4324/9780203401002

Ranke, L. (2011). *The theory and practice of history* (G. G. Iggers, Ed. & W. A. Iggers, Trans.). Routledge.

Rensmann, L. (2017). *Politics of unreason: The Frankfurt School and the origins of modern antisemitism*. SUNY.

Ricoeur, P. (1970). *Freud and philosophy: An essay on interpretation*. Yale University Press. (Originally published 1965)

Rogers, W. S. (2003). *Social psychology: Experimental and critical approaches.* Open University Press.

Rogers, A. (2016). *Incandescent alphabets: Psychosis and the enigma of language.* Routledge.

Rose, G. (1979). *The melancholy science.* Verso.

Rose, G. (1993). *Judaism and modernity: Philosophical essays.* Verso.

Roth, P. (2000). *The human stain.* Houghton Mifflin.

Rothberg, M. (2009). *Multidirectional memory: Remembering the holocaust in the age of decolonization.* Stanford University Press.

Rothberg, M. (2019). *The implicated subject: Beyond victims and perpetrators.* Stanford University Press.

Rothberg, M., & Lenz, R. (2024). We need an ethics of comparison. *Medico International.* Retrieved March 14, 2024, from https://www.medico.de/en/we-need-an-ethics-of-comparison-19392

Roudinesco, E. (1997). *Jacques Lacan* (B. Bray, Trans.). Columbia University Press.

Said, E. (1979). *Orientalism.* Vintage. (originally published in 1979)

Salamon, G. (2021). The place where life hides away: Merleau-Ponty, Fanon, and the location of bodily being. In D. Hook, L. Laubscher, & M. Desai (Eds.), *Fanon, phenomenology, and psychology.* Routledge.

Samuels, M. (2016). *The right to difference: French universalism and the Jews.* University of Chicago Press.

Santner, E. L. (2001). *On the psychotheology of everyday life: Reflections on Freud and Rosenzweig.* The University of Chicago Press.

Sartre, J. P. (1965). *Anti-Semite and Jew: An exploration of the etiology of hate.* Schocken. (Original work published 1946)

Sass, L. (2019). Three dangers: Phenomenological reflections on the psychotherapy of psychosis. *Psychopathology, 52*(2), 126–134. https://doi.org/10.1159/000500012

Schäfer, P. (1997). *Judeophobia: Attitudes toward the Jews in the Ancient World.* Cambridge University Press.

Scholem, G., & Adorno, T. W. (Eds.). (2012). *The correspondence of Walter Benjamin: 1910–1940.* (M. R. Jacobson & E. M. Jacobson, Trans.). University of Chicago Press.

Schraub, D. (2019). White Jews: An intersectional approach. *AJS Review, 43*(2), 379–407. https://doi.org/10.1017/S0364009419000461

Shapiro, D. (1984). *Autonomy and rigid character.* Basic books.

Sheskin, I. M., & Dashefsky, A. (2020). How many Jews of color are there? *eJewishPhilanthropy.* Retrieved April 30, 2024, from https://ejewishphilanthropy.com/how-many-jews-of-color-are-there/

Simmel, E. (Ed.). (1946). *Anti-Semitism, a social disease*. International Universities Press.

Sloan, T. (1995). *Damaged life: The crisis of the modern psyche*. Routledge. https://doi.org/10.4324/9780203407295

Stern, K. (2019). I drafted the definition of antisemitism. Rightwing Jews are weaponizing it. *The Guardian*. Retrieved December 28, 2022, from https://www.theguardian.com/commentisfree/2019/dec/13/antisemitism-executive-order-trump-chilling-effect

Strosberg, B. B. (2021). Adorno's negative psychology. *Social and Personality Psychology Compass, 15*(2). https://doi.org/10.1111/spc3.12578

Strosberg, B. B. (2022). Levinas and psychoanalysis: An antihermeneutic approach. *Journal of Theoretical and Philosophical Psychology, 42*(3), 146–157. https://doi.org/10.1037/teo0000193

Strosberg, B.B. (2022a). Reading Lacan *as* or *with* phenomenology: Implications for psychosis. *Psychoanalysis, Culture and Society, 3*(27), 235–249. https://doi.org/10.1057/s41282-022-00283-3

Strosberg, B. B. (2022b). Critical theory of anti-Semitism: Implications for politics, education, and psychoanalysis. In D. Burston & J. Mills (Eds.), *Critical theory and psychoanalysis*. Routledge.

Strosberg, B. B., Hook, D., & Leadem, S. (2023). Uncanny teletherapy: Working with extimacy. *Journal of the American Psychoanalytic Association, 71*(2), 237–258. https://doi.org/10.1177/00030651231170561

Tajfel, H., & Turner, J. C. (2004). The social identity theory of intergroup behavior. In J. T. Jost & J. Sidanius (Eds.), *Political psychology: Key readings* (pp. 276–293). Psychology Press. https://doi.org/10.4324/9780203505984-16

Babylonian Talmud. (N.D.). Shabbat 31a.

Teo, T. (Ed.). (2014). *Encyclopedia of critical psychology*. Springer.

Tuffin, K. (2005). *Understanding critical social psychology*. Sage. https://doi.org/10.4135/9781446217566

USDS. (2022). Working definition of Antisemitism. Office of the special envoy to monitor and combat antisemitism. https://www.state.gov/defining-antisemitism/

Vanheule, S. (2014). *Diagnosis and the DSM: A critical review*. Palgrave.

Vanheule, S. (2017). Conceptualizing and treating psychosis. *British Journal of Psychotherapy, 33*(3), 388–398. Wiley.

Vargas, R. A. (2023, August). *Jamie Foxx apologizes after Instagram post draws accusations of antisemitism.* The Guardian. Retrieved August 6, 2023, from, https://www.theguardian.com/film/2023/aug/06/jamie-foxx-apologizes-instagram-post-antisemitism

Verhaeghe, P. (2008). *On being normal and other disorders: A manual for clinical psychodiagnostics* (S. Jottkandt, Trans.). Karnac.

Vuong, O. (2022). *Time is a mother.* Penguin Press.

Walkerdine, V. (Ed.). (2002). *Challenging subjects: Critical psychology for a new millennium.* Palgrave.

Walzer, M. (1995). Preface. In J. P. Sartre (Ed.), *Anti-semite and Jew: An exploration of the etiology of hate.* Schocken.

Weiss, B. (2019). *How to fight anti-semitism.* Penguin.

Whitebook, J. (1996). *Perversion and utopia: A study psychoanalysis and critical theory.* MIT Press.

Whitebook, J. (2004). The marriage of Marx and Freud: Critical theory and psychoanalysis. In F. Rush (Ed.), *The Cambridge companion to critical theory* (pp. 74–102). Cambridge University Press. https://doi.org/10.1017/CCOL0521816602

Wiggershaus, R. (1994). *The Frankfurt School: Its history, theories, and political significance.* MIT Press.

Wilderson, F. B. (2020). *Afro-pessimism.* Liveright.

Wittgenstein, L. (2009). *Philosophical investigations* (G. E. M. Anscombe, P. M. S. Hacker, & J. Schulte, Trans.). Wiley-Blackwell. (Original work published 1953)

Wolin, R. (2023). *Heidegger in ruins: Between philosophy and ideology.* Yale University Press.

Wood, J. (2019). *Serious noticing: Selected essays 1997–2019.* Farrar, Straus, and Giroux. eBook.

Yuval-Naeh, A. (2018). The 1753 Jewish naturalization bill and the polemic over credit. *Journal of British Studies, 57*(3), 467–492. https://doi.org/10.1017/jbr.2018.82

Žižek, S. (2002). *Welcome to the desert of the real.* Verso.

Žižek, S. (2009). *Sublime object of Ideology.* Verso. (Original work published 1992)

Zwart, H. (2018). *Tales of research misconduct: A Lacanian diagnostics of integrity challenges in science novels.* Springer Open. https://doi.org/10.1007/978-3-319-65554-3

Index[1]

[1] Note: Page numbers followed by 'n' refer to notes.

Printed by Printforce, the Netherlands